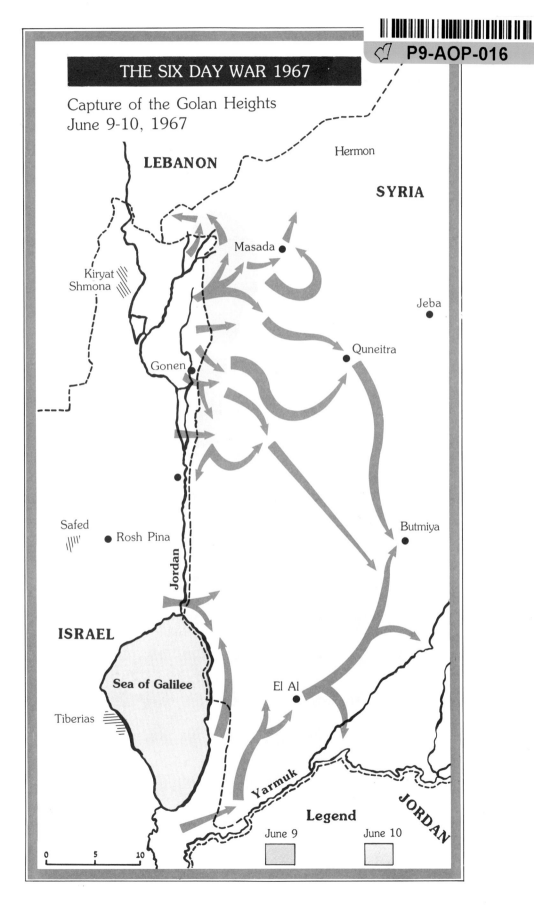

THE SIX DAY WAR 1967

Capture of the Golan Heights
June 9-10, 1967

THE ISRAEL DEFENSE FORCES
A PEOPLE'S ARMY

THE ISRAEL DEFENSE FORCES A PEOPLE'S ARMY

Lt. Col. (Res.) Louis Williams

MINISTRY OF DEFENSE
PUBLISHING HOUSE

ISRAEL DEFENSE FORCES
OFFICE OF THE IDF SPOKESMAN

This book is dedicated to all the men and women of the IDF who could not be mentioned in its pages - and to those who gave their lives that Israel could survive.

PHOTO CREDITS:
The photo at the top of page 15 is by Alex Libak.
All other photos are from IDF sources, and all rights are reserved to:
IDF Spokesman, Bamachane IDF Weekly, Israel Air Force, Israel Navy,
Bamachane HaNahal. Among the photographers are: Yuval Navon,
Michael Giladi, Carmi Galpaz, Ariel Yerozolomsky, Tal -Yodkovik,
Herzl Conessari, Ran Ravid, Yehonatan Carmi, Natan Alpert.

First published October 1989
Ministry of Defense Publishing House, Tel Aviv.

Printed in Israel
ISBN 965-05-0461-3

CONTENTS

Introduction	1
An Overview	5
The Making of a Soldier	31
The Family - Golani Brigade	59
Israel Air Force - Birth of Air Power	85
Combined Operations: Entebbe	119
Pages From the Diary of a Paratrooper	147
The Men Are the Steel	175
Merkava - A National Enterprise	215
The Artillery Corps - 1948 to the Present	231
Captain's Log - Israel Navy	247
The Cherbourg Boats	279
Not By the Sword Alone - The Nahal	297
Women in the IDF	319
Education Corps - An Obligation to Society	341

RANK BADGES
Ground Forces - Bronze on Olive Green
Navy - Gold on Navy Blue
Air Force - Silver on Blue

Lance Corporal	35
Corporal	35
Sergeant	35
Staff Sergeant	35
Sergeant Major	36
First Sergeant Major	36
Senior Sergeant Major	36
Command Sergeant Major	36
Second Lieutenant	39
Lieutenant	39
Captain	39
Major	44
Lieutenant Colonel	44
Colonel	47
Brigadier General	47
Major General	48
Lieutenant General	**48**

CAMPAIGN RIBBONS AND MEDALS

Hagana Ribbon, pre-May 1948   8

War of Independence, May 1948-March 1949   8

Sinai Campaign (Operation Kadesh), 1956   8

Six Day War, 1967   9

Yom Kippur War, 1973   9

Operation Peace for Galilee, 1982   9

Medal of Valor   12

Medal of Courage   13

Medal of Bravery   17

Operational Service Badge   81

CAP BADGES

Infantry   59

Air Force   89

Armored Corps   175

Ordnance Corps   215

Artillery Corps   231

Israel Navy   247

Engineer Corps   279

Intelligence Corps   297

General Service Corps   319

Education Corps   341

SHIRT INSIGNIA

Pilot	94
Navigator	99
Flight Mechanic	102
Medivac	107
Radio Operator	113
Parachutist	151
Senior Parachutist	152
Marksman	156
Sharpshooter	161
Armored Reconnaissance	188
Officer School Pin	193
Diver	265
Naval Commando	270
Submariner	275
Missile Boat Crewman	276

INTRODUCTION

Over four decades, the IDF (Israel Defense Forces) has fought four major wars (Independence 1948, Sinai 1956, the Six Days 1967 and Yom Kippur War 1973), three prolonged wars of attrition (Waters 1964-67, Egypt 1968-70, Syria 1973-74), two campaigns against terror organizations (Litani 1978, Peace for Galilee 1982) and thousands of actions against terrorists. All of these were forced on Israel by invasions, incursions or imminent threats. Throughout, the IDF has been pledged to the proposition that Israeli citizens have the right to live in security. In return for that pledge, Israeli society has been and is committed to sharing in the IDF's effort both physically through the reserve army and morally by support of the army's socially oriented programs and by providing for the welfare of its soldiers.

The same four decades have witnessed an unprecedented scientific and technological development in the art and weapons of war. And most of that development has been readily available to Israel's neighbors, both as a result of power and influence plays by major governments outside the Middle East and as a result of lust after a share of the immense wealth amassed by the oil rich countries. If the 1948 War of Independence was an amateurish scuffle, fought over 15 months with the hardware and concepts of World War II - the three weeks of the 1973 Yom Kippur War were waged amid firepower, intensity and technology that not so long before were only to be found in the pages of science fiction. Thus, the IDF, with rarely a moment free from maintaining the burdens of ongoing security, has been obliged to struggle to keep abreast of the new technologies and, wherever possible, to achieve that slight edge that is, in conditions of numerical inferiority, the difference between survival and extinction. The key to maintenance of that margin of quality versus quantity has always been the standard of the Israeli fighting man - his capacity for independent thought and innovation, his capability to develop, grasp and master the new technologies and, above all, his devotion to the defense of his nation and homeland.

This book is not a complete history of the IDF. No volume this slim could hope to cover all that has happened in the arena since 1948. It is an attempt to give the reader insights into the thinking and performance that has made the IDF an object of interest to friend and enemy alike, and into the special relationship between the army of Israel and the society from which it springs. The chapters on commitment and involvement, the making of a soldier, the role of women, education and the Nahal, will explore some aspects of the interface between society and the army. Those chapters of the book that deal with armor, artillery, paratroops, Golani Brigade, the Israel Air Force and the Israel Navy form a representative cross section of the combat echelons of the IDF. Though the choice of these units was not entirely arbitrary, it should not be taken as detracting from the performance and importance of other combat echelons. Nor should it be forgotten that no fighting man can perform effectively without intelligence, signals and electronics, combat engineering, logistics, maintenance, transport and other functions that support his presence in the field. And no military organization can exist without command and control, manpower management, planning, administration, research and development.

Most military historians would probably concur with the conception that there is no single absolute truth about the battlefield and the conduct of war. From different vantage points, the story of a battle or a campaign will develop along lines that far from converging may in fact be inconsistent or contradictory. The present purpose is not to resolve the riddle. Those battles that have been selected, and other writers might have made other choices, were chosen to illustrate the history and development of the combat units involved. To satisfy the appetites of those readers with a taste for the more exotic, the book includes chapters on the Entebbe raid and the Cherbourg boats - both of which represent, not isolated incidents, nor even past newspaper headlines, but rather illustrations of how the IDF has dealt with its specific problems. The chapter on the Merkava tank appears here as one example of how the IDF, and Israeli industry, have coped with the technological challenges of their environment.

This book would not have been possible without the willing cooperation of hundreds of men and women, officers and other ranks. It is impossible to mention all of them. However, a special debt of gratitude is owed to some people and institutions of the IDF who can be named. Israel Air Force History Branch generously supplied their own research material, not only for the chapter on the Air Force but also as it relates to the battle for the Mitla Pass and the lifting of the P12 radar out of Egypt in the War of Attrition. The Public Relations Department and Senior Historian of the Israel Navy were more than helpful with research material and comments. The story of the Cherbourg Boats is that of Commodore (Res.) Hadar Kimhi.

No less than five serving and retired generals of the IDF readily volunteered their time and knowledge for the chapter on Golani Brigade. Entebbe Diary could not have been written without the help of (then Defense Minister) Shimon Peres, Motta Gur, Maj. Gen. (Res.) Benny Peled, Col. (Res.) Muki B. and the commander of the IAF transport squadron involved in the operation. The chapter on artillery relies heavily on research done for the IDF Journal by Col. Shmuel Gordon and Sgt. Dan Petreanu. The chapter on the role of women in the IDF would not have been as comprehensive without the graciousness and generosity with their time of Brig. Gen. Amira Dotan, Brig. Gen. Hedva Almog, Col. Yisraela and Lt. Col. Yaffa (both the latter commanders of basic training installations).

Some of the material used in the book has appeared in slightly different form, by the present author, in the IDF Journal - a publication of the Israel Defense Forces Spokesman's Office. All the chapters have been read, and commented on, by the IDF units concerned. Last but not least, the author is grateful for the support, suggestions and comments of serving officers in the IDF Spokesman's Unit and, most particularly, the Film Unit and Public Relations Department. Needless to say, the final responsibility for the views expressed must rest with the author.

AN
OVERVIEW

Modern Israel has always been long on commitment and motivation but short on numbers. With too many challenges to meet, the nation has never been able to afford the luxury of a standing army large enough to cope with defense needs. Thus, Israel's military capability is based on a civilian militia. Conversely, where the scope of civilian problems has exceeded the resources of manpower and organization needed for their solution, the army has responded with an involvement in society at large unprecedented anywhere in the world - and which has in fact served as the model for other countries to follow. This chapter presents an historical overview of society's commitment to the IDF and national security, and the IDF's involvement in the country's social problems, some of which will be examined in greater detail in the chapters that follow.

Driven by the recognition that a nation must have its roots in the soil, the immigrants of a century ago, and those who followed, set about creating farming communities on marginal lands where their primary task was to clear away rocks and drain malarial-infested swamps. In the latter days of the Ottoman Empire and the three decades of the British Mandate that were to follow, the central authorities were incapable of - or unwilling to - provide the physical security required by a growing agrarian society that was constantly plagued by Arab bandits and marauders. Local defense began with the hiring of Arab watchmen who sometimes presented as much of a risk as the threat they were supposed to combat, then was gradually rebuilt on organizations of Jewish watchmen - reinforced by the settlers' willingness to bear arms whenever necessary. The picture of the farmer plowing his land by day and patrolling the perimeter of his community, rifle in hand, by night, became part of the pattern of life. The Arab riots of the 1920s and 1930s brought home the need for the same kind of self-defense in the urban communities of Jewish Palestine.

In May 1920, the Jewish workers' parties created the Irgun Hahagana Haivri Beeretz Yisrael - "Hebrew Defense Organization in Palestine" - or Hagana ("Defense") as it became popularly known, as the first countrywide attempt to provide security. The Hagana then

consisted of a loose knit web of local volunteers, responsible for the protection of their own communities.

During the 1930s, the Hagana - now under the control of the Vaad Leumi (the representative committee of the Jewish community) was widened to include representatives of all factions. In 1934, its constitution was amended from that of an ad hoc militia to a military organization, with a structure for training - after which its young men and women were transferred to a reserve, on call if needed. The Arab disturbances of 1936-39 prompted Yitzhak Sadeh, a Hagana commander in Jerusalem area, to reorganize his command on a mobile basis to move wherever needed and show more initiative. In 1937, the effort was augmented by the creation of the "Special Night Squads" - the brainchild of Charles Orde Wingate, a British intelligence officer who would later distinguish himself in the World War II Ethiopia and Burma Campaigns.

Wingate's SNS - composed of British soldiers and Hagana personnel mobilized within the Supernumerary Police set up by the British - and ostensibly founded to protect oil pipelines, was designed to seize initiatives as a deterrent to the Arab raiders. Its tactics were influenced by Wingate's belief in the use of night, and his reliance on Biblical precedents. In 1941, Rommel's Afrika Korps stood at the gates of Palestine and British contingency planning began to envisage a withdrawal northwards. A frame for possible guerrilla warfare was indicated, and the Hagana used the men trained by Wingate, and his tactical concepts, to create the Palmach ("Strike Companies"). The Palmach operated, together with the Allied armies, in the World War II campaigns in Lebanon and Syria. Towards the end of the war, considerable numbers of Hagana men also served in the Jewish Brigade, raised by the British Army in Palestine.

At the end of World War II, while much of the paramilitary force of the Jewish community was involved in the effort to smuggle the remnants of European Jewry across the Continent and the Mediterranean to Palestine, the Hagana and Palmach were reorganizing to meet the changing needs and possible future threats. The Palmach - by now a regular force of 2100 men and women, with 1000 reserves - was based mainly in the kibbutzim; by sharing in the farm work they could both hide their military training from prying British eyes and pay their own keep. The Hagana, with a small full-time staff, was building two distinct "corps"; the HISH ("Field Army") composed of men from 18-25 and the HIM ("Garrison Army") for the over-25 men, together with women nurses and signalers. By late 1947, the HISH numbered 9500 men, and the HIM could muster 32,000 - but the community could also count on Jewish Brigade veterans, who could be called in an emergency.

However, this manpower had not trained under one coherent doctrine of arms. The men and women of the Palmach - organized in four battalions - were indifferent to formal discipline and rank, but highly trained and motivated, and inclined to unconventional initiatives. The HISH and the HIM were primarily territorial or local in organization and their members, who trained at weekends or vacations, were oriented to community self-defense. The 1800 regular Supernumerary Police did function as a mobile force on call to help in the defense of the moshavot (farming villages), kibbutzim (communes) and moshavim (farm cooperatives), but they, like all the others, had never operated in anything larger than platoon, or at most company frames.

Though the trained and semi-trained forces of the Jewish Yishuv ("community") totaled some 45,000 men and women, this was no true indication of order-of-battle, since - by late 1947 - the Hagana could only call on 10,000 rifles; of these, 656 were in the hands of the Palmach, and 8700 were distributed among the settlements, many of whom had purchased the guns with their own money. When the time came to build an army, a lot of persuasion would be needed to get the settlers to turn over even a part of their weapons to a central arsenal. And there were virtually no weapons heavier than rifles.

On 29 November 1947, the United Nations voted to partition Palestine into a Jewish and an Arab state. The following day, Arab riflemen opened fire on a bus on route from Natanya to Jerusalem, and the Arab Higher Committee declared a three day general strike.

On the second day of the strike, an Arab mob broke into the old Jewish commercial center of Jerusalem, looting and killing under the eyes of British troops. The disturbances spread like wildfire across Jerusalem, Tel Aviv and Haifa, then on to the critical supply routes to the outlying communities. The "War of the Roads" had begun, and it would continue, with little interference from the 90,000 British troops in Palestine, through the next five months.

With the UN General Assembly resolution to partition Palestine, the Hagana High Command had to face two challenges. The British, having decided to leave Palestine by mid-May, 1948, were not willing or able to maintain security. Conversely, they were less likely to interfere with Jewish self-defense. The first task, up to the British departure, would be to protect road communications between the populated centers and outlying communities, and to defend the cities and settlements against Arab irregulars and local gangs. The second mission was to prepare to meet the Arab armies, who would no doubt invade as the last British troops left. Neither challenge could be faced by an army structured on platoons and companies, with no higher level of coordination.

In November 1947, the High Command ordered the creation of territorial brigades: "Etzioni" in Jerusalem; "Givati" in the south; "Alexandroni" north of Tel Aviv; "Kiriati" in Tel Aviv and environs; and "Levanoni" in the north. The Palmach was also organized in three brigades: "Yiftach" in the north, "Harel" to be responsible for Jerusalem and the corridor leading to the city, and Palmach Negev in the south. Within weeks it was recognized that these territorial boundaries were too large for efficient operations, and so - on 28 February 1948 - Levanoni was replaced by "Carmeli" Brigade in Haifa and Western Galilee, and "Golani" in the valleys and hills of Lower Galilee.

At first, the problems on the highways that connected upwards of three hundred Jewish communities were restricted to those places where the road passed through Arab towns and villages. This was the case, for example, on the Tel Aviv-Jerusalem road that ran through the town of Ramle, where the Hagana was compelled to find an alternative, if tortuous, route through a continuous chain of Jewish settlements as far as the hill gorge that climbed the Judean mountains. Protective methods began with wire screens on bus windows against stones and hand grenades, then required armor plate as the Arabs began to snipe. The early escorts consisted of one boy or girl per bus, armed with a revolver or stripped-down Sten gun. Then, as the Arab gangs started to plant mines and set up roadblocks, the escorts increased through squads and on to larger units. Gradually, the local Arabs organized into larger groups and began to harass transport in open fields and on the hills, and the response had to be convoys.

On 10 January 1948, the Arab Liberation Army (ALA) - which had been organizing across the frontiers under an Arab League decision - made its debut in an attack on Kibbutz Kfar Szold in Upper Galilee. A British armored unit assisted in the defense, but this was to be an exception rather than the rule; the main British preoccupation was with the needs of their own security and evacuation. From 10 January through to 15 May 1948 - the date of the British departure - the Hagana and the Palmach were faced with missions that would have daunted a regular army, free to function and maneuver openly. The War of the Roads was continuing, with the Arab villagers now reinforced by the well-armed and organized ALA. The Jewish communities in all the mixed communities of Palestine were under siege - and nowhere was this worse than in Jerusalem, with its special significance for Jews everywhere. The ALA was attacking outlying settlements and the available limited manpower and weapons had to be rushed from place to place to meet each new threat. On top of all this, the Hagana High Command was desperately trying to organize to meet the now inevitable invasion by five regular armies.

The organizational efforts were not limited to the recruitment and training of new formations alone. The work of clandestine immigration continued, in parallel with immense efforts to acquire and smuggle in whatever arms and ammunition could be found in Europe and America. Furthermore, since the necessary weapons were not openly and easily available, all possible resources were being devoted to the creation of an underground arms industry. The combination of sixty years experience of Zionist settlement, and the bleak circumstances of a population of 650,000 facing violence within the country and the threat of invasion from all four points of the compass, had made the war effort the concern of every man, woman and child. With the backing of the entire society and its representative organizations - soon to become the government of the State of Israel - the Hagana and the Palmach, with the later incorporation of the IZL ("National Military Organization") and LEHI ("For the Freedom of Israel"), had established a tradition of a civilian militia army that would survive the May 1948 transition to the IDF and the War of Independence.

In May 1948, the Hagana High Command became the General Staff of the IDF, with full powers of coordination. The brigades, of

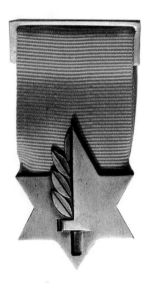

which there would be 12 by the end of the war, were operating as each understood best at the tactical level. There were, however, two prevailing doctrines: that of the Palmach, with a grand flair for improvisation, and that of the men who had served in the British Army with its traditions of organization, rank and tactics. On top of these were grafted a number of volunteer advisors - relatively senior officers experienced in foreign armies. The War of Independence, which lasted until March 1949, forged a single, united army from the component parts - but, under the pressure of events, left many major issues to be resolved after the dust settled over the battlefields. And, obviously, the most important issue of all was the need for an army large enough to face the hostility of Israel's neighbors who, though they had lost a war, were not ready to make peace.

In the aftermath of the war, serious thought began to be devoted to the maintenance of sufficient defense capability. Obviously, the population of Israel was too small to support a regular army large enough for current security needs or emergency situations. In addition, both political and military circles felt that a regular army based on the trained cadres of the pre-1948 community would exclude the new immigrants, who were arriving in their masses, from their share of responsibility for Israel's security, and this might in turn adversely affect their integration into Israeli society.

In 1949-50, three IDF generals went to Switzerland to study that country's reserve army structure, and decided to adopt it with minor modifications. From age 18, all Israelis, both men and (unmarried) women, were to be subject to national service - presently three years for men and two for women. Upon completion of conscript service, the men were to be liable for reserve duty of from 30-45 days a year (depending on rank) till the age of 48; the age limit is now 54, though it is no longer customary to call them after age 50. Women would serve in the reserves up to 24. In times of emergency the length of duty can be increased as the circumstances warrant. Consequently, many Israelis refer to themselves as soldiers on leave for 11 months a year. Unlike the Swiss example, where service is much shorter, Israeli reservists do not keep their personal weapons at home: the reserve army is supported by its own emergency stores of weapons and vehicles, which are maintained ready for combat by the standing army and the reservists themselves.

If the standing or "conscript" army has become a part of the process of growing up in Israeli society, then the reserve has become the symbol of the nation's commitment and determination. Though few rejoice at the need to leave work and family behind at sometimes inconvenient moments, mobilization in an emergency is quick and ungrudging - as the following 1967 war report by a correspondent (Abba Kovner) illustrates:

> I was leaning over a newsstand at the time. The owner, reaching for my journal, suddenly went rigid at the sound of the newscaster's voice. His eyes widened. Staring right past me, he uttered a surprised 'Ah! They've called me too!' He stacked his papers and left. Across the street a salesgirl was leaving her store. She stopped a moment in the doorway, her head tilted, then she buttoned her jacket, closed her handbag firmly and went off. The butcher next door whipped off his apron, pulled down the shutters and departed. On a nearby lawn stood a group of men huddled around a transistor radio. With the announcement of a unit code-name, one of them would slip away, then another...
> A silence like no other enveloped the city... I have seen nations going off to war. I have seen men marching to the blare of earshattering loudspeakers. I have seen them crowding the railway stations. I have seen them parading through the streets. I have seen them stomping off in their hob-nailed boots to the harsh sounds of their marching songs... But never, never have I seen a city rising to its duties in such silence, nor seen a nation go forth to fateful battle so hushed, so grim, so committed.

The same sense of commitment was expressed by Chief-of-Staff Rabin after the Six Day War:

> Our soldiers prevailed not by their weapons but by their sense of mission, by the consciousness of the rightness of their cause, by a deep love for their country and an understanding of the difficult task laid upon them: to ensure the existence of our people in its homeland, to protect, even at the price of their own lives, the right of the Jewish People to live in its

own state, free, independent and in peace. This army, which I had the privilege of commanding, came from the people and returns to the people - to a people which rises to great heights in times of crisis and prevails over all enemies by virtue of its moral and spiritual strength.

In that phrase "came from the people and returns to the people" lies the key not only to society's commitment to the army, but to the army's involvement in society. Such a national environment, reinforced as it has been by the need to fight five major wars and constant skirmishes over forty years, might among other peoples have led to a militaristic society and an endangered democracy. However, there is every evidence that Israelis, while they relate to the army with affection, consider its fighting role as a necessary evil forced upon us by the world in which we live. As for its influence on democracy, the best commentary was perhaps that of an Israel Radio reporter during a recent week when the IDF Armored Corps decided to give Tel Aviv children a treat by setting up in the city an exhibit of its history and equipment. Noting that thousands of children were happily clambering over tanks, the reporter went on to say: "When you stop to think about it, this is the only country in the Middle East, and one of few in the world, where you can place a dozen tanks in front of City Hall and it has no political implication!"

Soldiers of the reserve army are civilians in uniform, who bring their political opinions with them. No formal political activity is allowed within the army, but no attempt is made to stifle informal discussion. This is hardly the atmosphere in which an army could be used to exert political pressures on the democratic establishment. The reserve army has had other, profound influences on Israeli society, though these are largely ignored, or at best taken for granted by that society. Because the army cuts across all segments of the population, men and women come together to serve their annual duty year after year in a mix of all the ethnic groups that make up modern Israel. Thus, though they might not have "fraternized" outside the IDF, in uniform they gain a better understanding of the other man, his culture and way of life. Similarly, the army often turns the pyramid of civilian organization upside down. Thus, a university professor may find himself under the command of one of his students, or a plant manager subordinate to

one of his workers when they turn out for their periodic service in the reserve. There is little doubt that the army, in this context, has contributed massively to the prevention of the more negative aspects of class and social strata in Israeli society, and to the feeling of being one family with all its members sharing responsibility for each other.

Israel emerged from the 1948 War of Independence with other serious problems. The population of the country had doubled overnight and, with waves of immigrants continuing to arrive, food, housing and employment were in critically short supply. The IDF had problems of its own. Having been born in battle, it now needed time to convert the improvised structures created under the pressure of simultaneous war against the invading armies of Lebanon, Syria, Iraq, Jordan and Egypt into the regular establishment of a modern army. The army that had fought this war did not have standardized weapons and equipment, and even lacked a common language: few of the immigrants who had gone straight to the battlefield from the port of Haifa knew Hebrew, and training sessions or the giving of battle orders often sounded like the multilingual hubbub in the corridors of the United Nations. Prior to 1948, the Hagana and Palmach had been deeply involved in rescuing the remnants of European Jewry and bringing them to pre-State Palestine, but the task of absorption and immigration had fallen on other shoulders. This was now to change dramatically.

In 1949, the immigrant transit camps - where close to half-a-million people were living under canvas or in ramshackle huts - were swept by a wave of epidemics. The task was beyond the capability of the fledgling civilian authorities, so the IDF moved in. Thousands of conscripts and reservists "invaded" 24 transit camps to rebuild tents and huts, pave roads, dig storm drains and install sewers. Children were transferred temporarily to army camps (of which, thanks to the British Eighth Army, there were no shortage), and 200 army reserve doctors began a massive program of curative and preventive medicine. The campaign lasted four months, but the lessons of it set something far more permanent in motion. Firstly, the immigrants - who had come from an environment of inherent distrust of armies and police forces - came to trust the men and women in IDF uniforms. Secondly, the high command realized, as Chief of Staff Yigael Yadin put it, "we cannot treat the distress of our immigrant recruits while ignoring the distress of their home environment." From this point on the IDF was wholeheartedly involved.

A popular Israeli humorist once claimed that Israel is the only country in which the mother learns the mother tongue from her children. As the proportion of second and third generation Israelis in the total population has steadily grown, the problem of a common language has become less of an issue. But, in the 1950s, language was perhaps the major obstacle to the formation of the new nation. Obviously, no army can function efficiently without the ability to communicate freely and understandably between all its personnel - nor for that matter can any modern society. The first IDF effort to teach Hebrew to its immigrant recruits began in 1948, at Camp Marcus in Haifa, on an elementary school level. Camp Marcus was an experiment, provoked by the education gap between different immigrant communities. Its success was to result, in 1955, in the inauguration of a major drive to end illiteracy within the IDF.

Though the challenge of teaching Hebrew as a "new native language" is no longer relevant, the army has continued its war on illiteracy. All recruits who do not measure up to minimal educational standards are sent upon enlistment to special centers that aim at achieving at least an eighth grade level education. The aspects of schemes that deal with different categories of illiteracy, low social motivation and juvenile delinquency will be discussed in greater length in the chapter on the IDF Education Corps. Meanwhile, suffice it to say that, to drop out from an educational frame early in life is to drop out from society. And this is even more the case in a society where everybody serves, and potential employers are likely to reject job candidates with no army record: the assumption is simply that if the candidate could not satisfy the minimum requirements for entry into the IDF, how can he be suitable for employment? Thus, the army's effort with these groups is primarily aimed at salvaging productive citizens for society.

Within the constellation of an immigrant society lacking a common educational background, any serious attempt to upgrade the knowledge of the army-age generation was almost bound to cause friction between the recruits and their parents. This was particularly so in the case of immigrants originating from patriarchal societies, where the son's newfound formal education threatened the father's status in the family. Thus, the IDF found itself involved in support of the struggling education system of the young state. Women draftees who had completed secondary education were invited to volunteer for teaching assignments in transit camps, border and development areas, where their duties included adult education. Their efforts did not stop at formal education. The young women found themselves welcome, as members of the family, in situations where they were passing on know-how in basic home economics and tips on how to cope with the modern world to women who had originated in backward societies of the Middle East and Asia. They were also, inadvertently, introducing a new conception of the value of women to social groups where education, such as it was, had been the exclusive prerogative of men.

The role of women was not to be restricted to teaching, in the army or outside. Neither does the army's interest in education end with the underprivileged. At the upper end of the scale, for example, the IDF not only grants deferments to students of subjects of potential interest to itself (e.g., medicine, Middle East studies, engineering), but it also runs special programs for recruits of demonstrated exceptional intellect and creativity. Academic studies also feature in the army's approach to the officer corps: regular officers are encouraged to acquire a university degree at IDF expense.

Later chapters will deal in detail with the role of women in the army, not only in teaching, but also in social welfare and technologically oriented roles, and with non-military education in the IDF.

It might be natural to assume that the IDF is, by definition, an exclusively Jewish army. However, the army does number among its ranks representatives of the minority communities - some as conscripts and other as volunteers, both in the standing and regular echelons. The Arab community at large was exempted from the National Service Law, originally for two reasons: in the circumstances of the 1950s, it was strongly felt that a community finding itself a minority in a country that they had not chosen - and one at war with neighbors of their own religious and ethnic persuasion - presented a potential security risk; even where this was not the case, Arabs could hardly be expected to serve in situations where they would be required to fire on their own kin. Over four

decades, the first reason has tended to drop by the wayside as the Arab community, with all its problematics, has accepted its status as Israeli citizens. And there are voices that suggest the inevitability of accepting Israeli Arabs who choose to volunteer for the IDF. The advocates of this view are not indifferent to the existing legislation that offers social benefits, such as mortgages for young couples, to ex-servicemen. These arguments, which must ultimately be resolved, have never been relevant to the Druze, Circassian and Bedouin communities.

When the 1948 war began, the Druze in Palestine were faced with choices that were influenced both by their impressions of the performance of the outnumbered and outgunned forces of the Hagana and Palmach, and by their sometimes tense and even openly hostile relations with the Arabs. Though little is known about their religion, one commonly accepted precept calls on the Druze to be loyal to the regime of the country where they live - and this country was now Israel. Throughout the War of Independence, and immediately thereafter, they and other members of the minority communities all served in the IDF on a purely voluntary basis. In 1955, however, leaders of the Druze community proposed to the government that their sons be conscripted. This proposal was approved and legalized by an act of the Knesset. In May 1956, Druze were drafted for compulsory service. As Prime Minister David Ben-Gurion commented: "The pact between the Druze people and the Jewish people is not written on a scrap of paper. It is sanctified by the blood of Druze fighters." The following year conscription was introduced for Circassians. Bedouin continued to serve on a voluntary basis.

Following the War of Independence, the IDF established a "Minorities Unit" - 300 Brigade - consisting mainly of Druze, a few Circassians and some Bedouin. The Brigade was active against smuggling, spying and sabotage activities in the south - and later against fedayeen and PLO terrorism. The Brigade's Trackers Unit, made up mainly of Bedouins with some Druze, with their familiarity with the terrain and their aptitude as soldiers, played a key role in border patrols. After the Six Day War, the Druze Reconnaissance Unit shared in the pursuit of PLO terrorists who had infiltrated into the Jordan Valley. The Minorities Unit has distinguished itself in all the wars since 1967, when it participated in the campaign in

Samaria. In the Yom Kippur War, a small group from the Unit took part in the Golani Brigade assault on the summit of Mt. Hermon, displaying outstanding marksmanship and physical fitness. Operation Litani, in March 1978, was the first campaign in which the Minorities Unit was given its own objectives to assault and secure, followed by mopping-up operations. In the 1982 Operation Peace for Galilee, the Druze Reconnaissance Unit distinguished itself in the bitter fighting around Sidon, capturing its objectives ahead of schedule and making itself available to reinforce other units. In 1982, the General Staff opened almost all arms of the IDF to the minorities and decided to bring some Jewish soldiers into the Minorities Unit, ending its exclusive character.

Two organizational frames of the IDF have aroused considerable interest among the developing countries. The first is the Gadna ("Youth Battalions"), which were first created in 1940, when their main functions were the distribution of leaflets and the collection of information for the Hagana. By 1948 the organization numbered several thousand pre-army age youth, who served during the War of Independence in various support capacities - as messengers and so on, though some of its units saw combat in Jerusalem and Haifa. Following the 1948 war, Gadna became a joint venture of the IDF and the Ministry of Education. The Ministry is responsible for its organization within the schools, while the army supplies instructors and training facilities. The curriculum extends well beyond pre-military training. At one level it is comparable to a scouting movement, in which trainees are taught fieldcraft and learn more about the country in which they live. On another level, they are encouraged to take part in cultural activities such as debating clubs; within this frame, the Gadna also organizes and hosts an International Youth Bible Contest each year.

In times of emergency, Gadna members serve as hospital auxiliaries, deliver mail and help where they can to maintain essential services depleted by reserve mobilization. In relatively peaceful times, the boys and girls will spend a few days each year in projects that help build their national consciousness and sense of good citizenship; these can include, for instance, afforestation projects or archaeological digs. Gadna members have been trained to participate in the Israel Police Civil Guard, and youths resident in border areas have been trained for integration into the local defense network.

Aspects of the IDF such as its educational programs and the Gadna have aroused considerable interest from professionals abroad, but nowhere has that interest been keener than in the case of the Nahal ("Fighting Pioneer Youth") Brigade. The Brigade was established as a direct result of David Ben-Gurion's insistence on the inclusion into the National Defense Law of a clause requiring all soldiers to spend time in agriculture. The soldiers of the Nahal, therefore, spend a part of their time undergoing routine military training and sharing in the chores of ongoing security, and the rest - farming. The two are not unconnected. Their time on the land is spent either in existing kibbutzim ("communes"), or in exclusively Nahal settlements that prepare the ground for eventual civilian occupation - both in areas where a small military presence is essential to the maintenance of border security. The purely military portion of their service time is devoted to training in crack units such as the paratroops and armored corps. The formula has proven so successful that it now encompasses new immigrant recruits and disadvantaged youths as an aid to their integration into productive Israeli society.

Perhaps the most unique aspect of the Nahal seems to have escaped the notice even of those who have sought to emulate it in the developing countries. The Nahal, virtually alone among the military structures of the world, takes a peer group that have decided on a common future in a kibbutz or moshav ("cooperative farming village") from their days in high school and permits them both to remain together as a unit during their army service, and to utilize their time to gain practical experience for their chosen future life. The work done by these soldier farmers also means that they are the ultimate in rarities - military personnel who provide at least a part of their own upkeep rather than being a charge on the public purse. The IDF pays a price in that many of these Nahal soldiers would have been ideal officer candidates whom the army has voluntarily given up to the benefit of other national objectives.

The Nahal has existed since the 1950s, and had its ideological roots in the pre-State Palmach and kibbutz movement, but it has recently been joined by another organization with a somewhat similar nature in the wider sense, but very different roots. Traditionally, ultra religious Jews who were studying in yeshivas ("rabbinical seminaries") were exempted from military service. This

created bitterness and dissatisfaction among both non-orthodox youth, who felt that they were carrying an unfair share of the security burden while others were exempt, and among the Zionist-oriented yeshiva students, who sensed that they were being shut out of an important part of the process of becoming mature adults in Israeli society. As a result, the IDF agreed to accept entire yeshivas into the ranks under different conditions to those applicable to most enlistees.

The yeshiva students accept, voluntarily, a five year service (in place of the normal three), but spend 36 months of the total in their religious studies, in periods interspersed with their military training and service. The yeshiva soldiers serve either in Golani Brigade or the armored corps. In frames where they were originally welcomed somewhat suspiciously, and where consequently they had to perform better than anyone else in order to be accepted as equals, they have acquired a reputation of being among the best soldiers that the IDF has.

The IDF's link with religion does not begin and end with the yeshiva students, nor does it necessarily restrict itself to the stories of modern commanders who have sought their answers to pressing military problems in the pages of the Bible. Although the IDF does not involve itself in any way in a soldier's religious beliefs, or lack of them, considerable effort does go into ensuring the conditions that make it possible for religious soldiers, whether Jews or non-Jews, to serve without compromising their observances. All kitchen facilities are strictly kosher. All training stops for the Sabbath and religious festivals. Security needs permitting, as many as possible officers and men are given home leave for religious festivals. And for those who remain in camp, rituals such as the Passover Seder service and the building of tabernacles on Succot ("the Feast of Tabernacles") are observed. The Army Rabbinate has its own program of education and culture, and is responsible for attending to the spiritual needs of non-Jews (Christians, Moslems and Druze) serving in the IDF - and of prisoners-of-war.

At another level of care for the needs of the men and women of the army, each unit has two functionaries who are responsible for "education" and "service conditions." Both these functions are in fact misnomers. The Education Officer or Sergeant is not at all concerned with military education, but rather with bringing lecturers and organizing field trips on non-military subjects, and with organizing cultural and entertainment services. The Social Conditions Officer is primarily concerned with the soldier's problems outside the army. She, and it always a function of women soldiers, helps with postings near home for men with sick or incapacitated parents, allowances to supplement family income, foster homes for soldiers who have no family in the country, and so on.

It is perhaps not surprising that an army so concerned with the welfare and education of its men should also be sensitive to the individual's sense of justice or injustice. Acutely aware of the fact that military organization can lead to situations where a soldier believes he is being treated unfairly because it is difficult to appeal against superior rank, the IDF set up an office of Commissioner of Complaints, headed by a senior officer - the first of whom was a previous chief-of-staff with the rank of lieutenant general. This office deals with any complaint from soldiers - regulars, conscripts and reservists. From its statistics, this office has found more than half the complaints submitted to be justified, and has achieved whatever was necessary to redress the injustice.

One other aspect of social concerns at large is worth mentioning here, in that it touches on a basic, human value of the IDF. The army has always avoided the trauma of the impersonal telegram or phone call which is so much a part of other societies. When an IDF soldier falls in action, the family is visited by a team that includes an officer from the local town marshal's unit, a doctor or psychologist and - a woman soldier. This team is there not only to soften the blow as much as possible, but also to assist the bereaved kin through the traumas and problems of the ensuing period. The same human concern prevails in army-media relationships. The IDF Spokesman will not release names of the fallen to the media until he is sure that the family has been informed. Nor are Israeli tv cameramen allowed to film the faces of IDF dead or wounded on the field of battle. No family in Israel will learn about its tragedies from the ever-present box in the living room.

Beyond the normal technical, administrative, structural and tactical answers to current and future problems, every army develops its web of concepts and traditions that derive from its particular history, and sometimes from the legends surrounding one or other senior officer or enlisted man. In the case of the IDF, the concepts and traditions have developed rapidly on the fertile soil of a tiny nation, facing considerable odds, that has been compelled in the space of only four decades to fight five major wars and numerous skirmishes and counter-attrition actions - and yet has had the heritage of four millennia from which to draw its values.

Two particular concepts have dominated in the shaping of the IDF: an egalitarian attitude to rank; and an intense regard for human life and the individual human being.

The egalitarian aspect is rooted equally in the pre-State antecedents of the IDF, and in its present structure as a civilian militia. Rank is neither a privilege of class, nor a source of privilege - but solely the recognition of competence and of command ability. Officers and other ranks are issued the same uniforms and eat the same food. In line and field units, they will share the same mess halls and live in the same quarters. Commanders also know that, though disobedience is rare - and unheard of in combat - they may often be required by their men to explain the meaning and reasoning behind specific orders and regulations. In most reserve units, where men may have served together through two or three decades, the atmosphere is one of a comfortable, enlarged family or club of old friends where, duty apart, rank is of no significance.

In keeping with this atmosphere, the IDF has never tolerated the command approach of "Forward!" but rather that of "Follow me!" and the picture of the tank commander standing upright in an open turret has become part of the legend of the IDF. Obviously, it is an expensive legend - casualty lists are always top heavy with command ranks - but a training system and environment that encourages individual initiative has meant that there has never been a shortage of men to step forward and fill the gaps.

On the face of it, regard for the individual and for human life should not be worthy of special attention in an army. Yet the intensity of this regard, and the scope of effort that surrounds it, places the IDF on a plane by itself among military organizations. Ancient Jewish tradition teaches that "he who saves one soul is considered to have saved a whole world."

An IDF soldier going into battle knows that he is supported by the finest and most extensive system of military medicine of any army in the world. Not only does every unit have its highly trained corpsman, backed up by doctors at battalion level, but also the ready availability of tank and armored personnel carrier "ambulances," mobile operating theatres and helicopters staffed by fully qualified medical teams. The wounded soldier knows that medical aid will arrive within minutes and - perhaps most important of all - that the time hallowed tradition of the IDF cannot countenance the leaving of wounded on the battlefield. A study of the citations and medals awarded for courage and gallantry in battle reveals that a remarkably high number have been given for heroism in rescuing comrades, rather than for actual deeds in combat.

The IDF Medical Corps is so well oiled a machine that the organization and staffing of medical teams - including a fully equipped airborne operating theatre - for the Entebbe operation, based as it was largely on reserve doctors, was completed within hours of the day that the rescue team took off for Uganda. Apart from the intrinsic medical value of this effort, with the accompanying low rate of battlefield fatalities as compared with other armies, the contribution to morale and the sense of brotherhood in the ranks of the IDF is immeasurable.

The Medical Corps commitment is not restricted to the confines of the army, or indeed to the population of Israel. No distinction has ever been drawn between friend and foe in the giving of aid on the battlefield, or in the allocation of priority for evacuation to base hospitals. One day in June 1976, during the Lebanese Civil War, a peasant woman appeared on the other side of the fence that marks the length of Israel's frontier with her northern neighbor, bearing a wounded child in her arms and appealing for help. The IDF soldiers on the sector cut through the fence and called up a medical team to treat the child. That one isolated incident was the beginning of a major humanitarian enterprise. At what was to become known as the "Good Fence," the IDF Medical Corps set up three field clinics that have remained on duty night and day ever since. More than a quarter of a million patients from Lebanon have been treated for wounds received in the civil war, and for the more mundane and routine medical complaints of a civilian population without adequate medical service of its own. In their first two years, the Good Fence clinics treated, free of charge, 29,900 Christians, 13,500 Moslems and 1400 Druze - and sent 1600 patients on for hospitalization in Israeli hospitals. During Operation Peace for Galilee alone, 500 Lebanese were hospitalized in Israel for everything from maternity through to treatment for cancer. And this effort was not without precedent: from 1967 to 1982, the Medical Corps accepted responsibility for the medical and dental care of the Bedouin in the Sinai Desert.

The intensity of regard for the individual is not merely with the living. The IDF does not leave its dead on the battlefield, nor will it tolerate graves on foreign soil. Special units of the Army Rabbinate deal with the identification and burial of the dead. In keeping with this tradition, which is a major concern of Jewish religion, the Government of Israel has made the recovery of its dead a vital precondition to all armistice, ceasefire and peace agreements. Thus, for example, combined Israeli and Egyptian teams scoured the battlefields of Sinai for months after the Yom Kippur War.

The army's concern continues in its social and economic aid to its wounded veterans and to the families of its dead. Time may heal wounds, but it is not allowed to diminish the IDF's sense of responsibility for its own. Beyond the normal system of disability pensions, etc., considerable effort is invested in rehabilitation and job training, and the army will also help a disabled veteran with loans and grants for the purpose of creating a means of livelihood.

A measure of the special relationship between army and society is to be found in the voluntary organizations that raise funds and participate actively in programs that are beyond the means of the defense budget. Thus, the Soldiers' Welfare Committee not only raises moneys to build clubhouses and provide sports equipment, cultural needs and presents for soldiers for the festivals, but its volunteers are also to be found up on the battlelines bringing cakes, fruit, toilet articles, etc., and taking messages back to parents, wives and children. Schoolchildren write letters and send parcels to soldiers, and the national phone company provides mobile telephone vans carrying slogans such as "Soldier, phone home!" The Education Corps effort among the underprivileged is financed by a fund, Libi (a double entendre: the word means "my heart," the abbreviation is for Lemaan Bitachon Yisrael - "For Israel's Security").

Yet another field of concern for the individual in which the IDF has justifiably become legendary is that of the meticulous attention paid to safety and human engineering in combat equipment and systems. Not only are soldiers invited to submit their suggestions for design of personal webbing equipment, not only are they issued with fireproof coveralls and thermal clothing - but Israeli developed systems, such as the Merkava Main Battle Tank, are designed with a degree of consideration for survivability and comfort rarely matched in comparable systems elsewhere.

The IDF is a militia army in a democratic society. Its pre-occupation with the education and welfare of its own men and women, and of society at large, makes it unique among armies, yet it is no more than a reflection of the commitment and involvement of the society from which it comes and which it serves.

THE
MAKING
OF A SOLDIER

According to the Defense Service Law, all Israeli Jewish, Druze and Circassian male citizens are liable for military service at the age of 18. This service presently includes three years in the standing army and a further obligation to serve in the reserve army up to the age of 54. In some societies such a requirement might be viewed as coercive, possibly frightening, distasteful and contrary to personal convictions and conscience. Israel is not one of these societies. Because of the smallness of the country and its environmental conditions, the need for each and every citizen to contribute to the defense of the homeland is generally accepted as a necessity. This in no way makes of Israel a militaristic society, nor does it make joining the IDF a career decision in the same sense that the army is viewed in many other democracies. It is simply a reality with which Israelis know they must live - if indeed the country is to survive. And the awareness of need is not restricted to the army alone: in war time, Israelis not liable for military service flock to take over vital services depleted by mobilization. Volunteers can be found distributing mail, helping in the hospitals and bringing in the harvests.

In this atmosphere, it is hardly surprising that Israeli youth regard their forthcoming military service as part of the rites of passage to maturity. In every family, the father - and sometimes the mother - the brothers, sisters and cousins, have all traveled the same route, or will do so. Thus, the act of enlistment is a matter of anticipation rather than trepidation. Apart from the extensive treatment of the IDF in the Israeli media, children are almost certain to have been taken, by their schools or parents, to visit IDF bases and exhibits - and to have absorbed masses of information about the army from families, neighbors and friends. Primary school children are encouraged to write letters to soldiers, and to express their concepts of army, security and peace in essays and drawings. As the date for enlistment approaches, secondary schools invite senior officers to talk to the student body about the IDF in general and about some of its units in specifics. Some schools make a point of calling on recent graduates to speak about their army experiences.

Formally, the recruitment process begins somewhere between age sixteen and a half and seventeen, with an official notification - both by posters on public notice boards and by mail - of a date to report for enlistment. The timing of the notice is roughly one year before induction, which in turn is determined by date of birth. The familiar IDF envelope - somebody in the family has been getting them for as long as the youngster can remember - also contains a guidebook to enlistment and induction and a medical history form to be filled in and brought to the enlistment center. The first encounter with the center will last a few hours, and is devoted to basics. All enlistees are interviewed to verify the data passed on to the IDF from the Ministry of Interior register of all citizens: address, phone, parents, physical attributes, etc. To these are added an initial assessment of the enlistee's ability to read and write Hebrew, details of driving licenses (if any) and a summary of the latest school reports. At this stage, the IDF is also interested in knowing about any technological background and education that the enlistee might have. If there are any family or social welfare problems, the boy will be referred straight on to a Conditions of Service Officer.

There are two more steps to be taken on this first day: a preliminary check of medical records, aimed at establishing whether there are any problems or history that will require additional documentation later on; a two-hour psychotechnical exam to establish the "Initial Psychotechnical Classification" (IPC). The day ends with issue of a second notification - of the date to appear before an army medical board. The date will be set for around the enlistee's seventeenth birthday.

The second date is devoted to a thorough physical and medical examination, including medical history. At the conclusion of this stage, the examining doctors are ready to determine the recruit's "Medical Profile." Two ratings, 21 and 24, are "unfit for service"; the first is permanent, while the second is temporary and can be reassessed at a later date. The remaining eight profiles relate to limitations, or the lack of them, on the kind of service that the recruit is fit to perform. Profiles 31 and 45 denote conditions requiring constant and permanent medical treatment, usually dictating service in administrative capacities. Profiles 46 and 64 place physical limits, but do not prevent regular function; for example, these recruits can serve in technical trades, but will not be posted to jobs that might place them on the frontlines in combat situations. Profile 65 indicates unsuitability for the sustained physical activity of combat soldiers, but does permit roles in the battle area. Profile 72 usually indicates minor orthopedic or other defects that do not prevent service in the armored or artillery units. Profiles 82 and 97 are fit for service in infantry or special units. These profiles are not an indication of disabilities in civilian life, and all may be appealed to a higher medical board.

After the medical, the enlistee proceeds to an interview with a "psychotechnical interviewer." The interviewer, male or female, is a soldier specially trained in a four month course in evaluation techniques, psychology, inter-personal relationships and the recognition of mental problems or stresses. The primary purpose of this interview is to chart the personality traits of the recruit - motivation, ability to withstand stress, social or anti-social behavior patterns, degree of national pride - and assess suitability for specific roles in the IDF. The interviewer's assessment, together with the IPC results and educational attainments, give the "Quality Group" (QG) to which the enlistee belongs. The combined score will indicate suitability for junior command or officer training. Irrespective of unit to which the soldier will be posted eventually, the QG will determine the attention paid to his progress through the ranks. As a general rule, a decisive majority of the enlistees fall in the command groupings - junior or commissioned.

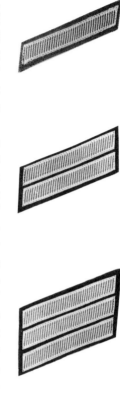

In theory, all the enlistee has to do now is wait for his final orders to report to the Induction Center. In practice, armed with the medical profile, QG rating and detailed interviews, the IDF is ready to evaluate candidates for some volunteer units of the army - the assumption being that the psychotechnical evaluation has already supplied data about suitability. These roles include aircrew, seagoing naval duties and some elite forces functions. Those found suitable are sent written material about the roles, and are invited for more complex psychotechnical tests, special medical checks and a series of interviews with psychologists and officers from the unit concerned. Though no one is forced to volunteer, the invitations are mandatory and the results will be used in further evaluation of the recruit. Each IDF unit in this category has its own criteria for acceptance.

The Air Force tests begin with a psychotechnical exam, followed by coordination and mechanical capability tests. If the candidate passes these, he will be summoned for a further series aimed at establishing personality traits, intelligence and general knowledge, basic familiarity with maths and physics and ability to absorb information flowing simultaneously from different sources - and to act on it according to the correct order of priorities. The next step is psychological and medical evaluation; here, the medical profile is not the determinant, but rather the detailed medical data. A profile of 65 might be acceptable, while a minor back or eye deficiency could cause rejection of a candidate with a 97 profile.

If all these stages have been negotiated successfully, the candidate will be called ten days earlier for induction, for a process called in the IDF "crystallization": ten days of highly intensive tests and activities - marches, weapons instruction, physical training, etc. - the purpose of which is to learn more about the candidate and establish performance under pressure. Those who do not qualify at this stage will return to the normal Induction Center process, but only after receiving an explanation of why they failed and the reassurance that this in no way damages their future in other roles in the IDF.

The successful ones, after induction, will continue through three weeks of basic infantry training and then - only then - receive Air Force uniforms and begin flying training. The course lasts 24 months, divided into six equal parts - at each of which some of the cadets will drop out. The pre-preparation consists mainly of classroom work, but does include ten flights in a Piper: the first nine are familiarization flights in which the instructor does the flying; in the last flight, the cadet will take the controls in the air. This stage is followed by an evaluation committee, which will fail a proportion of the cadets.

There follows a further period of advanced infantry training, culminating in navigation exercises on the ground. The third stage is the cadet's first introduction to jets - at this stage, two-seat trainers. Following classroom sessions on the structure of the plane, etc. - and provided the cadet passes exams - there are eight flights with an instructor, and another committee which usually fails one in five of the remainder. At this stage, decisions are made about who goes to jet fighters, who to helicopters and who to navigators' or flight engineers' course. The remainder of flying school is devoted to advancing flying skills, with a break in the stage before last for officers' school, where the cadet will qualify for parachute wings, exercise navigation on ground and at sea, undergo desert survival training and advanced infantry training - including a short period of active infantry duty. The last stage will take the cadet pilot to combat aircraft, but not to tactical combat flying. The school teaches flying; it is up to the squadrons, in a four month course, to teach the actual job of the fighter pilot. As a pre-condition to all the above, the cadet signs for two additional years in the regular army.

The Navy takes volunteers in three categories: ship officers, the Naval Commando and submariners. Crewmen on missile boats and patrol craft are theoretically not volunteers, but in practice no one is assigned to this duty unless he wants it. As a general rule, the Navy only seeks its volunteers from the officer-candidate Quality Group. The medical requirements are also not based on profile alone: 72 might be acceptable, where 97 is unsuitable if there are hearing or sight problems. Hearing must be perfect - difficult to achieve in the disco music age. Color blindness or the slightest limitation in scope of vision are disqualifiers. One other vital qualification is a love of water and the sea: sailors have to be born - they cannot be made.

The ship officers' course lasts 18 months, and carries with it an obligation to sign on for two and a half years in the regular army after the three years national service. Apart from psychometric exams, medical checks and interviews with psychologists, the Navy requires basic qualifications for each of the three disciplines of the course. Ships engineers and electronics systems officers have to be graduates of technical schools or of physics and maths from regular high schools. In the case of electronics, the candidate must have attained the level of technician at least. For deck officers, the minimum qualification is graduation from high school. Those who pass the initial evaluation will be called for five days of "crystallization" prior to induction. This will include evaluation of command ability, during which the candidate has to deliver a lecture, of over an hour, and hold the attention of his audience; the assumption is that the officer will command men whose QG is no lower than his own - and that command must emanate from respect. The candidate also submits to tests for seasickness. This disability is not a disqualifier in itself, but the criterion is the ability to continue functioning despite the sickness. The crystallization period is followed by appearance in front of a committee which measures not only performance to date, but also the candidate's determination to serve at sea.

The 18-month course begins, after induction, with four weeks of infantry training - up to Rifleman 2, the basic level of personal training. The next four months are devoted to familiarization with the sea in rubber boats and sailing craft. The cadet learns to function as crewman and finally qualifies as "boat commander." The next stage is a period of service on missile boats. This is the point at which the cadets begin to learn the specific professions for which they were accepted. Deck officer cadets are instructed in navigation, communications and seamanship. Electronics cadets are initiated in the systems in use on board the missile boats, while the engineer officer candidates learn the operating principles of the engines, technical draughtsmanship, metalworking, welding and thermodynamics.

In the following stage, the deck officer candidates qualify as watch commanders on patrol boats. Apart from sea service in routine security missions - where they will become acquainted with the weapons systems, navigation and detection equipment and shipboard and combat routines - they will spend time in the Navy's tactical training center exercising the principles of maneuver and warfare at sea. Their colleagues in electronics continue on the missile boats, while the engineer cadets are gaining their qualifications on patrol boat and missile boat engines. The final stage places all three categories of cadets as watch officers on missile boats, on the bridge, in the electronic nerve center or in the engine room. At the end of this stage, and after examination by professional boards, some cadets will be offered submarine duties, while others are posted as fully fledged officers to surface craft.

The Naval Commando requires perfect health and a high IPC score. Beyond these, the pre-induction interviews are aimed at determining degrees of integrity and initiative, willpower and willingness to withstand stress up to the outer limits. Here again, the candidate will undergo five days of crystallization before induction, mostly devoted to intense physical activity that includes a long and difficult route march. The instructors are looking, not only at who drops by the wayside, but at who helps his faltering comrades. Those who pass, and are willing to sign on for an extra

18 months of regular service, will spend their first few months after induction in the same training routine as paratroops. Their basic training - to the level of Rifleman 5 - will last four months. Immediately thereafter, the candidates proceed to a two-month course at the Infantry Squad Commanders' School to qualify as Rifleman 7. This is followed by another period of tough physical activity. Those who are rejected at this stage will retain the qualifications so far achieved as paratroopers, but will be freed of the commitment to regular service. The others begin their specific training as naval commandos. This stage lasts 18 months, at the end of which the cadets qualify with the rank of First Sergeant.

In some cases, the army offers courses, either before service or immediately after induction. In others, the enlistee may be granted deferment to complete his education outside the army before induction. In the latter case, the budding recruit will be expected to produce certification from a technical high school that he has been accepted for continuing studies to the level of technician. Those who wish to complete higher education in disciplines of interest to the army, such as medical doctors and some branches of science or engineering, must make special application to be assigned to the "Academic Reserve" where, in return for deferment, they will give the IDF extra years in their profession.

Intelligence Branch, having less interest in medical profiles, may earmark some of its potential volunteers even before enlistment. For example, the Branch keeps a watchful eye on students of Arabic, some technological professions, draughtsmen and model plane buffs while they are still at school. When it comes to Arabic, Intelligence is not satisfied with scholastic attainments alone: it invites candidates to sit for its own examinations. The Branch then puts in a request to the Induction Center to be assigned the candidates of its choice; the Center will comply with the request subject to the order of preferences for manpower assignment in the recruit's category. For those with knowledge of Arabic, but who have not majored in the subject in high school, Intelligence Branch offers pre-army courses, for male and female recruits, in advanced language studies and in other professional subjects. Other Intelligence occupations can be requested during the induction process.

Other non-combat military professions can be requested by enlistees whose basic data in advance precludes their service in line units. This group includes only sons - or sons of bereaved families, where a father or brother has fallen in action. In both these cases, recruits will be considered for combat units only if the parents have signed a declaration giving their permission (and it has to be both parents if they are alive). The professions or trades that can be chosen in this category sometimes involve intensive training, likely to be of use in later civilian life - and a commitment to additional months of service in the regular army; examples of these are trades involving electronics and computers.

Obviously, all the above occupations represent a minority of each year's intake of new recruits, but they all have the advantage that the recruits arrive at the Induction Center already knowing what their future will be. For the others, the first three or four days of army service still pose some question marks. In the interim period between enlistment and induction, those recruits who have set their aim on service in the combat units are advised to devote some effort to physical training - and one phenomenon of recent years has been the establishment of civilian courses to improve physical condition for those who feel that they need or want it.

The IDF has four distinct intake groupings a year, and the date on which the recruit will be called takes into account date of birth, school year factors, the start of courses for those already accepted for specific occupations, some attempt at homogeneity of groups by medical profile and so on. The recruits report, not to the Induction Center, but to their original place of enlistment, and are bussed to the Center: this eliminates the inequities of traveling time for those who live further away - and staggers the arrival of recruits at the Center to cut down the time spent sitting and waiting.

Even though the recruits are mentally prepared and generally willing, nevertheless the first hours in the army represent a sharp break with adolescence. In addition there are obvious tensions arousing from uncertainty about assignment: after all, the decisions taken at the Center are going to affect the recruit, not only during three years of conscript service, but for the next 36 years until he is released from the reserve army. With this in mind, the IDF Induction Center tries to make the transition as easy, pleasant and informative as possible.

Upon arrival at the Center, as they descend from the busses, the recruits are divided into platoons and companies. The groupings are

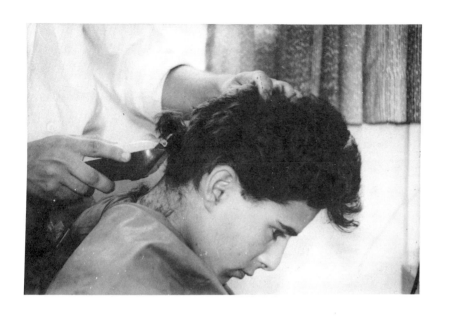

arbitrary and temporary - solely for the purposes of the first day's activities. Each platoon is greeted by the volunteer ladies of the Soldiers' Welfare Committee with a drink and cakes. They are also given, by the Committee, an overnight bag - which will be important in the next few days - and a set of postcards as a gentle hint to write home occasionally. They then settle down to watch a video film about the process through which they will be going in the next few hours.

The best part of the first morning is spent in the "Induction Stream." The first stop is the barbershop - but only for those whose hair is far too long: IDF regulations are relatively liberal when it comes to haircuts. Then, in fairly rapid succession they pass through processes of registration and identification, which include a photograph (rather unkindly, if accurately, referred to as "photo murder") complete with army identity number, yet another check of personal data, and the taking of fingerprints (purely for army identification purposes and held in IDF records). During this stage, the recruit has his first encounter with the Paymaster - at two levels. Firstly, since army pay is transferred directly to the soldier's bank account, the recruit must give details of that account: although enlistees are advised before induction to open accounts, if they did not do so, they will be helped at this stage to choose a bank branch near home and to fill in the necessary request for an account. Secondly, each soldier is given a cash advance against his pay (which will be deducted over a few months). Although no fuss is made about the point, the purpose of the advance is to iron out any immediately obvious economic inequities between those who arrived with pocket money from indulgent parents and those who did not.

The next stations in the "Stream" are medical. Dental technicians take X-rays and Polaroid photos of the recruit's teeth, again primarily for identification purposes: if the recruit needs dental treatment, that will come later. The recruit then receives injections - by air not needle: there are three of these (tetanus, smallpox and jaundice) in summer intakes, and two in winter (no anti-jaundice). The medics also take blood samples from those who are willing to give - there is no compulsion: these will be matched, for research purposes, against samples taken at the end of service. The last two steps in this section are fittings for earplugs and gasmasks. Recruits who

wear spectacles have an extra fitting for masks that will enable the wearing of both mask and glasses together.

The next two steps are probably the most significant for the recruit. At the soldier's first meeting with the quartermaster, he is issued a uniform and boots, kitbag and the other basics of personal equipment. The uniforms at this stage are standard issue IDF green combat fatigues. Dress ("walking out") uniforms are only issued after the decisions have been made about unit assignments. After a thorough check that everything that should be there was in fact issued, the recruits change into uniform - with the opportunity to exchange items that do not fit. Finally looking like soldiers, the recruits take the oath to the IDF and the State of Israel and sign a copy of the oath and an obligation to protect military secrets. The whole process so far has taken two to three hours. Now the soldiers will pack into their overnight bags whatever they will need for the next three or four days. All the rest of their kit, in the kitbags, will go into storage until they are ready to leave the Induction Center. In earlier days, the recruits had to drag their kitbags with them through every stage, with all the problems that this involved.

The process is interrupted, either at this stage or midway through the next - depending on the hour - for the soldier's first encounter with an army mess hall. IDF menus are standard throughout the army for each day. However, the variety of ethnic origins of IDF soldiers, and cooks, can make a meal something of an adventure. Great emphasis is placed on fresh fruit and vegetables: canned products are generally only for use in battle rations. At the Induction Center, particular care is taken to make the transition from mother's cooking as pleasant as possible.

Before or after lunch, depending on the hour that the platoon finished the Induction Stream, the soldiers are taken to the "Information Center." This is a slight misnomer: in fact, the Center is a large open area, around which are arranged exhibits of each of the combat arms of the IDF. The separate pavilions are the responsibility of the respective units and are manned by NCOs and officers from each. They contain personal and unit equipment, photo and map displays of the unit's history, some explanation of the way in which its soldiers are trained and serve and video films or slides that may relate to any of these aspects. The new recruits are taken around, shown the films and given an opportunity to hear, and question, the officers and NCOs about life in the unit. The pavilions include the Armored Corps, Artillery Corps, Combat Engineers, three separate infantry brigades (Golani, Givati and Paratroops: Nahal does not exhibit since its recruits have requested the brigade upon enlistment), and two missile units (ground forces anti-tank and Air Force surface-to-air).

This exercise, which takes some three hours, is designed to help the new recruit reach his own decisions about where he would like to serve. Experience shows that more than 50% of the recruits in fact make their decisions while going around the exhibits - or change their minds about previous selections. Those who already know where they are going, or whose medical profiles preclude service in combat units, do not need this tour, though many of them take it voluntarily to get a better idea of the scope of the IDF.

The evening, after the soldier's second army meal, is devoted to lectures to all the companies of the day's new intake. The first lecture is given by the base sergeant major: it relates to basic concepts of discipline - what constitutes an order, who should be saluted (important for new recruits, but relaxed in most units after basic training), how to wear a beret, the correct form of questions to avoid charges of insubordination and so on. If the sergeant major is dealing with matters of importance for the next three years, the second lecture is oriented to matters of concern during the next two or three days. The Head of Classification and Assignment outlines for the recruits the options open to them and describes the processes through which they will go on the following day. It is important that they start their interviews as relaxed as possible, and prior knowledge is the best way of relieving the almost inevitable nervousness.

The recruits spend the night in a tent camp organized by companies. The camp area includes a clubhouse and canteen, where they can buy snacks, soft or hot drinks and various necessities - at the reduced prices that will become part of their army life. In addition, the area is amply equipped with public telephones. The IDF is generally attuned to the fact that parents want to hear frequently from their sons and daughters (the army has been known to go to war with mobile Ministry of Communications phone trucks hovering in the background, bearing the legend "Soldier, Phone Home!").

Throughout the induction process, random polls are taken among the intakes about the experiences in the Center, in a constant effort to amend or improve services, facilities, food, etc.

The second day, after breakfast, begins with a parade of all the previous day's intake. The Center is now ready to redivide the recruits into more homogenous platoons for the classification process. The criteria are medical profile, quality group, previously expressed willingness to serve in volunteer units and decisions already made in the evaluation stages after initial registration for service. These platoons are now the groupings in which the recruits will go through their individual interviews. The classification officers with whom they will be meeting are reservists, who bring to this function years of experience, both in the IDF generally and in this specific process.

The interviewer has at his disposal, and has already read, the individual's "manila" - a folder that contains all that the IDF knows so far about the recruit: IPC, QG, medical profile, psychotechnical interviewer's report, competence in Hebrew, limitations on service because of social welfare problems, family status (if the recruit is an only child, or the family has sustained the loss of a father or son in service, he will not be sent to a combat unit without specific consent from his parents) and so on. Interviews invariably start with an attempt to put the recruit at ease before the serious questions begin.

The first question relates to the recruit's own desires. Provided that he is making a choice of unit that suits his medical profile and other data, he is asked to assess the intensity of desire on a scale of one to seven, and then state second and third choices. If the recruit's wishes conflict with his qualifications, or if the unit of choice is not presently recruiting - the interviewer will help him towards a more realistic selection. Although the classification officer is primarily seeking recruits for the field combat units, he is not at this stage forcing decisions on the interviewee. His duty is to guide the recruit to a choice - not make it for him. He will, however, note on the manila comments about willingness or the lack of it. If medical or social welfare problems not previously noted surface during the interview, the officer will note a need to refer the recruit to a medical board or a conditions of service officer. If the problem justifies alteration of already recorded data, the recruit will return later to the interviewer for another session. For example, a recruit who very much wants to serve in a field unit, but who has some recorded medical disability, might in certain circumstances succeed in convincing the doctors that desire can overcome disability. It is obviously somewhat harder for a recruit who is physically fit to convince the interviewer that his place is in an administrative capacity in the rear. In any event, the classification officer is not making decisions, but only recording facts and impressions.

Once the entire platoon has completed its interviews, it will move on to a second series of lectures. A medical officer talks about hygiene, preventive medicine and army procedures for dealing with sickness. He is followed by a conditions of service officer who, in general terms, informs the soldiers about their rights and obligations in the area of social welfare. The rest of the day is spent in physical training. Meanwhile, the manilas are being collected and sorted into two groups: those for whom the classification process seems to be at an end; those who are destined for additional evaluation because of expressed desires for service in volunteer units, requests for courses or a need for reevaluation by medical boards or conditions of service officers.

In the evening, while the recruits are enjoying a movie or relaxing in the club, senior officers of the Center are reviewing the manilas and deciding assignments. For them, there are three decisive criteria: the recruit's personal data, his expressed preferences and the current needs of the army. Obviously, the latter takes precedence over all else, but experience has shown that 50% of recruits will get their first preference and another 25% will be assigned their second choice. For some recruits, this will be the end of the induction and classification process. For others, the decisions taken at this session will lead to further evaluation by the units concerned or requested.

On the third morning, the platoons return to the parade ground for reconstitution according to destination. From the parade, the platoons destined for field units move on to medical checks by doctors from those units. This takes the best part of the morning, and anyone found unfit at this stage will be returned to the classification stage. The others go on to draw the personal equipment and uniforms of their assigned unit, reclaim their kitbags, and leave the Center for the basic training camps. They have one last chance before boarding the busses to question the assignment

and request an interview with a senior officer. Those who chose exclusively volunteer units, asked for accelerated officer training in communications, adjutancy, ordnance, etc., or who are deemed suitable for special courses (technical trades) will stay on in the Center for their next stage.

Evaluation at the Volunteer Center begins on the third afternoon. This stage is the responsibility of officers and NCOs from the unit requested, and each has its own procedures. A volunteer for the paratroops, for example, will fill in a detailed questionnaire and then go through a series of interviews. He will be asked why he wants to get into the paratroop brigade, and why he thinks he is suitable. He will then proceed to a thorough medical check, in which the doctor is looking for the specific disabilities that disqualify a soldier from parachute training. The following day, the budding volunteers will be put through physical tests against norms and a number of difficult team assignments. Each soldier is watched closely to see how he performs under criteria of willingness to extend a hand to others, leadership, clear thinking and physical ability. This is followed by a sociometric session, which assesses each volunteer's impressions of his comrades. At the end of the day, the recruit's scores will be matched with the other data in his manila. Good results are not necessarily a guarantee of acceptance: on an average, there are three or four applicants for every place in the brigade. If the recruit has passed and been accepted, he will depart next morning for the paratroop basic training base. If not, he returns to the classification process.

Volunteers accepted for the paratroops are destined for any of four echelons within the brigade: the paratroop battalions, the brigade anti-tank missile unit, combat engineers unit or the reconnaissance unit. Training routines are tough and long. The first month is spent in basics: the function of the infantryman as an individual, proficiency with small arms and physical training to bring all the recruits up to the standards set by the brigade. The second and third months are devoted to field training up to the level of company in various combat conditions - and including familiarity with armored personnel carriers. A three-week "time out" takes the companies to IDF Parachute School to qualify for their wings. Then, another month is devoted to recapitulation of things already learnt and in training to function in battalion situations. Basic paratroop

training ends with a 24 hour, 90 kilometer route march, culminating in award of the coveted red beret. The companies then spend nine months in line duties and training, before being withdrawn for three months training as squad commanders: all paratroops complete IDF Squad Commanders' School.

The notes unobtrusively made by the officer on the sidelines at the Volunteer Center, also included earmarking of candidates for the brigade's reconnaissance unit. Those accepted for this elite unit, after additional crystallization exercises, will join the other companies for basic training, but part company after six months for specialist training. They will spend another nine months in advanced training and will then proceed to a separate squad commanders' course tailored to this unit's own needs. A high proportion of soldiers in the reconnaissance unit will continue, after 24 months in the army, to IDF Officers' School.

The other infantry brigades of the standing army are in theory not volunteer units - although in practice at least 90% of the intake directed to Golani Brigade have in fact requested the assignment. Recruits to Golani transfer from the Induction Center to the Brigade's training base on the third day. However, formal basic training only begins two or three weeks later. The time is not wasted. During the first week, the recruits are given physical training and talks on the combat heritage of the Brigade and the areas of the country in which they will serve. Part of the second week is devoted to small arms training and the firing ranges. At the end of the two weeks, those recruits who want to join the Brigade's reconnaissance unit can apply and go through the selection tests and procedures.

Once the selection of candidates is complete, the combat engineering and anti-tank units of the Brigade make their choices from among the intake. Companies for basic training are constituted according to these selections, even though everybody goes through the same initial course. The recruits already know at this stage to which battalion of the Brigade they will be assigned. Recruit training is divided into two distinct stages. The first stage, which lasts two and a half months, is devoted to weapons training and steady improvement of physical performance. The second stage takes the soldier through combat training as an individual and up to company level tactics as mechanized infantry, with the capability of functioning as airborne. During this stage, soldiers will be assigned their eventual roles in their platoons - machinegunner, radio operator, etc. - and selection will be made of candidates for courses as medical corpsmen, sharpshooters and so on. Upon completion of basic training, the companies join their battalions, either in line duties in the north or in training.

After nine months in the battalion, all Golani soldiers proceed to three months in the IDF Squad Commanders' School, during which they will go through officer selection procedures. Those chosen - if they are willing to sign for an extra year in the army - will go straight to a six month course at IDF Officers' School immediately upon completion of their squad commanders' course. Outstanding soldiers in the Brigade may also go to IDF Parachute School to qualify for wings.

The route for soldiers in Givati Brigade is similar to that of Golani, with minor differences. In the course of basic training, in addition to mechanized infantry tactics, the companies will also specialize in seaborne operations. Though the IDF has never felt the need for marines as a regular entity, Givati is trained to function as such if the need arises.

Combat engineers also complete a full infantry course of 19 weeks - attaining the status of Rifleman 5 like their comrades in the infantry brigades. However, their training in the use of explosives, the laying or clearing of minefields and other techniques proceeds in parallel with infantry skills. Following the course, the engineers spend six months in a line battalion, continuing their training at company and battalion level and participating in combined exercises with armor, artillery, etc. By companies, with a few exceptions, they then proceed to IDF Squad Commanders' School, at the end of which those found suitable will continue at IDF Officers' School. The others - now Rifleman 7 - go on to a three month course to attain the grade of Pathfinder 8. At this stage they are getting advanced training in explosives and mine laying and clearing from the viewpoint of commanders. Upon completion of this course, while some report back to their battalions as squad commanders and others go to basic training or stay put in the advanced course as instructors, a proportion of the graduates will be selected for specialist training in bomb disposal, water crossing and bridging techniques and the use of heavy engineering equipment.

For recruits requesting naval seagoing trades, the Volunteer Center process begins with a series of talks or lectures on the roles open to the new intakes in the Israel Navy, followed by individual sessions with a naval psychologist: since a ship at sea is a close-knit family functioning in a confined space, a seaman's ability to fit in socially is a prime condition. Then come the inevitable psychological tests and medical checks. Those who pass all these obstacles are ready to be taken for six days "crystallization" in a naval training base. These days will be devoted, among other things, to finding out whether the recruit is suitable for service at sea and in the specific duty that he is requesting. At the end of the period, the recruits return to the Induction Center to draw their equipment and uniforms as sailors in the Israel Navy. However, there is one more step on dry land: basic infantry training.

All soldiers, sailors and airmen of the IDF undergo basic infantry training. Nobody expects all of them to function as infantrymen. For those not destined for the infantry, this form of training achieves other purposes that the army considers essential as the first building block. Rifleman 2 - the four-week course to which non-combat troops go - first and foremost transforms the recruit from civilian to soldier. He learns in rapid time the meaning of discipline within a system where everybody obeys orders from the general downwards. He also learns to function with, rely upon and help others who were perfect strangers - and who might have come from totally different backgrounds and environments.

The route marches (bearing a comrade on a stretcher) and runs, which get progressively harder, yet make allowances for those who really cannot achieve the peak, are designed both to bring the soldier to his potential conditioning and to give him a new awareness of his own capabilities. Weapons training, including the Uzzi sub machinegun and Galil assault carbine, is necessary for all soldiers: all IDF personnel might have to stand guard duties or need to defend themselves in a variety of circumstances. Unarmed combat, apart from instilling personal discipline and coordination, answers the same need for knowledge in self-defense. Acquaintance with army radio equipment and rudimentary first aid may stand a soldier in good stead no matter where he serves. The ultimate objective of the training is to produce a soldier with basic military skills, capable of functioning with others and ready, physically and mentally, to absorb the knowledge of his ultimate trade.

In all armies, and the IDF is no exception, basic training is wrapped in layers of popular legend and hearsay that all amount to one apparent "fact": "the purpose is to pound the recruit down to a submissive and humiliated jelly in order to refashion the soldier." Although reinforced by generations of books and movies about army life, the legend distorts the real objectives and dismisses the amount of serious thought that has been devoted to the soldier's first weeks and months in uniform. In the IDF, first of all, arrival at basic training camp marks a change of jurisdiction. Up to this point in time, the enlistee and inductee have been under the jurisdiction of IDF Manpower Branch. The Branch will continue to be an ever-present factor in the background of service, promotion and welfare of the soldier until he is released from reserve duty, at age 54, but other army echelons are now coming to the fore. If the soldier is destined for service in the ground forces, he is now the joint responsibility of Training Branch, Ground Forces Command (which guides and develops tactical and inter-arm doctrines) and of the unit in which he will spend the next years. Behind all these hover professional advisory echelons, such as ·the IDF Behavioral Sciences Department.

As for the legends, IDF regulations governing the treatment of recruits during basic training are extremely strict. Exercises and training sessions must be just that - and no more: in other words, soldiers may not be put through additional or repeat exercises as punishment or attempts at humiliation. Disciplinary infractions can only be dealt with under the provisions of the army code of laws. A soldier cannot be punished by hours on the drill ground or additional guard duties. If a squad commander or drill sergeant is convinced of the necessity to repeat a training session, because of unsatisfactory performance, he must have the permission of a training officer of the rank of lieutenant and up - and in no event may the repeat take place after 22:00 hours at night. Any excesses or attempts at humiliation of recruits by instructors are punishable offenses.

Within the context of basic training, the IDF departs from the pattern of many other armies: squad and platoon NCOs are not long-service regulars, but national servicemen and women who are only a few months older than the recruits. Consequently, they are not that far removed from the experiences of basic training to have forgotten the difficulties and traumas which they experienced. In recent years, a high proportion of the instruction in all basic training installations of the IDF has been given by women NCOs. Although this occasionally causes some initial discomfort among the "male chauvinists," it has softened the legends.

Tank crewmen, artillerymen, anti-aircraft gun and missile crews, medical corpsmen, radio operators and field intelligence personnel will spend two months in qualifying as Rifleman 3. Beyond the objectives of Rifleman 2, which all concentrate on the function of the individual, this course assumes that all soldiers in a battlefield environment might face a sudden or temporary need to function with, or as infantrymen. For most of these soldiers, the basic training will take place within the frame of their own ultimate units, and with specific inputs appropriate to their future assignment. Thus, for example, tank crewmen will have opportunity to watch tank exercises during basic training, and will receive lessons or lectures on the combat heritage of the Armored Corps: since assignments to brigades are made immediately upon arrival, and the recruits will train in the same companies to which they will belong through Armor School and field service, the accent will be on the history of their own brigade.The infantry course itself, in the Corps' own basic training installation, will bring the recruits up to a level of function as crews - parallel to that of an infantry squad. The course ends with a 50 kilometer route march and a ceremony at which the recruits are sworn in as fully fledged soldiers of the IDF and the Armored Corps.

For stage two of armor training, the recruits are assigned their jobs in the tank: the assignments are made according to expressed wishes matched against physical coordination abilities and the ubiquitous IPC and QG ratings. From here on, the tank crewmen will be escorted through the seven-week training course by the tank, platoon and company commanders with whom they will serve in their battalions. The course proceeds along three parallel routes, according to the assigned roles - drivers, gunners and loader-radio operators. Each route includes classroom theory, work with stripped down equipment and simulators and practical training on the tanks.

The training, much of which is again given by women instructors, does not include tank tactics and formations. The purpose of the Armor School is to produce crewmen proficient in handling the individual tank. Their training as combat soldiers will take another three months, which they will spend as the "in-training" company in their battalions. There, alongside the veteran companies, they will learn their function on the battlefield as coherent crews individually and in platoon and company formation. Upon completion of the three months, the company takes its place in the tank laager as a combat ready force. At this stage, the battalion begins its selection of future tank commanders, based on "Integrated Group Rating" (IGR). The IGR is a combination of the Quality Group score, the results of sociometric evaluation and the fitness rating given by the soldier's immediate commanders.

Here, as in other echelons of the IDF, the significance of sociometric evaluation is that soldiers are being given a voice in choosing their own commanders. As far as is practical, the IDF prefers to have officers and NCOs lead by virtue of respect accorded them by their fellows, rather than by dumb obedience to rank badges. Those chosen will spend a few weeks at Tank Commanders' School where, apart from training for command, they will learn the other two trades that complement their own basic knowledge: the assumption is that a tank commander should be familiar with all the functions of his crew. During this course, the Corps is conducting officer selection evaluation and tests. For those chosen, an officer's commission will come at roughly 15 months after induction into the IDF.

With minor variations, the training of all other IDF personnel follows one or other of the above patterns: basic training to the appropriate level of infantry skills, followed by professional training - with ample opportunity for advancement and promotion. No matter what arm of the IDF the soldier is going to serve in, the army wants its NCOs and officers while they are young. One side effect of this policy is that junior officers receive their commissions before higher education of the kind offered by military academies in some countries. On the other hand, the IDF is gaining officers who have served in the ranks and whose leadership capabilities have already been proven and noted. The system also implies that social background and influence carry no weight in officer candidate selection.

To compensate for the commissioning of officers at the age of nineteen, the IDF offers, and indeed encourages, captains, majors and upwards to take time out for academic education. This is often financed by the army on condition that university courses of three years duration are completed in two: in practical terms, the implication is a three semester academic year. Since promotion comes fast in this environment and in an army that is required by Israel's security circumstances to prove itself constantly, it is not unusual to find line battalion commanders in their late twenties or early thirties - and who already have academic degrees in subjects of their own choice.

Throughout their service, IDF soldiers are escorted by extensive social welfare services. Each unit of the army has a "Conditions of Service" NCO or officer, whose job it is to be thoroughly acquainted with all the men and women serving in the unit, and to see that they do get any assistance to which they are entitled. The pay for conscript soldiers is little more than pocket money, but the IDF does provide family support payments for wives, parents and other dependents. In cases where sickness or disability in the family justify it, the IDF arranges postings so that the soldier may be home almost every evening. For new immigrant soldiers with no family in the country, the Conditions of Service officer will arrange housing allowances, foster homes and a trip abroad to visit family, partially financed by the IDF, at least once during national service.

The care offered by IDF Manpower Branch to its soldiers is strongly reinforced by a very active Soldiers' Welfare Committee, which maintains hostels and recreation facilities for soldiers on leave, provides clubs and entertainment equipment to army units, gives presents to all IDF personnel on annual occasions such as Independence Day and the Jewish New Year. The Committee, which is supported by public subscription, also runs commissaries on bases and discount shopping facilities for families of soldiers. Local branches in various parts of the country staff free snack bars and other facilities at which soldiers are welcome to stop on their travels. Beyond the actual material comfort of these services lies the strong sense that Israeli society is supportive and caring about the men and women who protect and defend the country.

THE
FAMILY-
GOLANI
BRIGADE

On 28 February 1948, the Hagana High Command ordered the creation of a new brigade, to take responsibility for the valleys and hills of Lower Galilee: that brigade, Golani, was to become the only IDF infantry brigade to maintain an unbroken history as a regular unit of the army.

All the 1948 brigades were directly responsible to the Hagana High Command, yet their commanders wielded authority akin to that of local warlords. Thus, Golani, which inherited one Haifa-based Field Corps battalion and maintained two others in the Jezreel and Beisan valleys, now had to do its own recruiting and see to its own logistics. The obvious reservoirs of manpower for a brigade that was to operate in the valleys and in Galilee were the farming villages of the area - all of whom were experienced in self-defense. The Brigade Operations Officer, who was destined to take over as Brigade Commander in May 1948, also issued a special call for veterans of the World War II British army in order to benefit from their experience in organization and communications.

Golani would shortly spin off its Haifa battalion to form an independent territorial force in the Northern Galilee panhandle, and in turn would begin to receive recruits from the towns of central Israel, with a sprinkling of volunteers from abroad, but the character and lifestyle of the brigade was determined by its first intakes. The men and women of Golani possessed all the traits of farmers: they were obstinate, single-mindedly devoted to their objective, rooted in the soil and deeply attached to the areas in which they would have to fight, quiet-spoken and simple in their needs and attitudes.

There were no army camps, except for the few that would become available as the British withdrew from those areas firmly under Hagana control. The platoons and companies were based in the farming communities. They ate in the dining halls of the kibbutzim and with the families of the moshavim. In some cases the Brigade supplied food to the settlements, or paid for what its men ate. In others, no recompense was asked or accepted. Enlistment was not restricted to men of military age. Older settlers - men and women - helped out with the administrative and logistic functions. In one classic case, a battalion commander, later to be a brigade commander and major general in the IDF, recruited his mother to cook for his men.

Weapons were in even shorter supply than men and women to wield them. Hagana inventories listed a total of 10,500 rifles, 3500 submachineguns, 935 light and medium machineguns and 750 mortars. Golani's share of this treasure amounted to 45 rifles and seven light machineguns for each of its battalions. Over the years, some of the settlements had acquired their own small arsenals of weapons for self-defense. The Brigade commander, faced with a shifting battlefield, borrowed weapons from kibbutzim in relatively quiet areas for companies that were deep in combat with Arab irregulars or with the invading armies. Some rifles were loaned willingly, others hesitantly because the threat of attack could materialize virtually anywhere and anytime, but all were returned as soon as possible.

In May 1948, when the Hagana High Command became the IDF General Staff, with full powers of coordination, each brigade was making its own choice between two prevailing doctrines: that of the innovative and unorthodox Palmach, or that of the veterans from the British Army, with its traditions of organization, rank and tactics. Under the influence of the brigade commander, a Hagana veteran who had served in the British Army, Golani became a synthesis of both. The Brigade was better disciplined and organized than the Palmach, but more open to improvisation than the units modeled on the British pattern. One element was to prevail throughout the War of Independence: the unique contribution of the men and women from the kibbutzim and moshavim. Their entire life was one of deep commitment to their fellow settlers and to the principles of mutual aid. This inherent trait, combined with the "brotherhood of arms" of any good combat unit, were to forge a unique family; all cared about each, and an officer's ability to command was dependent on personal example and the care that he took of his men. This heritage was to pass down the generations, through all the peaks and troughs of Golani in years to come.

Within Golani's assigned area, two kibbutzim - Kfar Szold in the Galilee panhandle, and Tirat Zvi in the Beisan Valley - had already been attacked in the months between the November 1947 UN decision and late February 1948, when the Brigade was formally established. The High Command's instructions, emanating from David Ben-Gurion, were very clear: no settlement, no matter how desperate its position, was to be abandoned. This order could not be obeyed without control of the roads. The sole main road connecting the north of the country with the center ran through Wadi Millich - the only route that avoided the Arab "Little Triangle." Deeper into Golani's area, the east-west roads past Mount Tabor and along the Jordan Valley were constantly harassed by the Arab villages that straddled them. In the mixed towns of Tiberias and Safad, the Jewish populations were under constant attack. In addition, the Arabs were preparing to seize the evacuated British bases at key points.

Throughout March, units of Golani participated in local actions, some very fierce, to repel Arab attacks on outlying settlements, and on the roads. On 4 April, soldiers of Golani's Dror Battalion reinforced the members of Kibbutz Mishmar Haemek, in the face of an all-out assault by the Palestine Liberation Army. The kibbutz occupied a strategic hillside at the western entrance to the Jezreel Valley close to Wadi Millich, and had been chosen by Kaukji, the PLA commander, as the place to demonstrate the true might of his forces by cutting off the northeast. It was a landmark battle in many senses. Firstly, Kaukji used artillery for the first time in the conflict between Jew and Arab. Secondly, it provided proof that Hagana units could coordinate efficiently: the relief of the siege called into play elements of Golani, Carmeli and Alexandroni Brigades, and a battalion of the Palmach, supported by two light planes of the Hagana Air Service. At the tactical level, the battle supplied valuable information on Kaukji s doctrines for the use of artillery, daylight assaults and so on, and conversely demonstrated the defender's ability to make use of terrain and deceptive feints by small forces.

Meanwhile, the situation in Tiberias had worsened. The town resembled a many-layered sandwich: a small Jewish community in the old city by the lakeside surrounded by hostile Arabs, and cut off from the main Jewish population higher up the slopes of the town, who in turn were dominated by a chain of Arab villages along the hilltop. For some nights, the old city defenders had been supplied, first by swimmers, and then by fishing boats coming in from the lake. On April 18, after almost a week of fighting, Barak battalion of Golani, and a Palmach company, smashed through to re-establish contact between the old and new towns - and Arab resistance crumbled. British convoys that had been standing by to evacuate the Jews were put to use for the same purpose by the Arabs, though no one was asking them to go.

In the ten days that followed, the same battalion staged an attack on Zemach, with its police post that controlled a vital crossroads to the south of the Sea of Galilee, and reinforced Kibbutz Gesher on the road between Beisan and the kibbutzim of the Jordan Valley. Meanwhile, Allon Battalion seized the recently vacated British police station and army camp at Rosh Pina. On 3 May, in preparation to meet the coming invasion, elements of Dror Battalion demolished the bridges linking Arab Nazareth in Lower Galilee and Shfaram at the exit to the coastal plain north of Haifa. On 6 May, Barak Battalion fought a bitter but successful engagement at Sejera, to relieve the pressure on the road from Jezreel to Upper Galilee.

On 11 May, Allon Battalion joined Yiftach Brigade of the Palmach in relieving the siege of Jewish Safad, thereby creating one of the legends of the War of Independence. During the battle, the Hagana force used a Davidka homemade mortar, which made much more noise than it did damage. The police fortress above Safad, which was in Arab hands, was virtually impregnable. On the morning after the battle in the lower town, a 17-year-old from a nearby kibbutz, convinced that the fortress must already be in Hagana hands, and unaware that his comrades were regrouping to assault it, walked up to the huge iron gates and knocked. There was no answer; the Arab garrison had fled, apparently convinced that the Hagana had atom bombs.

On 12 May, with only hours remaining to independence and invasion, Gideon Battalion completed the occupation of the town of Beisan. Not only was the eastern line, facing the invaders, now intact, but in mopping up the area the Battalion had laid its hands on considerable quantities of desperately needed arms and ammunition.

In the afternoon of 14 May, in the name of the Provisional State Council, David Ben-Gurion proclaimed the independence of Israel. The invasion of Israel by five regular Arab armies was underway mere hours after Ben Gurion's proclamation. On the night of 15 May, the Syrian Army began a systematic bombardment of the kibbutzim around the Sea of Galilee, followed in the morning by aerial attacks. Syrian troops and tanks began to move down from the

Golan Heights to the south of the lake, in a move aimed at Tiberias and Lower Galilee.

The Syrian force - an infantry brigade supported by an armored car battalion, a regiment of artillery and a company of tanks - were held through two critical days at the fences of Masada and Shaar HaGolan, and by three Golani platoons in the town of Zemach. Time was vital for preparation of the defenses of the twin kibbutzim of Degania Aleph and Degania Bet, on the Syrians' road to Tiberias and the north. During the night of 17 May, Golani mobilized every available truck and tractor from the nearby settlements, and ran them time and again down the steep road west of the Deganias with headlights on, then back up in darkness. The ruse convinced the Syrians that tanks were pouring into the area. A few more hours were gained. But, on the morning of 18 May, a Syrian armored car column dislodged the defenders of Zemach. The survivors struggled back to join the men and women on the fences of the Deganias. That night, Masada and Shaar HaGolan were also evacuated.

At dawn on 20 May, the Syrians reached the perimeter of the Deganias, where they were held by a mix of dogged determination and some home-made Molotov cocktails. A delegation from the Jordan valley kibbutzim had gone on 19 May to explain their desperate plight to Ben Gurion; the Prime Minister ordered up to the sector two of the IDF's five French field artillery pieces. These 65mm 19th century guns - nicknamed "Napoleonchicks" - which had arrived in the country only six days earlier, lacked sights and rangefinders. They were placed on the hills above the lakeside kibbutzim, while their gunners assessed range by lobbing shells into the water and watching for splashes. The use of artillery took the Syrians by surprise. By 23 May, they had withdrawn from the Deganias, Zemach, Masada and Shaar HaGolan, leaving behind quantities of artillery, armored vehicles, arms and ammunition.

Meanwhile, following seizure of the Naharaim electric power plant by the Jordanian Arab Legion, nearby Kibbutz Gesher had feverishly prepared its defenses, which included a company from Barak Battalion. Two nearby bridges across the Jordan were demolished. However on 15 May, the Iraqi Army reached the river and, under cover of heavy artillery bombardment on the kibbutz, began to construct a pontoon bridge. They soon desisted, since they had found a shallow ford further south. By the morning of 16 May, the

Iraqis had encircled Gesher and occupied a high hill to the northwest. Supported by artillery, they began a series of assaults on the kibbutz and the neighboring police fortress. But all were repelled by the kibbutzniks and by Golani. Unable to break the perimeter defenses, the Iraqis settled down to a steady bombardment, with occasional aerial bombings. On 18 May, a Golani company made a futile attempt to regain Carmel Hill to the immediate northwest. Then, on 22 May, a detachment of Gideon Battalion occupied the Crusader fortress of Belvoir, which towered over the shallow ford that the Iraqis were using. An Iraqi force that was climbing to take Belvoir was taken by surprise and routed. The Iraqi army promptly withdrew across the Jordan, and then left the area completely when the "Napoleonchiks" from Degania were brought up and began a bombardment.

Apart from occasional artillery clashes and patrol activity, the battle for the Jordan Valley was over. But its significance was far greater than the actual achievements on the ground. The success of Golani and the settlers in driving back two invading regular armies raised morale in all the kibbutzim and army units that had doubted their own ability to face the Egyptian, Lebanese, Syrian, Iraqi and Jordanian onslaughts.

From 28 May to 30 May, units of the Brigade swept the western and southern slopes of the Jezreel valley, to contain any Iraqi Army breakout from Samaria towards the coast, and to pave the way for an offensive against Jenin. Early in June, Golani battalions participated in an unsuccessful counter-offensive around Jenin. In July 1948, after an uneasy truce, there were ten days of bitter fighting against the PLA in lower Galilee, mostly in defense of the strategic Sejera crossroads, that would become known as "Golani Junction," while other elements of the Brigade participated in the operation that secured Nazareth and the roads north. The main battles for Galilee were over, but mopping up would continue until October. In November 1948, Golani was ordered south to join in the last major offensive to clear the Egyptian army out of the western Negev and push them back beyond El-Arish - an operation that lasted well into January 1949.

In early March, there were clear indications that the Jordanian Arab Legion intended to lay claim to the southern Negev. In what was to be the last dramatic operation of the War of Independence,

two IDF columns raced southwards through the desert to Eilat. The westerly route, over rough terrain, was taken by Palmach Negev Brigade, while Golani infantry and mechanized units headed down the Arava Valley. Golani had the easier route but had to contend with the Arab Legion. The IDF's last operational message of the War of Independence was radioed in the early evening of 10 March 1949, to Southern Command hq. It read: "Relay to Government of Israel: ...Palmach Negev and Golani Brigade present the Gulf of Eilat to the State of Israel."

The kibbutzniks and moshavniks, some of whom had been in uniform since the early 1940s, went home. In keeping with the General Staff recognition that the population of Israel was too small to maintain a large standing army, Golani was chosen to be one of only two regular infantry brigades; the rest of the IDF infantry force would be reservists. Within the tiny manpower pool available, the induction system was channeling the few who had completed secondary education to administration, logistics, intelligence and the technical trades. Golani and the other standing army brigades got a very high proportion of new immigrants, straight from the transit camps. On the average, their education level and motivation was low, and few even knew Hebrew - the language of their new home. In addition, with too few men to go around, IDF Manpower Branch was sending all three basic medical classifications - Combat Fitness 1 and 2, and Fit for Service Occupations only - to the line units. Even then, some of the companies were little more than skeletons of their full strength.

The Brigade senior officers were mostly veterans of the 1948 war, transferred from units that had ceased to exist. Each brought with him the tactical concepts, standards of discipline and military vocabulary of his previous command. And some of the junior officers and NCOs operated on the time-worn principle that good soldiers are made by breaking raw recruits, then remolding them into the required shape. This brutal approach was neither uncommon, nor restricted to the infantry. The new refugee recruits, though fiercely loyal to the country, were reluctant soldiers. There were economic and social problems "at home" in the transit camps. Theft of personal possessions and even some military equipment was a daily occurrence. One Golani company awoke to a new day at Zemach camp to find that all their boots were missing. A soldier had sold them in Haifa during the night to send money to his family.

Within the limitations of tiny defense budgets, and the reticence of potential suppliers to deal with Israel, the available weapons were Czech rifles, with a built-in magazine that held only five rounds, and Sten machineguns, originally conceived as cheap throwaways for British paratroops to use until their "real" weapons were dropped. As for transport, each battalion had one stationwagon, a tender and a single truck. Personal equipment was of decidedly inferior quality. One company had their leave stopped by their commander because they dared respond to the battalion CO's interest in their problems by showing him boots that were tied with string to hold the soles on.

Despite all the problems, including desertions and absences without leave, the senior officers of Golani determined to make do with the human and material resources they had. Within the concepts of those days, training meant route marches and runs, and repetitive platoon and company assaults on fortified positions. More often than not, the recruits were worked to exhaustion simply to keep them busy. But alongside the purely military aspects, tremendous efforts were made to teach the boys Hebrew, reading, writing and the rudiments of arithmetic - this by a few hardy souls among the officers and NCOs - and attention was paid to their home environment and problems.

In parallel with the poor state of affairs in IDF combat units, it was becoming clear that the Arab armies had recovered from their trauma of defeat in the 1948 war. On 2 May 1951, a reserve platoon, on a routine training exercise, discovered that a Syrian force had crossed the Jordan near its junction with the Sea of Galilee, and had dug in on Tel Motile and two other hills in the demilitarized zone on the Israeli side. In the first clash, four soldiers were killed. A Golani company was called up, then a battalion. The battle escalated as the Syrians brought in mortar and artillery fire, and Golani received air support from four Spitfires that were under orders not to open fire. The battle raged, with frequent assaults by both sides, and with a short cease fire organized by UN observers, through to 6 May. After fierce fighting Golani drove the Syrians back across the border, but the cost was heavy: 40 Israeli dead and 72 wounded.

Tel Motile lit some red lights in the IDF. The soldiers of Golani had fought well and obstinately. The senior officers performed magnificently, in the best IDF tradition of "Follow me!" But something was sadly wrong with the standards of leadership at the squad and platoon levels. The implications were to rock the foundations of IDF thinking. The General Staff took a series of decisions that were to change the entire structure and performance of the IDF. The combat brigades began to get their fair share of secondary school graduates and recruits from the kibbutzim and moshavim. If Golani had been a cross-section of the new immigrant population, it was to become a mirror reflection of Israeli society. More emphasis was placed on the training of NCOs and junior officers for combat duties, and the level of leadership began to improve accordingly.

In the interim, officers were transferred into Golani from among kibbutz and moshav youth, of the same background from which Golani had been raised in 1948. The new officers brought with them a repugnance for the callousness of their predecessors. Their soldiers were to be treated as human beings. If some company commanders had previously kept their distance, the officers and men now ate, slept and trained together. If problems back home in the transit camps had been dealt with by the army bureaucracy, the men were now to find that their own company commanders were visiting their families to see if anything could be done to help.

Simultaneously, the standard of equipment, both personal and unit, was upgraded within the limitations of the available resources. Then, in 1954, a decision was made that was to revolutionize the face of the IDF. Young women conscripts began to be channeled to the combat units as clerks, radio operators and teachers. The presence of women humanized the atmosphere - but it was destined to do other things as well. Firstly, the teaching of Hebrew and basic schooling for immigrant recruits could now move into high gear. And what the women taught was backed up by platoon, company and battalion commanders, who made a point of acquainting their men with the history and lifestyle of the areas in which they trained and through which they marched. Golani like the other combat units was becoming a powerful force in the integration of its recruits into the life of their new country. Secondly, the women were setting a new standard of performance. Of their own volition they took part

in the route marches and runs, and even in the assault exercises. True, they did not carry a full pack, but even so a soldier would think twice before dropping out when a woman was marching alongside him.

One innovation aimed at improving IDF performance was to prove a mixed blessing for Golani. The General Staff ordered the creation of an elite unit named "101," which was a cross between a commando unit and a long-range penetration group. The new echelon, which would shortly be merged with the paratroops, set completely different, much higher standards for the entire IDF to emulate. But until 1955, it was assigned virtually all the combat missions against terrorists, who were becoming a serious factor in daily life, and the Arab armies. Within Golani, a feeling began to develop that all their intensive training was meaningless, since their red-bereted comrades were doing all the work and reaping all the glory. Even worse, and through no fault of their own, Golani and the other standing army units found themselves the butt of ridicule because the paratroops were making all the headlines. Despite the protests of successive brigade commanders, from 1951 through 1954, Golani was only assigned routine security and guard duties in the north of the country.

At dawn on 25 October 1955, in a move reminiscent of the Syrians at Tel Motile, the Egyptian Army crossed the demilitarized zone and seized an Israeli police post in the Nitzana area. After the Egyptians refused a request from UN observers that they withdraw without a fight, a small IDF force pushed them back: the intruders now dug in at a number of positions inside Israel. The IDF was ordered to remove them. To gain the necessary time for the organization of the operation, an immediate counterstroke at Quntilla, further south, was decided upon; this took place on the night of 28 October. Meanwhile, the main operation - the largest staged by the IDF since the 1948 war - was assigned to paratroopers and Golani, under the command of the latter. After a forced cross-country march of 16 kilometers, units of the Brigade moved straight in to assault the two main strongholds of the Egyptians. The battle lasted all of 25 minutes, with two more hours needed to mop up.

On 29 October 1956, the IDF moved into Sinai, with the dual objectives of eliminating terrorist bases and throwing the Egyptian

Army off balance before it could complete absorption of the vast quantities of war materiel flowing in from the Eastern Bloc. Golani was given the mission of securing the vital road from the frontier up to the key Rafiah crossroads, to allow the 27th Armored to breach the Egyptian lines and break through to western Sinai. The task necessitated approach in three battalion-strength columns through extensive minefields, and the dislodging of the Egyptians from a fortified network of positions - all this under heavy artillery fire. The Brigade distinguished itself, not only by its obstinate adherence to mission, but also by the improvisation and initiative displayed by all ranks in a battle that defied the initial planners at every stage. Golani's achievement was later described by the Chief of Staff as vital to the success of the northern prong of the IDF offensive.

The Brigade had earned its rightful place in the front line of the IDF. But it would still be plagued, in the years to come, by the public assumption that it was the red berets who handled the tough assignments. Within Golani, however, the 1956 Sinai Campaign came to be seen as the turning point. It did not matter that the paratroops were the idols of the public. The men and women of Golani were developing a pride of unit that even their airborne comrades could not match. And entirely in keeping with this was an unusual incident in 51 Battalion of the Brigade. Shortly after the war, at a demobilization party for soldiers whose service had been extended for three months because of the emergency, the battalion commander - recognizing the social problems of some of his men - announced that anyone who had no home to go to was welcome to stay on as long as he wanted. Golani was, after all, their home.

The 1956 Sinai campaign gained for Israel and the IDF a temporary respite in the war of sabotage and terrorism. Golani used the time well. The Brigade was preparing itself to cope with every foreseeable situation, and training now included water crossings, mountaineering, and airborne and seaborne combined operations, both by night and day. If this training was deepening the mutual trust between officers and men - it was also increasing the Brigade's familiarity with the terrain of Galilee and Israel's northern frontiers.

In late 1959, Syrian implementation of the Arab League decision to deny Israel use of the waters of the Sea of Galilee and the River Jordan moved into high gear. Throughout December there were shooting incidents, mostly at farmers working their fields on the

Israeli side. Then, on 31 January 1960, Damascus radio announced that Syrian troops were moving into the demilitarized zone. While the Government of Israel debated how to react to the announcement, an Israeli armored car approached to within 400 yards of a group of Syrian "peasants" who were plowing land belonging to Kibbutz Tel Katzir. In response to a shouted warning to move off, the Syrians opened heavy and disciplined fire. Clearly, these were soldiers and not peasants. Elsewhere along the frontier, Syrian positions began a sustained bombardment with 120 mm mortars. The Government decided that the time had come to destroy the deserted village of Lower Tawfiq on the slopes above Tel Katzir. The village and its heavily fortified neighbor, Upper Tawfiq, had been used for some time as cover for Syrian troops on the sector. The two villages were at front center of a line of Syrian strongpoints, equipped with long-range weapons and covered from the Golan Heights above by artillery and searchlights that had been frequently used to harass the Jordan Valley kibbutzim. A paratroop unit was available in the area, but Northern Command gave the assignment to Golani.

The Brigade commander chose the squad leaders' course, supported by a platoon from Golani reconnaissance unit, for the main assault mission. Other tasks were allotted to units from all the battalions: setting up of roadblocks to the east, southeast and northeast of Tawfiq; transporting and laying of the demolition charges; and tank and artillery fire to destroy those strongpoints likely to interfere with the mission. At 11:20 p.m. the assault force set out, on foot, followed by halftracks carrying the explosives. Within 40 minutes, and after a short fight, the objective had been obtained and the Syrians were gone. Meanwhile the Syrian upper positions, gathering what was going on, opened up with a heavy artillery barrage, which only served to cover the noise of the approaching halftracks. The last lap of their climb to the village was exposed and covered by a Syrian searchlight. Tank fire was called in to douse the light. By 2 a.m. the explosive charges were in position, and IDF artillery had silenced the barrage from above. Elsewhere, there had been light resistance, which was quickly overcome. After a quick review of the situation, the mission commander decided to advance the planned time of demolition by an hour, and the units began to withdraw at 2:30. At 3:00 a.m. the charges were exploded. It had been a quick and clean job and, as an additional bonus, the units brought back masses of discarded Syrian weapons, including Goryanov machineguns, a rare item for the IDF arsenal. The total cost was three dead and seven wounded.

After more than a year of anger and frustration while the men of Golani watched the Syrian harassment, by shell and mortar fire, of the kibbutzim and moshavim and of fishermen on the Sea of Galilee, the Brigade was ordered into battle again. On 16 March 1962, the Syrians fired on a police launch on the lake; orders came through to teach the Syrians on the eastern shore a lesson, and to do it that very night. The target was chosen only late in the day, and the men were pulled out of a pop concert to be briefed for their mission: the elimination of the Syrian strongpoint of Nukeib on the eastern shore of the Sea of Galilee, just over a mile from Kibbutz Ein Gev.

Nukeib was a tough nut to crack, and there was little chance of achieving surprise since the approach would have to be along the narrow lakeside strip under the towering Golan Heights. The mission was accomplished largely due to superb coordination between the two companies that were assigned the main missions, and the ability of their commanders to improvise under changing conditions on the battlefield. At one stage, the assault teams temporarily halted to allow Syrian civilians from the village of Nukeib to leave without harm. Golani sustained casualties - seven dead and 43 wounded - but the Syrian punishment was far worse.

In the years that followed, the IDF had to contend with a new enemy, the PLO. Golani was in action against PLO bases and installations, some of them in Jordan. Golani's busy schedule brought the Brigade a reputation for perfectionism in performance. Meanwhile, the battalions were training intensively as mechanized infantry, with the use of surplus World War II halftracks.

There was another no less significant revolution. Early in the 1960s, the brigade commander, during a periodic visit to the IDF Infantry Officers' School, struck off the list of subalterns that he was being offered all those who had not served in Golani. During his tenure of command, the Brigade's junior officers would come from its own ranks and traditions. If the course could not supply enough qualified candidates, then Golani would manage with NCOs until it did. The brigade commander's view was not acceptable to the school commandant, but he stuck to his guns and got the backing of the

Chief of Staff. His insistence created a precedent that has become common practice throughout the IDF.

Though the ranks of Golani were drawn from all over the country and from every segment of Israeli society, a special relationship was developing with the towns and villages of Galilee. Two towns, Acre and Naharia, had formally adopted the Brigade. And the kibbutzim, some of which had contributed men and women to the ranks of Golani since 1948, could always find hot water for showers for the boys, or coffee and cakes and a place to relax when time permitted. For their part, the soldiers of Golani shared in the agony and anguish of settlers compelled to bring up their children in air raid shelters because of the constant harassment from the Syrian lines on the Golan Heights. And perhaps this was nowhere worse than in the shadow of Tel Aziziyat - "the Monster" as it was called by the farmers of northern Galilee. From the loopholes of the Syrian fortifications of Tel Aziziyat, the garrison fired at random at tractors plowing the fields, at men and women bringing in the crops, and into the very centers of the kibbutzim. The constant threat of mortar, bombs and machinegun bursts made it hazardous to take the short walk to the communal dining hall, or to go about daily chores.

It was this feeling of partnership in a common destiny with the settlers that was to cause Golani its greatest agonies in the first days of the Six Day War. The war began on 5 June 1967. By late morning of the first day, the IDF was deep in battle with both the Egyptians and the Jordanians, but the Syrians, who had provoked the entire situation that had made war inevitable, now sat back like disinterested onlookers. Golani saw action on the second day, when they joined an armored brigade for the assault on and mopping up of Nablus. One day later they were back facing Syria, in what would be described by the GOC Northern Command as the worst days of his life, while the war tapered out in the south and the Syrians remained unscathed. His feeling was shared by Golani. Finally, on 9 June, the brigade commander received orders to take the line of Syrian fortifications on the Golan Heights. The camps of the brigade's battalions presented a remarkable sight. Soldiers who had witnessed in torment the destroyed houses and burning fields of the kibbutzim and moshavim, and who had agonized for four days over their inactivity, were hugging their officers, some with tears of relief rolling down their cheeks.

All along the northern sector of the front with Syria, together with their comrades of the 8th Armored Brigade, the battalions of Golani swept into action. Speed was vital, as no one knew when the UN Security Council might intervene. In the north, in a classic infantry action, completed on foot because of minefields that hampered their APCs, a Golani battalion stormed "the Monster" and cleaned out its trenches and firing points. Thirty Syrians were killed and 26 captured. Golani's casualties were one dead and three wounded. Behind Tel Aziziyat stood the sector command post of Tel Fahar. The opening assumption had been that Tel Aziziyat would present problems, while Tel Fahar as a second line position would be easier. However, a vast net of minefields and barbed wire fences made it impossible to approach Tel Fahar with tanks and armored personnel carriers (APCs). While Tel Aziziyat had been taken by flanking maneuvers, its neighbor to the rear, contrary to plan, was subjected to a frontal assault. The assault battalion crossed hundreds of yards of fences by running over the backs of comrades who deliberately dropped on the coils of barbed wire to provide a human bridge. In the bitter fight that followed, many of the battalion officers, including the commander, were killed or wounded. By sheer determination and, as some were later to admit, a fierce dedication to Golani and their comrades, the infantrymen persisted in their mission, battling their way through the trenches for more than three hours, many of them with no officers to tell them what to do.

By the end of a two-day battle, the flags of Golani proudly fluttered over 13 fortresses on the Syrian frontline. The brigade records list a private who had been punished for an infraction of discipline. His punishment: he would not be allowed to take part in the battle for Tel Fahar. He stood before the battalion commander and begged, with tears streaming down his face, until the lieutenant colonel relented. Others of his comrades "deserted" hospital beds to rejoin their companies. Golani's mission was not over at Tel Fahar. The battalions swept on to mop up through the next day and, in a race against the hands of the clock, joined an armored column in a brief battle to take Kuneitra, the deserted town from which the Syrians had controlled the Golan Heights. Then, in the last action of the war, elements of Gideon battalion landed from helicopters on the southern peak of Mount Hermon, which towered over Golan and northern Israel.

The years that followed the Six Day War were not peaceful. In 1969 the Egyptians to the south waged a "War of Attrition" across the Suez Canal, and Golani did its share of duty and action on the line. In the north, PLO terrorism became a daily fact of life, and here the Brigade was to have a virtual monopoly for six years. In 1969, for example, the terrorists, operating from bases in Jordan, killed eight Israelis and wounded another 59 in the Beisan and Jordan Valleys. They bombarded villages and towns, attacked patrols and traffic on the roads, and staged five raids into kibbutzim close to the frontier. At first the IDF responded to the terror actions when and where they took place. But it soon became obvious that the initiative could not be left to the PLO.

A series of low-key operations, including the mining of roads used by the terrorists and nightly searches of outlying buildings and farms known to be used by them, were the openers in a campaign that eventually led to three major raids against targets in Jordan. The objective was dual: to punish the terrorists, and to remind the Hashemite Kingdom of Jordan of its responsibility to police its own frontiers. The latter objective was attained by the demolition of a Jordanian irrigation canal in June 1969. Golani's hard work and professionalism restored a relative quiet on the Jordanian frontier, but the PLO - who had in any case overstayed their welcome in Jordan - moved elsewhere, helped on their way by an all out onslaught by the Jordanian Army.

In the face of a Lebanese government powerless to stop them, the PLO took over an area along the western slopes of Mt. Hermon, which was to become known in IDF jargon as "Fatahland." Using this as their base, the terrorists bombarded towns and villages with Katyusha rockets, reaching a peak in May 1970, with a bazooka attack on a school bus, killing eight children and three adults and wounding 29 more. From October 1969, Golani was in almost constant action against the new source of threat. Units of the Brigade struck wherever and whenever it could be established that the PLO was using a launching area for its terror teams. A series of daring and deep penetrations succeeded in neutralizing the PLO for the time being.

There was a growing recognition that Golani was no longer just a brigade; it had become a family. There were soldiers whose fathers had served in Golani. There were weddings of men and women who

had served together. There were even business partnerships in
civilian life that had grown out of comradeship in the ranks of Golani.
The Brigade and its veterans began to plan a family reunion - all of
those who were serving and had served, together with their own
families - to celebrate Golani's first 25 years. It was set to take
place in a large Tel Aviv Park, immediately following the Day of
Atonement, 1973. Meanwhile, some of the companies were
enjoying a well-earned leave. On Friday, 5 October, leaves were
canceled and the Brigade was put on alert. The flags and bunting
were left to wave in the autumn breeze around the reunion site. It
would be days before anybody thought to take them down.

At 1:50 p.m. on the Day of Atonement, the armies of Syria and
Egypt, in a surprise attack, swept across the IDF lines on the Suez
Canal and the Golan Heights. On Golan, the Syrian attack plan
comprised three reinforced mechanized infantry divisions and two
armored divisions. Their primary objective, to be achieved within 24
hours, was to secure the whole of Golan and establish a defensive
line along the River Jordan. From there they would choose targets
of opportunity in Northern Israel. As the attack began, Syrian
commandos seized the Israeli outpost on top of Mount Hermon. The
13 men of Golani, who were the outpost's only combat troops, had
no chance.

The forward strongpoints on the northern Golan line were
manned by Gideon battalion of Golani and paratroop detachments,
and it was against them that the Syrians threw the lead infantry
brigades, whose mission it was to open up an eight kilometer-wide
corridor through which the armor would race westward. First 20
Syrian aircraft bombed and strafed Gideon's positions, and then
waves of infantry - supported by tanks - moved in to finish the job.
But Golani thought differently. The positions, some manned by no
more than 10-15 men, held. The Brigade reconnaissance unit got
through to some of the strongpoints with reinforcements, individual
tanks, ammunition and medical aid. The positions continued to hold,
and to pass back information on the Syrian columns that were
pouring through the breach - information that was vital to their
comrades to the rear who were fighting desperate tank battles to
halt the Syrian avalanche until the reserve army could arrive. On the
second day of the war, orders were received to withdraw, but the
battalion replied that there was no reason to retreat. Their verdict

was upheld by the brigade commander and accepted by the OC Northern Command.

Meanwhile, other elements of the Brigade were securing the roads and junctions that were vital for the continued stream of men, ammunition, fuel and other supplies to the front. Containment actions were taking place between the men of Golani and vastly superior infantry and tank forces across the whole length of the Heights. And wherever Golani fought, they held. For example, at Nafah, a few hundred yards from the crest of the Heights overlooking Galilee, a Golani platoon armed with bazookas stopped two companies of Syrian tanks.

The first hours of the Yom Kippur War were to destroy a myth that had become part of IDF folklore. Traditionally, it had been believed that the standing army's function was to keep everything clean, tidy and ready for the reservists - veterans of '48, '56 and '67 - with their vastly superior combat experience. It did not matter where the legend came from, or even whether it was true. The reserve army believed it, just as older generations have always considered the youngsters to be less than they once were. But, this time, eleven hundred 18-year-old conscripts of Golani and the 7th and 188th Armored Brigades were standing and fighting like lions to hold back five Syrian divisions, while the reserve army struggled to reach the frontlines. The lesson did not go unnoticed.

Slowly the tide of battle turned, and the reinforcements reaching Golan enabled the IDF to sweep the Syrians back off the Heights and a long way down the roads leading to Damascus. Israeli armored columns moved forward, and Golani went with them. The battle for Golan and the counter-offensive that followed lasted three long weeks and involved some of the fiercest fighting that the world had ever known. It was a battlefield of massed armor, missiles - used in quantity for the first time in modern warfare - commandos and airpower. And in its first stages, virtually the only resistance was the dogged determination of exhausted and outnumbered men. Golani did all that was asked of it, and more. But when the battle of the Golan Heights was over, one task still remained.

On 8 October, the third day of the war, two companies of Golani, supported by two tanks, had attempted to retake the Hermon Position - one company on foot and the other mounted on APCs. After losses numbering 25 dead and 57 wounded, the assault force came back down the mountain. For 13 days the Syrian incursion remained undisputed while Golani was busy elsewhere. On the night of 20-21 October, three battalions set out on foot to scale the 9000 foot mountain, while a force from another brigade prepared to be dropped by helicopter in the Syrian rear, where they would take the enemy's Hermon outposts. It was hard going: a long uphill climb with Syrian snipers entrenched on every peak. The battle raged through to midday of 21 October, as Golani fought for each yard of the steep slopes. At 11 a.m. on 21 October, the flag of Golani was hoisted above the Hermon fortress. It had cost 55 dead and 79 wounded, but there had never been any doubt in the minds of the men who climbed the Hermon that they would reach the top no matter what the cost. Not only was the fortress vital to Israel's early warning capability, but its loss had symbolized the trauma of the Yom Kippur War and its recapture would symbolize Israel's survival and victory.

In the years that followed the Yom Kippur War, Golani was not allowed to rest on its laurels. The Brigade fought in the War of Attrition waged by the Syrians, took part in the battles to release the hostages in the PLO attacks on the children's house of Kibbutz Misgav Am and elsewhere, staged raids against terrorist bases and took part in the 1978 Litani Campaign. But all these were almost a return to routine compared with one special assignment in 1976.

Golani had received recognition before. In any army that attaches little importance to uniforms and medals, the Brigade had been granted the right to wear a distinctive brown beret of their own, in place of the khaki worn by infantry and administrative echelons alike. To outsiders it perhaps meant little, but this was a brigade, as one brigade commander fondly related, whose wounded refused to lie in a hospital bed unless their flag - or a brown beret - decorated the wall above. Now the Brigade was to get recognition of another kind. In the early morning hours of 4 July 1976, an IDF force that had flown 2500 miles into Africa, released the hostages taken off a hijacked Air France plane and held at Entebbe Airport in Uganda. Three elite units of the IDF had been called on to supply elements of the assault force, and Golani was one of them. This was not a prize for past achievement but simply acceptance that only the best would go on this mission, and Golani were the best.

The Brigade was still to play a prominent part in the ongoing

security of northern Israel, and in some of the fiercest battles of
Operation Peace for Galilee, where they took Kfar Sil and Beirut
Airport. But for the people of Galilee, the most important and
symbolic battle of all was the one fought by Golani at the beginning
of the 1982 war: the conquest of the Crusader fortress of Beaufort,
on a mountain top towering over the valley of Upper Galilee. It was
from Beaufort that the PLO had directed its artillery and rocket fire
on the towns and villages of northern Israel - a barrage that had
made many of them seriously consider leaving the homes and lives
that they had built for themselves. And it was no less symbolic that
Golani, which had become so much a part of the life of Galilee, was
the brigade to which the task of driving the PLO off Beaufort was
entrusted.

Golani troops were the last to leave Beirut in 1983, and the last
to withdraw from southern Lebanon in 1985, to resume their
traditional duties on Golan and in Galilee, having added another
chapter to their proud record of determined dedication to the safety
and security of the people of Israel wherever they may be. The
brigade that returned to line duties was largely a volunteer force.
Fully eighty percent of the Brigade's numbers are now chosen from
amongst youngsters who fight for the privilege to serve in Golani.
The bulk of the remainder are immigrants who need the chance for
integration into Israeli society that the family and home which is
Golani can offer. Perhaps for this reason every spare moment is
spent in acquainting the new recruits with the farms and industries
of northern Israel, showing them the way to a productive life and
reminding them of the values in the defense of which the men and
women of Golani, and their brothers and sisters in the IDF, have
fought so devotedly.

ISRAEL AIR FORCE - BIRTH OF AIR POWER

On 10 November 1947, the Hagana High Command created an "Air Service" from the available 11 light planes of a local civil aviation company. Early in 1948, they were joined by 21 surplus RAF Auster trainers. By no stretch of the imagination was this an air force. For months, its missions were confined to mail delivery, air lift of supplies, evacuating wounded and reconnaissance flights - though the pilots were occasionally tempted to strafe attacking Arabs with their revolvers, and to drop "bombs" by hand. But the air drops of mail and sacks of flour made besieged kibbutzim feel less isolated and primitive "medivac" in the back seats of Austers and Piper Cubs saved lives.

On 9 May 1948, ten pilots were flown to Czechoslovakia to train on Messerschmitt 109s - sold in total secrecy to the Hagana. Four were "Palestinian" Jews who had served in the World War II RAF; two were Palmach veterans; the others were volunteers - come to the aid of the country about to be born. Impatient at the news of the Arab invasion and air attacks on Israeli targets, some of the pilots decided to cut short their training and return home. On 21 May, they arrived in Israel - with the first fighter plane, stripped down and crammed into the belly of a C-54 transport, acquired by equally clandestine means.

Reassembling planes was more complicated than stripping them down, and the first four 109s were only ready for service on 27 May. The High Command decided not to use them just yet: since the enemy was unaware that the IDF had warplanes, their debut would be in a surprise strike planned for the Egyptian airfield at el Arish. However, the ground battle was becoming desperate. An Egyptian column of some five hundred vehicles, including tanks and artillery, was advancing north along the coast road to Tel Aviv. Twenty miles south of the city, the few available infantry companies were digging in for a last ditch stand, and their plight was serious enough to postpone the plans for the el Arish strike; the four as yet untested Messerschmitt 109s were committed to strafing missions on 29 May. The sudden appearance of Israeli planes so unnerved the Egyptians that the column scattered and began to dig in. The advance on Tel Aviv had been stopped, but at a heavy price: one Messerschmitt was lost - 25% of the IDF's effective aircraft and 20% of its available combat pilots - and one more plane was damaged.

On 3 June 1948, the Israel Air Force - no longer the Hagana Air Service - got its first taste of aerial combat. Towards dusk, two Egyptian Dakotas appeared over Tel Aviv for routine bombing runs - this time on the Central Bus Station and Sde Dov Airfield in the north of the city. A single Messerschmitt scrambled to intercept, and shot both down. This was the delighted Tel Avivians' first hint that Israel had an air force. Somehow a rumor swept the city that the pilots were quartered in a seafront hotel; the room of the solo pilot was swamped with flowers, boxes of chocolate, bottles of cognac and champagne.

On 4 June, all the available "bombers" - a Bonanza, a Fairchild and a Rapide - were scrambled to deal with three Egyptian warships that were bombarding Tel Aviv. With no bomb sights, only one hit was scored from six bombing runs. It was sufficient. The Egyptian ships turned tail. The Arab forces - with considerable numerical superiority - were demoralized by the sudden appearance of "Israeli airpower," and were beginning to concede the aerial initiative.

That initiative was not limited to tactical targets. On 29 May, the IAF's only Dakota hand dropped two tons of bombs on enemy concentrations at Ramallah and, on the evening of 1 June, three aircraft damaged a military base in Transjordan. The latter raid provoked a written threat from the British Ambassador in Amman. His letter was forwarded, via the Haifa consulate, to "the Jewish authorities in Tel Aviv," and returned unopened as "incorrectly addressed." On 11 June, to emphasize IDF ability to retaliate against Arab air raids, the Dakota spent 30 unhindered minutes over Damascus, again dropping two tons of bombs. Little damage was done, but the psychological impact was immeasurable.

By mid-June, the Israel Air Force had eight fighter planes and a dozen combat pilots. Frequent air raids and artillery fire on the ex-RAF airbases in the center and south of the country made their use a risky business. So the fighter squadron moved, lock, stock and barrel, into a citrus grove north of Tel Aviv: their runway was a hastily leveled dirt track.

The first truce in the War of Independence, which took effect on 11 June, gave the IAF a much needed breathing space in which to

get organized. Planes were arriving steadily from Czechoslovakia, and volunteer pilots were trickling in from abroad. By the end of the War of Independence, the volunteer force from abroad would amount to 700 pilots, mechanics and technicians, mostly from the United States, South Africa, England and Canada. Everything else that the squadrons needed was acquired by a time-honored military method: if it isn't bolted down, take it! The fighter squadron acquired their first adjutant by loading him on a jeep and whisking him away from another unit.

Early in the morning of 9 July, the first truce ended and war was renewed with a ferocity that was to last ten days till the second truce. The Egyptian Air Force bombed Tel Aviv, a number of outlying communities and even Jerusalem on 11 July - a raid that shocked world opinion. But the IAF was now ready to retaliate in kind. The procurement effort abroad had come up with three surplus B-17 Flying Fortresses. On 14 July, on their way to Israel, they made a detour to bomb the area of King Farouk's palace in Cairo and military installations in el Arish and Rafiah. Air Force bombers flew the same number of sorties in the last five days of battle as they had in the first, but the total payload was five times greater.

The growing number of transport planes, acquired surreptitiously, was also beginning to have an impact. C46s and DC4s were bringing in arms, ammunition and volunteers from abroad. They were also easing the problem of maintaining contact with besieged areas. In August 1948, during the second truce, IAF transports airlifted 1700 men of a Palmach brigade to the Negev, brought back 3200 men and carried 2200 tons of food, weapons and ammunition in a total of 410 flights. In recognition of the growing importance of these functions, an Air Transport Command had already been created on 1 July. The flow of experienced volunteers from abroad to the transport, bomber and fighter squadrons also enabled the Air Force to pull out some of the Palestinian-born pilots and send them abroad for advanced training.

The first Spitfire to enter service was built from discarded parts found at the old RAF bases, but it was joined by three more from Czechoslovakia in September. Equipped with reserve fuel tanks, good for eight hours flight, and receiving navigation instructions radioed by walkie-talkie from a C-46, six planes took off from Czechoslovakia and flew via a Yugoslav airfield - but one crashed on landing in

Yugoslavia and two were forced to put down in Rhodes.

By the end of the war, in March 1949, the IAF's one and only fighter squadron had 20 Spitfires and a few Mustangs; the Messerschmitts had been retired to make way for the much more pilot-friendly Spitfires. IAF planes had shot down 22 enemy planes - a sizable number in the 1948 conceptions of air power - and had gained aerial supremacy. The last dogfight against Egyptian pilots had taken place on 5 January. But two days later, IAF pilots had clashed with RAF Spitfires - which were behaving as though Israel's skies still belonged to them - and shot down four of them.

The IAF came out of the War of Independence in disarray. It had demonstrated not inconsiderable abilities in aerial combat, in ground support, in bombing and in transport missions. But it lacked formal organization, combat doctrines, instruction and technical manuals. Above all, the IAF lacked manpower. Most of the 700 volunteers were returning home, and only a handful remained to help the fledgling force put its house in regular order. Holding on to the Israeli pilots was also not without problems. One veteran, Moti Hod, was under pressure from his kibbutz to return home and farm the land. He asked his squadron leader, Ezer Weizman, for help in convincing the kibbutz general meeting to let him stay on. Confronted by the obvious disapproval of the sunburnt communal farmers of Degania, the "bourgeois town-dweller" played his trump card: "We need an air force. Would you really like to see it left to characters like me?" Weizman's argument was convincing and Hod remained with the squadron.

Other units of the IDF had started the war with the organization, traditions and training routines of the Hagana and Palmach. The Air Force had started from scratch, with no time to build an effective machine to cope with everyday routine. In addition - a phenomenon not unfamiliar to Allied aviators after World War I - the IDF General Staff was not impressed with the need to maintain a powerful, independent air arm.

In the face of the staggering economic burdens of absorbing immigrants, and General Staff priorities that favored the ground forces, the IAF put its initial efforts into manpower. In October 1949, the Air Force took possession of its first flying school facilities: an advanced course for 30 pilots, who had received their basic instruction in Czechoslovakia and Italy, began on 14 February

1950. Under an ad hoc compromise, Israelis gave the instruction, while a few of the remaining volunteers supervised and awarded grades. In these circumstances, much of the teaching was in English. On 1 August, the school graduated its first 15 advanced level pilots. Meanwhile, the IAF Technical School was finding its feet in what had been the RAF technical school in Haifa Bay, after a temporary start in borrowed space at the Haifa Technion.

In the background, a war of philosophies was raging within the General Staff. Maj. Gen. Aharon Remez, the 28-year-old Officer Commanding (OC) Air Force, believed that the Arabs would quickly develop their air power; the IDF, therefore, could not afford to relate to its Air Force as a support echelon alone. The prevailing General Staff thinking was that the role of the IAF was to assist the main IDF force - the infantry. On 27 October 1949, Defense Minister Ben Gurion ruled that there would be a single General Staff, responsible for land, sea and air. In the view of Lt. Gen. Yigael Yadin, the incumbent Chief-of-Staff, that made the IAF subordinate to the General Staff branch heads responsible for manpower, logistics, ordnance, etc. Yadin saw the Air Force as yet another IDF brigade, which happened to operate in the air instead of on the ground.

The OC Air Force held that the air arm must be free to use its own technical and professional discretion, while he personally should report directly to the Chief-of-Staff. The argument was submitted for resolution to the Defense Minister. Ben Gurion shared Remez' conviction that air power should be more than support for infantry. He even stated that victory - the domain of ground forces - would depend on an efficient air force from the very first moments of war. But he accepted Yadin's view that the General Staff branches did not exist only for the ground forces.

Remez submitted his resignation, but agreed to remain until a replacement was found; he was promised that the proposed subordination to the General Staff branches would await the new OC. Eleven months later, on 14 December 1950, Maj. Gen. Shlomo Shamir was transferred from command of the Israel Navy to the IAF. While Remez had flown with the World War II RAF, Shamir was an infantryman - though he had completed a civil pilot's course in 1940. The appointment, and the orders that he brought with him - to effect the integration of the Air Force into the General Staff

branches - did not sit well with the senior IAF officers, some of whom left the service.

General Shamir's first preoccupation was with organizing IAF headquarters. Early in 1951, he transferred the staff from scattered buildings in Jaffa to tents and temporary quarters alongside a RAF airfield in Ramle. He then set up a logical manpower establishment, by eliminating duplication of functions and shedding some units that should not have been attached to the Air Force. Shamir also applied himself to a number of projects that remained from his predecessor. The IAF shared with other IDF units the responsibility for children from the immigrant transit camps; 1000 of them were housed in a specially built camp at Ekron airbase. The reserve force of the air arm was properly organized and the reservists were assigned to squadrons and support echelons. And the IAF began to look to its next generation of aircraft; Mosquito fighter bombers were purchased from France, and the first IAF pilot was sent to the UK to train on jet Meteors and Vampires.

Shamir's tenure lasted eight months until he retired, in August 1951, because of ill health. He was replaced by Maj. Gen. Haim Laskov, who was expected by Chief-of-Staff Yadin to speedily complete the integration of the IAF into the General Staff. Laskov was also an infantryman, who - like Shamir - had attained the rank of major in the British Army, which was about as high as the British allowed Palestinian Jews to rise in their ranks. He brought with him a reputation for instilling order and organization, but he knew nothing about aircraft and aerial warfare.

Laskov began by dealing with still pending business, then restructured Air Force headquarters into logically organized branches to handle air operations, administration, training, equipment and engineering. As chief of this staff he recalled Col. Dan Tolkowsky who, after flying as a sergeant pilot in the RAF and serving in staff and combat roles in the IAF, had left the service only six weeks before Laskov took over. The new OC then set about learning all there was to know about air power and its uses. He made his views clear in a September 1951 status report: "The operational objective of the force is not clear; the command is not properly trained, administratively or operationally, for its tasks. There is a shortage of commanders. Staff work vis-a-vis the General Staff is unclear. Tactical and administrative discipline in the units is in a sorry state. So is morale. The professional level of job holders is insufficient, as is the state of readiness. The fighting capacity of the Air Force does not exceed 48 hours." On 24 September, Laskov was to receive an object lesson about the level of General Staff awareness: the Air Force was ordered to provide 12 Spitfires to support a ground forces exercise, though only four planes were serviceable.

Tolkowsky's November 1951 readiness report showed a desperate shortage of aircrew; most of the operational fliers were either training new pilots or in the UK learning the newly purchased Mosquitoes. Of 137 fighters and bombers, 52 were grounded by shortage of parts; of 63 fighter pilots only 27 were available to the squadrons. As if that wasn't bad enough, procurement problems were forcing the IAF to fly 17 different aircraft - a maintenance nightmare.

The aircraft situation was soon to ease, as a result of procurement deals made during Remez' tenure. Sixty Mustangs arrived from three different sources - either in parts or as planes that were being phased out by other air forces. A similar number of Mosquito bombers were purchased from the French Air Force. These wood frame planes, bought from the British at the end of World War II, were now handed on for a price of $13,500 per plane. By late 1953, the IAF could expect to have two Spitfire and two Mustang squadrons, two squadrons of Mosquito tactical bombers, its three Flying Fortresses and two squadrons of transport and reconnaissance planes. But the planes and early warning and fire control radars were posing a serious manpower problem. Laskov urgently needed 500 more air and groundcrews to maintain immediate readiness, free of the delays involved in mobilizing reserves. Yadin, on the other hand, was involved with an economy cut - under which the IDF was to reduce its regular payroll by 5000 - and he saw no reason why the Air Force should be exempt.

A joint ground-air exercise, in September 1952, in which all the squadrons participated, only served to strengthen Yadin's view that the Air Force was not yet to be reckoned with. Laskov agreed that the IAF performance was not what it should have been, but placed the blame firmly on lack of manpower, spare parts, air intelligence and ground facilities. Later, he also noted that control and communications - supply of which was not an Air Force responsibility - were inadequate.

In October 1952, the OC Air Force was confirmed by a General Staff order as air advisor to the Chief-of-Staff, which effectively made him a full member of the General Staff forum - and no longer a mere "air brigade" commander. The same order placed his staff under his direct command, the implication being that they were to report to him rather than to the General Staff branches. But the order was not executed, and IAF needs continued to be one item in a ground forces oriented order of priorities. In discussing the IDF work program for the next two years, Lt. Gen. Makleff, the new Chief-of-Staff - who faced further budget cuts - insisted that absorption of new squadrons had to be at the expense of the old. The only manpower concession was an additional 250 unskilled national servicemen, rather than the 500 professional regulars that Laskov claimed the IAF needed. Laskov requested leave to study in Oxford.

Convinced that the OC Air Force should be an officer with aircrew experience, the outgoing commander recommended Tolkowsky as his successor. In May 1953, after having created order and effective staff work in the IAF, Laskov handed the baton of command to Dan Tolkowsky. Originally appointed, like Shamir, to keep the airmen in their "rightful place" - as viewed from the office of the Chief-of-Staff - Laskov had become a convert to Remez' view of the need for air power independent of ground considerations. Tolkowsky was known to share those views. Consequently, his appointment was as "Acting OC pro tem." - together with his functions as Chief of Air Force Staff. In his letter of acceptance, the new "temporary" OC stated his reading of the October 1952 General Staff order: IAF headquarters is to be seen as paralleling General Staff responsibilities - not subordinate to them.

Dan Tolkowsky was taking over in grim circumstances. The Egyptian Air Force possessed 90 World War II vintage fighter planes and 15 Lancaster, Halifax and Stirling bombers. In addition, under the terms of a 1949 agreement, the British had delivered to Egypt 25 Meteor and 26 Vampire jets. The Iraqis, who had ended the 1948 war with 18 Hawker Furies and Hurricanes, were building their air force on 35 Furies, 15 Vampires and 15 Venom jets. The Syrian Air Force had just signed a deal for 40 Spitfires. All three were giving clear preference to the building of air power, and had worked out a common strategy. The Egyptian Air Force, making use of Syrian and Jordanian airfields, was to achieve aerial supremacy by destroying the IAF in the opening move of the next war. The Syrians and Iraqis would then join in tactical bombing of targets in northern and central Israel. Their procurement policies were guided by this strategy.

Late in 1952, in keeping with a "Tripartite (US, British and French) Declaration" on maintenance of the Middle East balance of power, Britain announced willingness to sell 14 Meteors to each country in the arena. At that stage, Egypt already had 49 jets. Under the peculiar mathematics of "balance of power," Egypt, Syria and Iraq were to get 42 modern jets - to Israel's 14. By 1954, Israel's Arab neighbors could expect to have a total of 360 fighter planes, of which at least 120 would be modern jets - a vastly superior air power both in quantity and quality.

Shlomo Shamir had been concerned with a frame of organization. Haim Laskov had established norms of staff work. Dan Tolkowsky's initial preoccupation was with the basic principles of force building. The objectives were easily defined: Israel's lack of strategic depth necessitates constant readiness and fast response; limited resources ordain multi-purpose aircraft, for defense and attack; aerial control is vital for real-time changes of mission; qualitative inferiority dictates attainment of aerial supremacy by destroying the Egyptian Air Force on the ground at the beginning of a war. The IDF General Staff was not overly impressed, but IAF headquarters was determined.

The immediate task was absorption of the Meteors, the first of which were delivered on 17 June 1953. Three pilots, trained in the UK, now began to process others through the steps of adaptation to jets. In parallel, ground and logistic crews were developing techniques for fast turnaround of the new aircraft; shortened time between sorties would reduce numerical inferiority. The Mosquito squadrons - with their edge over the Meteors in operational range and payload capacity - were developing new skills in aerial photography and intelligence.

All this effort paralleled regular operations to protect Israel's air space and assist the ground forces. On 2 March 1954, the light aircraft of the IAF were briefly to seize the limelight. A naval craft ran aground on a reef on the Saudi Arabian coast, 79 miles south of

Eilat. Seven sailors were stranded a long way away from home, and Saudi police boats were already showing interest. Under cover of a quartet of Mustangs, seven Piper Cubs landed on the shore, picked up the sailors and deposited them in Eilat.

There was a message here for the General Staff about the IAF's ability to react quickly and function far from home in unconventional circumstances. But the struggle over philosophies was far from resolved. The new Chief-of-Staff, Lt. Gen. Moshe Dayan, though more sympathetic than his predecessor, persisted in his belief that nothing old should be procured; he needed to be persuaded that readiness and technology could not switch overnight exclusively to jet age conceptions - when there weren't enough jets. The debate between the General Staff and the IAF was to reach a new high with the transfer of a senior Air Force officer, head of Air Operations Division, to a job in General Staff logistics. Tolkowsky could not stop the posting, but he did extract a promise of no more transfers without the agreement of the OC Air Force.

Manpower transfers were not Tolkowsky's only problem. A new Minister of Defense, Pinhas Lavon, had taken over from Ben Gurion at the beginning of 1954 - and his first interest was in economy. One early result of Lavon's policies was a written caution from his office to the OC Air Force not to exceed eight hundred thousand dollars for spare parts. The senior IAF officers protested that this entailed grounding most of the aircraft. Tolkowsky himself told a General Staff meeting: "You want an air force that is both good and cheap. There is no such thing. You must choose which you want." There was support from Ministry of Defense Director General Shimon Peres, and the attitude to procurement did change slowly during the year.

In April 1954, the IAF was ready to specify its shopping list for the next two years. The choice was a compromise between quality aircraft, suited to the arena and better than the Arab planes, and those that would actually be available to Israel in the given time frame. Negotiations for Saab J-29s failed when the Swedish government backed down on an earlier promise to extend credit. The first choice was now the US Sabre, which had proved itself against MiGs in Korea, to be purchased from the Canadian licensees. However, in July 1954, the United States - which was pursuing a policy of mutual defense with the Arab countries against Communist

expansion - refused consent to the deal. With no other acceptable alternatives, the choice now fell on the French Mystere, of which the IAF wanted 15 Mark IIs and another 15 Mark IIs or Mark IVs. In August 1955, influenced by Egyptian support for the Algerian revolution, the French Government finally agreed to supply 30 Mystere IIs.

Meanwhile, Ezer Weizman - now the wing commander at the Ramat David fighter base - was initiating changes of his own that would, eventually, affect the entire IAF. He had concluded that the 15 months of active duty remaining to conscripts after their pilots' course was no way to staff fighter squadrons. So he refused to accept any pilot who did not sign on for three years after the course; a pilot who didn't like that could serve in Mosquitos or B17s, but was not going to be trained on Weizman's Spitfires, Mustangs and Meteors. He also persuaded key groundcrew to sign on for regular service and, despite heavy opposition, got housing built on the base so that pilots and senior technicians would live in with their families. This, added to the time that he devoted to getting to know all the groundcrews, was the beginning of a social atmosphere that would soon become the hallmark of all IAF bases.

The year 1955 was one of dynamic change in the Middle East. A mutual defense agreement, the "Baghdad Pact," signed between Iraq and Turkey in February, widened to include Great Britain in April, Pakistan in September and Iran in October. The United States supported the initiative, aimed at confining Communist expansionism, in the hope that Egypt would join. But President Nasser saw the pact as a threat to his leadership of the Arab world. Egyptian intelligence had been actively supporting large scale terrorist incursions into Israel, but now Nasser was ready for more direct involvement. On 12 September 1955, he announced intensification of the partial blockade on the Gulf of Eilat: all ships and planes bound for passage through the Straits of Tiran were required to request permission 72 hours in advance - and no Israeli craft would be allowed.

Three months before Nasser's announcement, in the knowledge that, sooner or later, it might be necessary to take steps to break the blockade, the IDF had taken a look at the terrain along the west coast of the Gulf of Eilat. A Mosquito returned from a reconnaissance mission over eastern Sinai with indications of negotiable routes for vehicles. Following up on this, six army scouts made a three-day trek on foot through the desert to check conditions on the ground - while maintaining contact with an IAF Dakota, which also dropped them water and other supplies. They were brought out on the third night by six Pipers. Again the Air Force had demonstrated capability in complex combined operations over enemy territory.

Aided by inadequate IAF early warning control, the Egyptians had, since August, been flying regular penetrations of Israeli airspace by Vampire jets based in El-Arish in the Sinai desert. To overcome the problem, a mobile listening post was moved up to the edge of the Gaza Strip. In the early morning of 1 September, the forward station reported Egyptian air activity, and two IAF Meteors were scrambled to intercept. Within minutes two Egyptian Vampires had been shot down over the Negev - and the IAF had its first victories in aerial combat since the 1948 war.

On 27 September, Nasser announced conclusion of an arms deal with Czechoslovakia. The British Foreign Office hastened, the next day, to release details of the agreement: apart from armored vehicles, artillery and ships, the Czechs were to supply Egypt with 100-150 MiG 15 and 17 fighters, 70 Ilyushin 28 bombers and 20 Ilyushin 14 transports. This was the first Soviet-bloc move into the arena - and it was the largest arms deal ever made in the Middle East. Furthermore, rumor had it that a similar deal had been made with Syria. On 17 October, Egypt and Syria signed a military pact. Renewed Syrian gunfire on fishing boats in the Sea of Galilee was promptly added to the Egyptian-inspired terrorist problems and aerial incursions in southern and central Israel.

On 2 November, David Ben Gurion voiced his concern in a speech to the Knesset, then noted: "If our rights are harmed by acts of violence on land or sea, we shall reserve our freedom of action to protect those rights in the most efficient manner... We look forward to peace, but not to suicide." Chief-of-Staff Dayan was proposing military action to stop Egyptian interference with shipping in the Straits of Tiran and to upset Nasser's timetable for absorption of the new weapons; his argument was rejected by the Prime Minister as an untimely invitation to British intervention and an arms embargo.

In December 1955, the Royal Air Force - under the terms of an October 1954 agreement - turned over the ultra modern Fayid airbase and Abiyad logistic installations, both on the banks of the Suez Canal, to the Egyptian Air Force. The RAF presence had offered an element of early warning; while the British were there, the Egyptians had to leapfrog squadrons and logistic support to forward fields in Sinai. Now they could operate, with no advance warning, directly from Fayid into Israel. In the evaluation of the IAF, within one year - with the absorption of the Russian equipment - the Egyptians would dominate the skies over Israel.

Meanwhile, the IAF was having second thoughts about the French aircraft deal. Six pilots had gone to France in August to learn the new aircraft. They had been provided with six Mystere IIs and two Ouragans. The senior pilot, Capt. Benny Peled, reported back to Dan Tolkowsky that the Mystere II was unstable at high speed, needed a long runway and suffered from short operational range and payload limitations. The OC Air Force promptly recommended to the Chief-of-Staff to wait for the Mystere IVA. In September, a Defense Ministry mission to France, headed by Shimon Peres, consulted with Peled and supported Tolkowsky's recommendation. Since the balance of power in the air was already tilted dangerously, the French agreed meanwhile to sell Israel 12 Ouragans - on condition that the IAF also bought three Nord 2501 transport planes.

Neither aspect of the deal was greeted with universal acclaim. IAF transport was based exclusively on Dakotas; the Nords promised maintenance and training headaches. Ouragans, though they carried more ordnance than Meteors, were inferior to the Egyptian and Syrian MiG 15s. And, finally, Chief-of-Staff Dayan was annoyed with Tolkowsky for initially choosing the readily available Mystere II instead of waiting for the IVA. Nevertheless, on 6 October 12 Ouragans, withdrawn from a French squadron, were ferried to Israel in two flights of six each; the first was led by a French deputy squadron commander and the second by Benny Peled, but the Frenchman made a navigational error and Peled took over. For the first time, Israeli fighter pilots navigated their own ferry operation - a precedent for the future.

One month later, a further deal was signed with France for another 12 Ouragans and 12 Mystere IVAs. The Mysteres were withdrawn from the French Air Force and prepared for transfer, but US pressure caused the French to revoke that part of the deal. The Ouragans were in Israel by the end of November, followed in

January by the three Nord transports. By March 1956, the IAF mustered a combat force of 44 Meteor and Ouragan jet fighters, 72 Mustang and Spitfire fighters, 55 Mosquito fighter bombers, three B-17 bombers and 13 transports. The increased proportion of jets called for redeployment of squadrons, retraining of air and groundcrews and a reshuffle of control and communication systems to deal with higher speeds and possible mission changes for aircraft already airborne.

The situation appeared somewhat better, but neither available jet was a match for MiG 15s and Ilyushin 28s. In addition, the only known performance data on the MiG 15 was from the published stories of American pilots in the Korean War - and they were impressed with it. The IAF work program called for higher-level operational training - without impairing constant combat readiness - and gradual conversion to advanced jets, away from Mustangs and Mosquitos. But there were no advanced jets. Then, in early April 1956, a ray of sunshine appeared among the black clouds on the horizon. The US administration withdrew its veto on the supply of Western-made weapon systems to Israel. Renewed negotiations for the Canadian Sabre progressed too slowly. France, however, approved the sale of 12 Mystere IVAs. By 11 April, the same six pilots who had gone to France in August 1955 went again to accept and transfer the Mysteres. Twelve days later, the French agreed to supply a dozen more. Within a month, all 24 were in Israel.

On 26 July, angered by the withdrawal of American finance for construction of the Aswan Dam, Nasser announced the nationalization of the Suez Canal. Britain and France began to plan a military takeover of the Canal Zone, and the French discreetly put out feelers to Israel about possible cooperation. By August, Paris was prepared to sell another 36 Mysteres. Twenty-one IAF pilots and 13 groundcrew were withdrawn from two squadrons "for operational exercises with the French Air Force in North Africa." The pilots, some with only eight hours logged time on Mysteres, learnt the true purpose of their trip on the transports en route to France. Security was so tight that only 11 IAF officers were aware of the deal and transfer details. The planes needed to refuel on the way from France to Israel. The Italian authorities at Brindisi Airport were told that 18 aircraft were returning to France for repairs. To cover two flights of 18 aircraft each, each identification number was duplicated - so the planes would appear to be making the two way trip. In Israel, Hatzor air base was locked down tight to prevent any leaks when the planes arrived.

The IAF had its state-of-the-art aircraft, but there was still a long road to travel. In September, only 12 were ready for combat duty, and their sole usable armament was 30 mm cannons. The few pilots trained for Mysteres still lacked the experience that can only come from flying hours. And, since the plane was new even to the French Air Force, nobody yet knew enough about its performance and limitations.

IDF contingency planning for the operation now being discussed with the French called for an air drop of a paratroop battalion. The existing 12 Dakotas and three Nords did not have the necessary carrying capacity, but Paris had offered the loan of ten Dakotas as part of the August deal. On 11 October 1956, a joint team of regular and reservist pilots, again in conditions of total secrecy, ferried the first five planes via North Africa. They were fitted for the nine hour flight with extra fuel tanks in the cargo hold, and flew at ten minute intervals. On 23 October, the remaining five Dakotas were flown to Israel, by two separate routes and under the cover of a fictitious civil airline.

Alongside training of pilots and groundcrews for the new jets, the IAF was developing the means and tactics to meet the new threats. Target priorities were set at enemy aircraft first, then airfield runways and installations. In the event of war, every airworthy craft - with a few exceptions to protect Israeli airspace - would be assigned to a simultaneous surprise attack on enemy airfields. The techniques had been exercised, early in the year, in dummy raids on IAF bases.

For ground support missions, Air Force officers, with their own communications, were to be assigned to all echelons from battalion upwards, while ground forces liaison officers were attached to the squadrons. However, exercises drew attention to failings in the system - some of which related to the ever-present "fog of war," the heavy burden of missions requested and the inadequate level of air operations controllers. In parallel with efforts to overcome these problems, Air Force headquarters was devoting thought to independent interdiction missions against enemy forces behind the battlefield, to disrupt the flow of reinforcements and supply intelligence on forthcoming intentions.

The World War II Mustangs, Mosquitos and B17s were gradually being transferred to emergency reserve storage. Work was progressing feverishly on updating IAF airfields to the jet age. And, in August 1956, air operations control was moved into a new facility more capable of supervising high speed changes in the aerial picture. The IAF was preparing for a new kind of war that now seemed inevitable. All this needed to be done without impairing constant readiness, which had dropped unavoidably in August - as a result of withdrawal of pilots from the squadrons for ferry missions from France.

On 5 October 1956, General Staff Operations Branch ordered, on a strict "need to know" basis, detailed planning of Operation Kadesh 1, which envisaged the dropping of a paratroop battalion at el Arish, the ultimate forming of a defense line facing the Suez Canal, and an attack on Egyptian airfields to gain air supremacy. The deadline was three weeks, but the General Staff was not satisfied with the submitted plans. Among other aspects, the Staff did not share IAF confidence about its ability to eliminate Egyptian airpower on the ground.

While Kadesh 1 was still on the drawing board, Ben Gurion met secretly - at Sevres near Paris, on 22-24 October - with the French Prime Minister, Ministers of Defense and Foreign Affairs and the British Foreign Secretary. The French and British wanted an Israeli "tangible threat" to the Suez Canal Zone to justify their intervention. Ben Gurion, who was accompanied by Moshe Dayan and Shimon Peres, was concerned about possible Egyptian bombing of civilian targets. The result was an agreement to produce the "tangible threat," in return for French promises of two squadrons, plus pilots for an unmanned squadron of IAF Mysteres, to protect Israeli airspace. Neither Dayan nor Tolkowsky shared Ben Gurion's concern, though the OC Air Force did concede that a French presence would allow the IAF to achieve aerial supremacy by a shorter timetable.

At midday on October 25, all units of the Air Force were alerted for quiet mobilization starting that same evening. During the night, Operation Order Kadesh 1 was replaced by Kadesh 2 - which was now dated for execution on 29 October 1956. The Order, distributed in only 12 copies, listed the objectives: creation of a military threat on the Suez Canal to satisfy the British and French; occupation of the Straits of Tiran to break the blockade; overthrow of the Egyptian dispositions in northern Sinai to remove the military threat.

Although the Order assigned the IAF the initial role of destroying enemy airpower, this was amended in a meeting between Tolkowsky and Dayan on October 26. The British and French air forces had scheduled bombing raids on Egyptian airfields for 31 October. Till then, all IDF actions would be designed as a "local retaliatory operation," from which forces could be withdrawn if anything went wrong with the Franco-British Operation Musketeer. Accordingly, the IAF would drop paratroops at the Mitla Pass - closer to Suez than the originally planed el Arish - and would supply air cover for the ground forces and the skies over Israel. In other words, the aerial role was to be defensive - unless the Egyptian Air Force took the initiative. In keeping with that thinking, the Air Force was prohibited from attacking Egyptian ground forces, unless Egyptian planes bombed and strafed the IDF on the ground.

To cover the IAF alert, while maintaining strict "need to know," the squadrons began "Operation Avshalom" - a ten-day training exercise that necessitated redeployment of squadrons, recall to service of the mothballed B17s, Mosquitos and Mustangs and air-to-ground sorties for pilots who lacked that experience. All routine training was shelved for the exercise; the instructors were posted to squadrons, while pilot cadets were assigned to light aircraft - where they would fly communication missions and transport senior officers.

At 20:00 hours on 28 October, all the wing and squadron commanders were convened for a briefing on the paratroop drop and the objectives of the war. For the majority of the officers present, this was the first indication that "Avshalom" was cover for something else. The promised French liaison and maintenance contingent arrived in Israel on the night of 28 October. At 13:30 hours on 29 October, a French Mystere squadron landed at Ramat David. They would be followed the next day by a squadron of F84 fighter-bombers.

At 14:00 hours on 29 October, four Mustangs flew low across Sinai, under total radio silence. They were towing weighted cables and their mission was to cut the Egyptian telephone lines. The cables did not work, but the aircraft completed the job with their propellers and wings. At 15:00 hours, 16 Dakotas took off with a full load of paratroops and their equipment. They flew south over the Negev 100 feet above the ground, using the gullies for concealment from Jordanian radar. Two Meteors, meanwhile, crossed Sinai towards the Canal to distract the Egyptian Air Force - but there was no reaction. At 16:30 hours, the Dakotas turned west into Sinai, escorted by ten Meteors and six Ouragans, while 12 Mysteres started to patrol over Kabrit airbase to prevent the Egyptian MiGs from interfering. By 17:00 hours, the paratroop battalion was on the ground to the east of the Mitla Pass, and 15 of the Dakotas were on their way home. The sixteenth circled to maintain radio contact until the paratroops completed their deployment.

By 5 November, the day the 9th Brigade completed its cross Sinai trek to reach the Straits of Tiran, the IAF had flown cover for the ground forces in north, central and eastern Sinai, dropped supplies to all units involved and had maintained constant contact - by use of its Piper squadron - with all commands. It had even taken part in a naval action that led to the capture of an Egyptian destroyer. At first, the Air Force had been restricted by the order to avoid air-to-ground action until the British and French dealt with the Egyptian airfields. Once this order was amended, the pilots played their part in close support and aerial combat.

However, the IAF came out of the Sinai Campaign with mixed feelings. The pilots had demonstrated that the training and doctrines were correct - even though they had fought with one foot in the jet age and the other in World War II vintage piston aircraft. They had flown a thousand sorties, downed enemy jets and destroyed twenty percent of the Egyptian Army's vehicles in Sinai. On the other hand, because of political limitations - resulting from the British and French operation - and the presence of the French squadrons, the IAF was not allowed to exploit its full capability. Perhaps the IAF's greatest achievement of the Sinai Campaign lay in convincing the IDF General Staff that airpower had come of age. The Air Force had not only gone to war with better equipment than ever before, but it was now high on the list of priorities for future procurement.

On 25 July 1958, Ezer Weizman received command of the IAF from Dan Tolkowsky. Weizman had a reputation for flamboyance and speaking his mind, and the appointment was greeted with some trepidation in the IDF General Staff. From the point of view of the Air Force, the pilots had a spokesman who would not be silenced. Not longer after taking over, Weizman installed Air Force Headquarters in the General Staff Compound; there would be no more "exile" at Ramle airfield. But, if the staff generals thought that this would bring the IAF under their administrative thumbs, they were sadly mistaken. Symbolically, a fence went up around air headquarters, and their own pennant flew over their section of the compound. As his next step, the OC Air Force insisted that IAF officers up for promotion or new appointments would be interviewed by him - not by the Head of IDF Manpower Branch. It was revolutionary, but he made it stick.

Within two years, the IAF was planning to move into the supersonic age with French Mirage aircraft - which would begin to arrive in 1962. For the time being, Weizman was not allowed to buy as many as he wanted; in place of the requested 90 planes, he was told to start with a dozen and prove that his pilots could master them. Not only did they master the planes, but began to make changes that astonished the French. The Mirage had been designed as a blind, all-weather interceptor based on missiles. The IAF installed guns and bomb racks and turned it into a day and night interceptor and ground support plane. This philosophy of multi-purpose planes and pilots, as an answer to the limitations on size of the Air Force, would influence all future procurement. Nevertheless, to carry out the slower bombing missions, the IAF acquired Vautours. The new planes added a new dimension. No other air force had long experience in supersonic doctrines and tactics, so the IAF could pioneer its own free of preconceptions. Indeed, Weizman insisted that air organization and tactics are a reflection of national characteristics; the IAF could learn from others - but should not copy.

Ezer Weizman was determined to convince his pilots that they could be the best in the world. He had already built a social atmosphere that made of the Air Force something akin to a kibbutz. Now he had the chance to apply his beliefs about the essential qualities of pilots; he wanted "flying warriors" who would take the war to the enemy. To this end, he hand picked his commanders from among pilots who demonstrated combat initiative, and insisted on drawing senior IAF officers, as far as possible, from the ranks of fighter pilots rather than administrative and support echelons. All this gained him a reputation for arrogance, but that was a price he was prepared to pay for aerial supremacy, under which the ground forces could operate without having to watch the skies above them.

Weizman added other practices to the IAF lexicon. He encouraged his young officers to speak their minds, and was willing to listen to their criticism and suggestions. This was to bear rich dividends in future years and be the envy of many pilots in other air forces. Effectively, it allowed a fighter pilot who had come up with a new tactical concept during a morning exercise or operation to climb out of his cockpit, go straight to a phone and be talking directly to the OC Air Force within minutes. If the concept made sense, it would become accepted practice within hours or, at most, days. In parallel, groundcrew handling of planes was exercised and amended, time and again, until the refueling and rearming of an aircraft could be held down to seven minutes. With only 210 fighter bombers, the turnaround time on airstrips could effectively expand the number of sorties flown to the equivalent of a much larger air force.

Weizman sat in the driver's seat for eight years, during which all his fighter squadrons converted to jet aircraft. For the first time, IAF pilot cadets were moving straight from Harvard trainers to jets, without serving in Mustangs and Spitfires. The new recognition won in the Sinai Campaign began to influence General Staff thinking in earnest during the War of Waters. From 1964 to 1967, the Syrians attempted to divert the Hazbani and the Banias - two of the three tributaries of the River Jordan - in order to deny water to the National Water Carrier. Each time the work began, the IDF intervened, at first with tank and artillery fire, then with the long arm of the Air Force. There was no longer any question about the IAF's equal partnership in the ground war.

In April 1966, Maj. Gen. Ezer Weizman moved on to become Head of General Staff Division of the IDF. His successor, Maj. Gen. Moti Hod, had been one of the first Israeli pilots to convert to jets - and had commanded an Ouragan squadron in the Sinai Campaign. He was, therefore, a jet oriented combat pilot taking over a jet minded air force. And he was inheriting a force that was ready for what it must do in the event of war. Hod did not have the advantage of a quiet transfer of command in relatively peaceful times. The IAF

was constantly on call to silence Syrian guns and prevent the diversionary works in the War of the Waters. Indeed, the event which initiated the chain of circumstances that made the 1967 war inevitable was an aerial battle over the canal that Syria was building from the Banias across the Golan Heights. On 7 April 1967, IAF planes on a routine mission, against the Syrian earthmoving operations, were met by MiGs - and shot down six of them. It was the stories of Israeli mobilization, spread by Syria as a result of that dogfight, that led to the Egyptian Army's move into Sinai, on 15 May, and Nasser's blockade of the Tiran Straits a few days later.

Of the 830 combat aircraft facing Israel in Egypt, Syria, Jordan and Iraq, the greatest immediate threat was posed by the Egyptian Air Force's 240 fighter bombers, 30 Tu-16 long-range bombers and an equal number of Il-28 medium bombers. Beginning late in May , Egyptian planes were flying sorties over the Negev, and the IAF was well aware that MiG 21s based at el Arish were only seven minutes flying time away from Tel Aviv. Maj. Gen. Hod's staff began to up-date in fine detail a pre-emptive strike that would deal first with the Egyptian Air Force, on the assumption that the Egyptians would take hours to digest, and then inform their allies of damage done to their airfields and planes. Though there were still some skeptics in the General Staff, the Air Force was prepared, in the first hours of war, to commit almost its entire strength to the plan that had been shelved at el Arish in 1948 and again, over Sinai and Egypt, in 1956.

On the night of 4 June 1967, the pilots of the IAF's fighter-bomber squadrons were ordered to get an early night's sleep since "the Egyptian Air Force could be planning to take action the next day." Between 03:45 and 04:30 on 5 June, they were all awoken and prepared for their missions. The strike plan called for a simultaneous attack on all the airfields in Sinai and across the Suez Canal; the airfields in southern Egypt would have to wait for the second wave. The IAF was taking a calculated risk by committing all but 12 of its combat aircraft to the pre-emptive strike.

At 07:10, the first squadrons were airborne. Flying out to sea, they descended to wave-top height - vanishing off any watchful radar screens - and turned south towards the Egyptian coast. The time had been chosen carefully; the Egyptian Air Force could be expected to have relaxed its dawn watch and its senior and staff officers would probably be in their cars on the way to work (both assumptions proved to be correct).

Sweeping in through the early morning mists, at 07:45 the IAF jets struck simultaneously at runways and planes parked on the ground at el Arish, Bir Gafgafa, Bir Thamada, Kabrit, Fayid and Abu Suweir. Minutes later, Inshas and Cairo West were under attack. By 07:55, the first six airfields were already receiving their second visit of the morning. At 08:10, the last planes of the first wave were dealing with the runways and aircraft at Beni Suweif. At each target, the pilots bombed the runways, then circled to strafe with cannon fire the parked planes. At 09:00, the planes - rearmed and refueled - were airborne for their second visit of the day to the Egyptian airfields. Within two hours of the outbreak of war, the Egyptian Air Force had lost 309 combat aircraft and had ceased to exist as an effective force. Israeli losses totalled 19 planes, none of them in aerial combat.

True to Hod's basic assumption that it would be hours before the Egyptians digested the truth, and passed the news on to Syria, Jordan and Iraq, the other Arab air forces began to take action in the late morning. At 11:50, Syrian MiGs began a series of attacks on targets in northern Israel. Some of them were shot down - and none of them did damage to their assigned targets. At 12:00, the Jordanians - whose artillery had been bombarding Israeli airfields since 11:40, despatched missions against Netania and Syrkin airfield. At 12:45, IAF squadrons took off to deal with Amman and Mafraq air bases. One minute later, another mission was on its way to five Syrian airfields. Both air forces virtually ceased to exist. At 13:15, the Iraqi Air Force showed up, with Hunters and a lone Tupolev bomber, over the Jezreel Valley and Netania. By 15:00, the IAF had sent three planes to deal with H3 airbase in Iraq. By sunset on 5 June, the combined Arab air forces had lost close to half their effective forces.

The IAF had total control of the skies and could turn to air-to-ground support that was of decisive help to the tank and infantry columns racing across Sinai, Judea and Samaria and the Golan Heights. IDF tanks and infantry arrived at some places only to find that their flying comrades had already removed the threat of enemy armored columns. In the battle for Jerusalem, Arab Legion attempts to reinforce the city with armor and mechanized infantry

from the Jordan Valley were thwarted by sorties that left the Jericho-Jerusalem road looking like a vast miles-long scrap yard.

By the end of the war, the IAF fighter-bombers had flown 3280 sorties - close to three per pilot each day. A total of 469 Egyptian, Syrian, Jordanian and Iraqi aircraft had been destroyed, 391 of those on the ground and 60 in aerial combat. The price to the IAF was 69 aircraft hit, of which 46 were a total loss. Twenty-four pilots lost their lives and seven were taken prisoner. It was a heavy price to pay, but the Arab air forces were decimated and the IDF ground forces had been free to operate without aerial interference. Though Maj. Gen. Weizman was no longer OC Air Force, he and Maj. Gen. Hod could be satisfied with the knowledge that the Israel Air Force had written a new and unprecedented chapter in the history of aerial warfare.

The June 1967 war lasted six days. At the end of it, the IDF was deployed on the Suez Canal, the Jordan River and the Golan Heights. However, and despite the extent of the defeat of the Arab armies, the lull that followed the war only lasted one month. Sporadic Egyptian artillery bombardments, in July-October 1967, and again in September and October 1968, were followed on 8 March 1969 by the outbreak of an Egyptian "War of Attrition" that was to last 17 months. Nasser was convinced that he could erode the morale of the Israeli public and the IDF by inflicting constant casualties: in his own words, "seven dead a day will be enough." Faced with incessant heavy bombardments and commando incursions across the Suez Canal, the IDF General Staff decided to respond where it hurt most - and not necessarily by direct fire across the water. Inevitably, that policy brought the IAF into play - initially in "flying artillery" operations against the Egyptian heavy gun batteries and tanks that were pounding IDF positions - and in the airlifting of raiding parties in its new helicopters. In January 1970, with no sign of a let up in the Egyptian bombardments, the IAF began a series of deep penetration bombing raids, some of them on military installations close to Cairo.

As the War of Attrition moved towards its second year, the IAF was to score two coups that would have a profound effect on Nasser's ability and willingness to continue. On 26 December 1969, acting on photo analysis in Air Intelligence, a combined IAF and ground forces operation was mounted to remove a radar station from the desert south of Suez and bring it back behind Israeli lines. This escapade led directly to a Soviet decision not to supply any more first line equipment to Egypt. The operation had been a perfect example of the informal communications and openness to suggestions from below that had developed under Weizman (see Chapter - Paratroops).

In the early months of 1970, it was obvious that Soviet squadrons were operating on the Egyptian southern sector - along the Gulf of Suez. Through April, May and June, the Russian pilots attempted to intercept IAF planes. Finally, in July, the Chief of Staff, Lt. Gen. Haim Bar Lev, got government approval to accept the Soviet challenge. In the early afternoon of 30 July, a pair of IAF Phantoms began a seemingly routine bombing raid on an Egyptian radar station. The Soviet squadrons took the bait. Six quartets of MiG 21s arrived on the scene from three airfields. High above, Israeli Phantoms and Mirages were waiting for them. The battle only lasted four minutes, but at the end of it the Russians had lost five planes. There were two direct results from the encounter. Firstly, the shocked Soviets told Nasser that they could not guarantee the protection of his airspace. Secondly, and ironically, the pilots of the Egyptian Air Force were delighted; for months they had been listening to Russian taunts about their inability to master sophisticated combat jets. Now their teachers had the egg on their own faces. Seven days later, Nasser gave in to US pressures to accept a ceasefire.

The War of Attrition cut a number of milestones in the transition of aerial warfare to a completely new age. For the first time, the IAF was flying in US-made aircraft. As a result of the Six Day War, Charles de Gaulle - offended by Israeli determination to fight the blockade of the Tiran Straits, despite his advice to give in - imposed an embargo on the supply of weapons to Israel. Though some spare parts seeped through the wall of embargo, there could be no more new French aircraft. Ironically, the reputation of the French aircraft industry had been built on the performance of IAF pilots, even though the planes were prone to malfunctions that needed to be corrected in Israel. During 1965, President Johnson had agreed, for the first time, to sell American aircraft. Despite delays, the first Skyhawk A4Hs arrived in Israel in 1968. They were followed, in 1969, by Phantom F4Es. The switch to American planes opened up a dialogue between the IAF and the American aircraft industry that was to lead to joint projects in development of Israeli avionics capabilities.

The war had a profound effect on the levels of inter-arm cooperation between the air and ground forces. Prior to the War of Attrition, ground-air coordination had been limited to conventional functions; the calling in of air strikes by ground commanders, paratroop and supply drops and medivac by small planes. The coming of the helicopter to the IAF had opened up new vistas. Now, ground forces could enjoy enhanced mobility. The helicopters could transport infantry and other units close to target, over large distances and according to precise timetables. The choppers had made possible a number of daring commando raids well outside the immediate battlefield of the Suez Canal. In addition, evacuation of casualties and rescue missions - sometimes behind enemy lines - were taking on a previously unknown dimension of speed and flexibility. As a direct by-product, the Air Force and the ground forces were learning to speak each other's language, and were developing direct lines of communication at all levels, relatively free of the need to go through the channels of inter-arm hierarchy and bureaucracy.

Last but not least, the war was an introduction to the technologies of the future. Ground-to-air missiles and sophisticated anti-aircraft guns were appearing on the battlefield. The pilots were learning to evade SAM2 and SAM3 missiles and were developing techniques to neutralize and destroy missile batteries. In parallel, smart munitions, electronic warfare and electronic countermeasures were becoming a part of the daily lexicon. A fighter pilot was no longer simply the jockey who placed his craft in the right position to press the machinegun button. In a direct violation of the August 1970 ceasefire, the Egyptians promptly moved missile batteries closer to their frontlines - and, thereby, served notice that the new age had come to stay.

Although the Air Force was not exactly idle in the next three years, as terrorism out of Lebanon increased, the end of the War of Attrition allowed a chance to perfect the organizational and technical changes from French to American made aircraft. The Skyhawks and Phantoms had played a part in the war, but they had been absorbed and put to work in a force that was involved in daily combat. In addition, the advent of Hawk surface-to-air missiles had finally brought resolution to a debate that had lasted years. In late 1969, the Head of IDF Operations Branch, Maj. Gen. David Elazar, resolved to let the officers of the anti-aircraft units - guns and missiles - decide for themselves whether they should remain part of the Artillery Corps, or should transfer to the IAF. Although some of them would have liked to be an independent corps, the majority decision was to become part of the Air Force. By February 1971, the new framework was complete and functioning - and the IAF had total responsibility for aerial defense. The new concept of ground-to-air defense necessitated an upgrading of the level of manpower to cope with the greater sophistication of the new weapon systems. Though the missiles and anti-aircraft guns were a separate entity, training and integration were obviously within the domain of the IAF staff.

On Saturday, 6 October 1973 - the Day of Atonement - at 05:00 the OC Air Force, Maj. Gen. Benny Peled, was informed by the Chief of Staff, Lt. Gen. David Elazar, that Syria and Egypt intended to attack at sunset on the same day. After a short discussion, it was decided that the IAF should plan a pre-emptive strike against the Syrian missile batteries, to take place some time after 11:00. Shortly before 11:00, Elazar again called Peled to inform him that the Prime Minister Golda Meir had ruled against pre-emption. In conditions of a surprise opening, the initiative was to remain with the Syrians and the Egyptians - because it must be clear to the world that they, and not Israel, had fired the first shot in the new round of war.

The 1973 Yom Kippur War came as a surprise to Israel and the IDF in more ways than one. Although the 1967 ceasefire lines had given the IAF more maneuvering space, the supply lines that needed to be protected were much longer than ever before. In addition, the Egyptian and Syrian missile arrays now included SAM 6 and 7 anti-aircraft missiles and short and medium range surface-to-surface missiles. The missile umbrella was denser than any encountered by any air force in previous wars; the intensity of war, the numbers of tanks and aircraft and the quantities of munitions expended, were without precedent in any conflict. The option of pre-emptive air strike was denied to the IAF, both by the surprise of war and by political decision. In these circumstances, the IAF's first mission was to protect Israeli airspace and find operative answers to the missiles.

Under a very effective air cover, the IDF mobilized its reserves without interference. In fact, in 18 days of war the IAF shot down 450 enemy aircraft and played an effective role against strategic targets.

The missiles had exacted a heavy price; the IAF lost 104 aircraft. But aerial supremacy, though impaired in the opening stages, had been maintained and did prove vital to ground operations. Inevitably, the war led to debates about whether the days of battle tanks and aircraft were not at an end. However, as the dust of battle settled, it became clear that the prophets of doom were mistaken: the future had to lie in different combinations of the conventional weapon systems and high technology. The new generation of aircraft needed to be faster and more sophisticated airborne weapon platforms, equipped with better protection against the threats of the modern battlefield. The IAF began to absorb F15s and F16s - planes that added a new dimension to war in the air. In parallel, the Air Force accelerated its joint projects with Israeli industry to develop the new technologies of electronic warfare and countermeasures. From 1975, the IAF began to absorb Bell HueyCobra and Hughes Defender helicopter tank destroyers - tiny craft which could stay longer on the battlefield.

July 1976 offered the IAF an opportunity to prove its capability in long-range complex operations that required meticulous planning, pinpoint precision and absolute rapport with ground forces. Four Hercules transports, accompanied by two Boeing 707s - a flying control center and an airborne hospital - transported a raiding force deep into the heart of Africa to release the hostages from a hijacked airliner at Entebbe. Apart from the success of the mission itself, it was to serve as a model to other countries plagued by the cancer of terrorism. A few years later, the transport pilots' comrades in fighter bombers would have their chance to prove an equal capability in taking out a nuclear reactor in Iraq and a PLO Headquarters in Tunisia.

The 1982 Operation Peace for Galilee provided proof that the new mix of fixed wing aircraft with smart munitions and electronic countermeasures and helicopter gunships was an effective force. In aerial combat, the kill ratio was 87 to zero. In the early stages of the operation, the IAF destroyed 18 missile batteries, and provoked a Syrian news broadcast that defied conventional missile age doctrine:

"Our brave fliers are flying in defense of the missiles" - so much for the 1973 pessimists who were prophesying the end of the aircraft. The operation also emphasized the correctness of a theory that pilotless vehicles - "drones" - could contribute invaluable intelligence without risking expensive aircraft and pilots.

The peace treaty with Egypt, and the subsequent withdrawal from Sinai, relieved the IAF of the need to police a considerable expanse of airspace. On the other hand, it reduced maneuverability and posed new problems in the speed of early warning. In parallel, the long arm of airpower became a major factor in the ongoing war against terrorists operating out of Lebanon. Fixed wing aircraft and helicopters became an extension of the ground forces in striking at terrorist concentrations, with the added advantage of surprise and total mobility.

Though the Israel Air Force has no more hunger for combat than any other arm of the IDF, it continues to upgrade its capabilities, ready at all times to meet any threat to the security of Israel's airspace and population. For some years now, the IAF has been in the forefront of world airforces in the development of tactics appropriate to the new battlefields. It may have taken decades to prove its point, but there are no more doubters in the IDF General Staff, neither about the Air Force's ability to protect airspace, nor about its place as an independent arm capable of enhancing the ground function.

COMBINED
OPERATIONS:
ENTEBBE

At 06:45 on the morning of 27 June 1976, Singapore Airlines flight 763 landed at Athens Airport en route from Bahrain via Kuwait. Of the five disembarking passengers, four headed for the transit area to check in for Air France 139 to Paris, then settled down to a long wait in the transit lounge.

At 08:59 on the same morning, Captain Michel Bacos, at the controls of Air France 139, took off from Ben Gurion Airport on what promised to be a routine flight to Paris via Athens.

As the Airbus made its final approach to Athens, the boarding passengers, 58 in all, were being processed through passport and customs formalities. Nobody was on duty at the metal detector in the passenger corridor, and the policeman at the fluoroscope was paying little attention to the screen at his side. In the line passing through to the bus that would take them across the tarmac to flight 139, were a 25 year old woman traveling on an Ecuadorian passport in the name of Ortega and, a few places behind her, a young blond-haired man whose Peruvian passport identified him as A. Garcia. Further back in the line were two dark-skinned youngsters with Bahraini and Kuwaiti travel documents.

The Airbus completed its approach on flight path "Red 19" and touched down at 11:30, to taxi to its parking spot, disgorge its 38 Athens-bound passengers and take on its 58 newcomers.

At 12:20 the flight was airborne and climbing steadily to its cruising height of 31,000 feet. The stewards and stewardesses were already busy in the galleys preparing lunch for their 246 passengers. Eight minutes after takeoff, "Ortega" and "Garcia" and their two Arab companions made their move. The young woman left her first-class seat and took up station at the front of the cabin; in the tourist compartment, the youngsters were already on their feet with guns in their hands. The blond youngster, a revolver in one hand and a grenade in the other, burst through the unlocked cockpit door.

Within minutes of the takeover of flight 139, Ben Gurion Airport management and the Air France station manager were aware that radio contact with Captain Bacos had been lost. The news was passed on to the Prime Minister, the Minister of Transport and the Defense Minister, all of whom were at the regular Sunday Cabinet session. At 13:27, IDF Operations Branch put into motion the pre-planned procedures for coping with possible emergencies at Ben Gurion Airport. IDF Central Command promptly moved to establish a command post at the airport, and to alert the necessary army units.

Shortly after 14:00 hours, Air France 139 radioed Benghazi control tower, in Libya, demanding fuel for at least four hours onward flight, and requesting that the local Popular Front for the Liberation of Palestine representative be summoned to the airport.

The immediate destination was now clear, but everything indicated that the plane would be traveling on - and Ben Gurion Airport was a possibility. At 14:58, the airliner touched down in Benghazi and was directed to a remote runway. Nobody was allowed off the plane, with the exception of one young woman who succeeded in convincing both the terrorists, and a hastily-summoned Libyan doctor, that she was pregnant and in danger of miscarrying. The woman, who was in fact on her way to her mother's funeral in Manchester, England, spent an anxious few hours in the airport terminal, and was then put on a plane to England.

Meanwhile, in Jerusalem, Prime Minister Rabin passed a note to the Cabinet Secretary to convene, in his office after the Cabinet session, a small team of ministers: Defense Minister Peres, Foreign Minister Allon, Transport Minister Yaakobi, Justice Minister Zadok and Minister without Portfolio Galili. Whichever way the Air France 139 episode would develop, these were the men who would have to take the decisions. The meeting, which convened at 16:05, decided very quickly on a number of immediate measures. Yigal Allon was to contact his French counterpart and demand that the French government do everything in its power to obtain the release of the passengers; 139 was, after all, an Air France plane. Gad Yaakobi would approach the international civil aviation authorities with a similar request, and would establish liaison with the families of the hostages and with the communications media. All the arms of Israeli security would take the necessary steps in the eventuality that the plane was destined for Israel.

After a long wait on the deserted runway at Benghazi, the Airbus, having taken on 42 tons of fuel, started its engines, gathered speed and, at 21:50 on the evening of 27 June, was airborne.

At Ben Gurion Airport, where it was now known that 77 Israeli nationals were on board the plane, IDF Chief-of-Staff Lt. Gen. Mordechai ("Motta") Gur phoned Shimon Peres, who decided to come to the airport himself. It was becoming clear that the aircraft, with its range of 2500 miles, was heading away from the Middle East in a southerly direction. Nevertheless, all the security preparations were kept in force.

With only a few minutes fuel left in its tanks, Air France 139 landed at Entebbe, in Uganda, at 03:15 local time on the morning of 28 June. The units at Ben Gurion Airport were ordered back to their bases, and the command post disbanded. Whatever would happen from here on, it would not require elaborate preparations at Ben Gurion Airport.

Monday, 28 June, was a day of questions - but no answers! Was Entebbe the final destination, or only a refueling station in the onward flight of Air France 139? Were the Ugandans unwilling hosts or active partners in the hijacking? Idi Amin, the Ugandan dictator, had not been exactly friendly to Israel since March, 1972, when he had been refused a squadron of Phantom jets with which to bomb Kenya and Tanzania, and had countered by expelling all Israelis from his country.

On the ground in Entebbe, the situation was clearer. At daybreak, the hostages had been able to see, through the windows of the plane, several additional terrorists, as well as Ugandan soldiers massing on the lawn alongside the runway. Idi Amin had put in a personal appearance during the morning, arousing a brief optimism on board the Airbus. But, at midday, the hostages had been transferred to the Old Terminal building through a cordon of Ugandan soldiers, whose weapons were pointing ominously at them. Later in the afternoon, Amin had paid a visit and made a speech in support of the Popular Front for the Liberation of Palestine.

Despite the uncertainties, some steps were taken in Israel. The French Government had been contacted, and had accepted responsibility for the safety of the passengers, and for the diplomatic efforts that would be made to obtain their release. Transport Minister Yaakobi persuaded the press and the electronic media not to publish lists of names; the chance existed, however slim, that some of the Israeli hostages might be mistaken for citizens of other countries. The Military Censor was roped in to delete any inadvertent hints that could help the hijackers.

Defense Minister Peres told his assistants, in an afternoon session, that if Amin was helping the hijackers, this would be a dangerous precedent; so far, no aircraft hijacking had enjoyed the overt assistance of any president, army or state. If this was the case, and it did succeed - no aircraft would be safe again in African skies. Therefore, it was vital to know what was actually happening at Entebbe.

Within the IDF no command decisions were being taken - or were called for. Nevertheless, in the joint air and ground staffs of Combined Operations, questions were beginning to be asked and ideas raised - almost as a matter of routine. There was no problem involved with the range; up to March 1972, Hercules aircraft of the IAF had flown regular flights with supplies for the Israeli mission in Uganda. But the Air Force needed to know - against any eventuality - whether any changes had been made to runways and other airport installations, and whether any anti-aircraft measures had been taken at the airport or on its approaches. There would also be a need for information about normal practices with runway lights, radar and all the other details concerning access to an international airport.

At the end of the day, the biggest question of all remained unanswered: What were the hijackers going to demand in return for the release of their prize?

At dawn on Tuesday, 29 June, the only available new information was a brief description of the hijackers, which had come in from Maj. Gen. Rehavam Zeevi in London. Zeevi, the Prime Minister's Advisor on Terrorism, had been in Europe when the hijacking took place, and was asked to remain there to coordinate contacts with the French government and efforts to obtain any relevant data.

At 08:30, Prime Minister Rabin met with the Foreign Affairs and Security Committee of the Knesset, Israel's Parliament, to bring its members up to date on the hijacking and the decisions taken on the previous day by the ministerial team. Later in the morning, in keeping with his awareness that critical security problems transcend party barriers, Rabin sat in private session with Menahem Begin, the leader of the Likud opposition. At the end of their meeting the Prime

Minister offered to keep Begin posted on any developments in the situation.

A meeting of the ministerial team was set for five in the afternoon. In the early afternoon, the Prime Minister asked that IDF Chief-of-Staff Gur be summoned to take part in the session. A routine exercise was in progress in Sinai, and the call to Gur caught him as he was about to board a helicopter at Dov Airport in north Tel Aviv, on his way to watch the maneuvers in the south. Before ascending the hills of Jerusalem, the C-o-S called Deputy Head of General Staff Branch, Brig. Gen. Avigdor Ben-Gal, and told him to "start thinking about plans for Entebbe..." The Air Force and Combined Operations officers, who had been "thinking" since the day before, were now free to move into higher gear. The Prime Minister opened the five o'clock meeting with a direct question to Lieutenant General Gur: "Has the IDF any proposal on how to extricate the hostages?" The General replied that it was too early, but options were being examined. There followed a few moments' debate on possible tactics, but this was cut short by Shimon Peres, who suggested that this was neither the time nor the place to discuss operational matters before they had been properly examined.

Minutes before the meeting, both the Foreign Ministry and the Defense Ministry received, from Paris, a preliminary list of terrorists, held in Israel, France, Germany, Switzerland and Kenya, whose release was being demanded by the hijackers in Entebbe. The Director-General of the Foreign Ministry phoned the list through to the cabinet room. Now the price was clear and now there was hard information on who was responsible. The ministers were given a briefing by the intelligence consultant who was sitting in, on the PFLP and its head, Dr. Wadia Hadad. The Prime Minister closed the meeting with an announcement of a special government session at eleven the next morning.

Early in the evening, another cable from the Paris embassy was placed on Foreign Minister Allon's desk. This one contained all the technical details of the proposed exchange of terrorists for hostages, and set a deadline - 14:00 hours, Israel time, on Thursday, 1 July. If their demands were not met, the terrorists threatened to blow up the plane and its passengers.

At 21:00 hours, a small group of IDF generals sat facing Shimon Peres and Motta Gur, while each in turn outlined his preliminary

ideas. Maj. Gen. Kuti Adam, who henceforward would be the coordinator and motive force in planning any operation, spoke briefly of three possible options, then turned to Maj. Gen. Benny Peled, GOC Air Force, for his evaluation of the logistics involved in getting to Entebbe. Peled, whose planning officers had been working on the problem for 36 hours, explained all the problematics, then stated that the necessary force ("1200 men with all their equipment, if you want") could be flown, nonstop, to target. It was too early for operational decisions, but the Air Force had said, loud and clear, that it could be done.

Unknown to the officers in Tel Aviv, Ugandan soldiers in Entebbe had spent part of the afternoon cutting an opening from the hostages' hall in the Old Terminal through to the next room, and had nailed planks in the shape of a "T" across the opening. The hostages were encouraged to believe that more space was being made available to alleviate their cramped conditions. But, in the late evening, Wilfried Boese, the blond-haired hijacker, appeared and announced that he was going to read a list of names, and that all those mentioned should crawl through the opening into the next room. Despite his assurances that the list had nothing to do with nationality, it was clear that he was only naming Israelis and Jews. The German word "Selektion" was muttered around the room - a reminder of Dr. Josef Mengele at Auschwitz choosing those who would live and those who would die!

During the late evening, and into the night, an Israel Air Force officer was making phone calls to senior Air Force personnel, serving and retired, who had seen duty in Uganda. All received the same message: "Report to the Deputy Chief of Intelligence Branch at one a.m.!" From elsewhere in the General Staff, similar calls were going out to officers who had enjoyed a personal relationship with Idi Amin, to meet in the P.M.'s office at 08:00 hours; to transport command pilots for a meeting with Peled also at 08:00 hours (their squadron leader, Lt. Col. S., was called out of a wedding party in Haifa to receive his summons); and to ground forces combat officers, whose input was now required by the planning team.

Ehud Barak, the deputy head of IDF Intelligence Branch, had two meetings scheduled during the early hours of Wednesday, 30 June. At 01:00 he met with senior Air Force officers who had spent time in Uganda, to find out everything they could tell him about Entebbe

Airport, other airbases in Uganda, Idi Amin's air force - and anything else that came to mind. At 04:00 hours, he chaired a meeting of the planners to survey progress. There were ideas, but nothing concrete so far; in fact, both meetings were more concerned with listing the gray areas where information was needed, and with compiling a checklist of possible sources. Among the officers now present in the meetings was Muki, a young paratroop major, who had been called in that night; his assignment would be to consider all the possibilities of seizing the Old Terminal and eliminating the terrorists.

The strangest meeting of all to take place during that day was in Shimon Peres' office, where the Defense Minister was picking the brains of a handful of IDF officers who were personally acquainted, and even friendly with Idi Amin. Slowly but surely, Peres was putting together a psychological profile of the African dictator - including details like Amin's ambition to be awarded the Nobel Prize for Peace, and his mother's appearance to him in a dream to warn him against ever harming the Jews. As a direct outcome of this session, a retired IDF colonel, Burka Bar-Lev, was led into a nearby room to wait while an international call was placed to Kampala. In the ensuing conversation with Idi Amin, and others that followed over the next few days, Bar-Lev was instructed to play heavily on Amin's ego and their personal friendship to extract every bit of useful information and gain as much time as possible. Through most of the conversations, Peres listened in on an extension phone, taking note of everything of importance that Amin let slip.

The Government of Israel convened, in full session, at 11:00 hours in the Cabinet Room of the Knesset. The only really new developments to report were the refusals of the French and West German governments to give up terrorists from their prisons. The French had, however, quietly intimated that they would follow Israel's lead. The consensus of the meeting, as summed up by Prime Minister Rabin, was that there was still time to decide; the Cabinet would be summoned again either later in the day or the following morning, a few hours before the ultimatum was scheduled to expire.

At Air Force Headquarters, Maj. Gen. Peled and his officers were fitting together the pieces of data to make a full picture. Peled's most basic concern was not with the logistics of reaching Entebbe, but rather with the possibility that unidentified aircraft might be fired on.

He had already concluded that little was to be feared from radar detection on route. Even if the planes did show up on hostile radar screens, it was unlikely that they would be believed to be Israeli aircraft so far from home.

At Entebbe, 47 hostages of the non-Israeli group were being herded onboard a waiting Air France plane. Captain Bacos and his crew from flight 139 refused to leave. They were adamant about staying with their passengers to the very end. A French nun also insisted on staying and giving up her place to someone else, but the Ugandans took no notice of her protests, and she was shoved on board the plane.

During the afternoon, two officers of the IDF returned to central Israel from the exercises in the south, to find that they were urgently required to report to the General Staff. One of them was Brig. Gen. Dan Shomron, Chief Paratroop and Infantry Officer, and his summons was to a briefing by Maj. Gen. Kuti Adam at 15:30 hours. The second officer was Lt. Col. Jonathan Netanyahu, and his meeting was with his own deputy, Muki, who wanted to bring his CO into the picture. Neither of these men had been aware of the frenzied activity taking place within the small inner circle. They were not alone in this: the requirements of security had even left most of the generals of the IDF General Staff in the dark about the search for a possible military option.

It was a busy evening. At 21:00 hours, Dan Shomron convened a planning session at his headquarters. Two hours earlier, Prime Minister Rabin met the editors of Israel's daily press to discuss with them aspects of the terrorist ultimatum and the diplomatic efforts, and to urge restraint in covering the story. From that meeting, Rabin went straight into session with the small ministerial team, again opening the proceedings with a direct question, "do we have a military option?" addressed to the Chief-of-Staff, and again receiving a terse "not yet!" After hearing reports from Foreign Minister Allon on the diplomatic scene, Shimon Peres reviewed the ideas already produced in the IDF - but there were still gaps in the available intelligence data. The team would meet again in the morning, before the Cabinet session that would have to decide about the 2 p.m. ultimatum.

At Orly Airport outside Paris, Foreign Minister Jean Sauvagnargues welcomed the 47 hostages from Entebbe in the name of the President of France. A number of men circulated in the crowd, discreetly collecting names and addresses. Late into the night, there would be knocks on the doors of families celebrating the safe homecoming of their kin, and questions would be asked: the number of terrorists, what weapons were they carrying and what were they wearing, how were the hostages housed, how many Ugandans were around the building and how were they behaving? Despite the lateness of the hour and the strangeness of the circumstances, none of the nocturnal visitors were turned away empty-handed.

Meanwhile, in Tel Aviv, Defense Minister Peres was sitting in his crowded office, listening to Kuti Adam, Benny Peled, Intelligence Branch chief Shlomo Gazit and their assistants. Three possible plans were taking shape: a parachute drop into Lake Victoria and a quiet landing at Entebbe from rubber boats, a large-scale crossing of the lake from the Kenyan shore - using whatever craft could be rented, borrowed or stolen, and a direct landing at Entebbe, a quick assault and a fast removal of the hostages by air. Both of the first two plans depended on releasing the hostages, then relying on either Idi Amin or UN intercession to get them out. They would drop by the wayside over the coming hours, both for military reasons and because the data coming in from Paris would confirm that the Ugandans were active partners in the hijacking. In the meantime, the problem was still insufficient information - and the clock was ticking away the vital minutes to midday on Thursday, 1 July. At the early morning, 1 July, meeting of Intelligence Branch planners, one of the points that came of light was the fact that an Israeli building contractor had built installations at Entebbe, including the Old Terminal.

At 08:00 hours, when the normal working day was beginning in Tel Aviv, young officers, in civilian clothes, paid visits to tourist agencies and airline offices to inquire about flight schedules in East Africa. Another small group descended on the headquarters of one of Israel's biggest building companies to borrow, in strictest confidence, their blueprints of Entebbe Airport and, most particularly, of the Old Terminal building.

Shimon Peres sat at his desk, reading over the transcript of the previous night's phone call to Idi Amin, and refreshing his memory about the information that the Ugandan leader, perhaps inadvertently, had let slip to his old friend, Burka Bar-Lev. Peres was convinced, based on his last session with the officers of the General Staff, that there had to be a military option and that it was only a matter of time till all the pieces fell in place. He was absolutely certain that giving way to terrorist extortion was not the path that a sovereign state should choose. At 07:45, when the ministerial team convened, Peres stressed his convictions, but the clock on the wall - which showed 08:40 as the meeting ended - was against him.

All 18 ministers in the Cabinet meeting that began at 09:00 hours were very conscious of the limited time remaining. But the issues were too serious to let pass without some debate. After hearing the opening round of discussion, Yitzhak Rabin apologized to his colleagues, and departed for a brief session with the members of the Knesset Foreign Affairs and Security Committee, at which he read out the proposed text of a government solution in favor of negotiation for the release of the hostages, and asked the opinions of the men present. He went out of his way to state that the Minister of Defense, and some other ministers, were on record as saying that they would vote for negotiation solely as a means of gaining time. After a brief recess, requested by the head of the opposition in order to allow consultation, the Prime Minister was assured of the Committee's agreement for what he felt the Government had to do.

Returning to the Cabinet Room, Rabin called for a vote, insisting that each man must vote "yes" or "no"; there could be no avoidance of responsibility by abstention. The vote was unanimous in favor of negotiation, it being recorded in the minutes of the meeting that Shimon Peres and Shlomo Hillel, the Minister of Police, regarded the decision as a tactic to gain time. Yigal Allon placed an urgent phone call to the Ambassador to France, and asked him to inform the French Foreign Minister immediately. There were ninety minutes to spare to the expiration of the ultimatum.

The answer was not slow in coming. Idi Amin told Burka Bar-Lev that the PFLP would broadcast on Uganda Radio at two p.m. Israel time. He would say no more than that. The PFLP had extended the ultimatum to 14:00 hours on Sunday, 4 July, a fact that Amin had already announced in yet another personal visit to the hostages in the Old Terminal.

The tension of the morning hours and the relief of temporary reprieve in the afternoon made little difference to the IDF. The air and ground forces teams had achieved substantial progress now that the required - and requested - information was pouring in. There was still one major gap in intelligence: any changes that might have been made to runways, taxi paths and other installations at Entebbe in the four years since the Israel Air Force had last visited Uganda. However, assurances had been given that every effort was being made to get an up-dated picture; in any case, the ground plans of international airports were not exactly top secret.

At 10:00 hours, while the members of the Government were agonizing over their decision, Chief Paratroop and Infantry officer, Brig. Gen. Dan Shomron, was presenting his preliminary ideas to Maj. Gen. Adam. At 15:15 hours, a group of senior officers convened in Shimon Peres' office to listen to the minister's report on the decision to negotiate. But that was not all. Peres went on to provoke a discussion on the probabilities of success of a military operation - though it must have seemed in conflict with the political situation. Despite the general atmosphere of caution, Benny Peled and Kuti Adam were optimistic. Forty-five minutes later, Maj. Gen. Adam formally ordered Shomron to flesh out the details of a military operation to rescue the hostages.

At 17:00 hours, Dan Shomron and his team were in joint session with the Air Force planners and, at 18:30, a more detailed conception was presented to Shimon Peres, as a result of which the Defense Minister approved the preparation of operational orders. Dan Shomron was appointed to command the operation on the ground.

Throughout the evening, the circle widened. Lt. Col. Netanyahu was again summoned from the south by his deputy, to be brought up to date, in a late night session, on the various ideas for an assault on the Old Terminal. They adjourned at 03:00 hours - Yoni Netanyahu to get some sleep, and Muki to draw up the assignments for their men and to list the equipment they would need. The Senior Medical Officer, and the Head of Communications and Electronics Branch were called in to be briefed, then departed to set their own wheels in motion. At Air Force headquarters, lists were being drawn up of pilots and aircrew, some of them reservists, the main criterion being experience in long range flights over Africa. Brig. Gen.

Shomron instructed his headquarters to bring in troops, drawn from three units, to a relatively quiet base in central Israel. The units would be drawn from Yoni Netanyahu's paratroops, another paratroop unit and Golani Brigade. Meanwhile, strict instructions were being issued to maintain communications silence; there was to be no hint in telephone conversations or among the uninitiated, about what was in the wind.

During the night, Kuti Adam ordered the erection of a full-scale model of Entebbe Old Terminal, based on the available blueprints and photographs, at the base where Yoni Netanyahu's men were now assembling; they would exercise on the model, with the help of a Hercules aircraft parked nearby. Almost as an afterthought, the Computer Center was asked to provide a code name for an operation: after rejecting their first offering, Shomron accepted "Operation Thunderball."

Meanwhile, a second group of 101 non-Israeli hostages had arrived in Paris. There was a double implication: there were fewer hostages to bring out of Entebbe; on the other hand, the knowledge that the terrorists were now holding Israelis and Jews exclusively, had to raise doubts about the sincerity of their negotiations. In any case, they had already intimated, via the Somali Ambassador to Uganda, who was serving as go-between for the French, that they were not interested in negotiation - only in total satisfaction of their demands. One supposition was that the ultimatum had been extended only to save Idi Amin embarrassment at the meeting of the Organization of African Unity scheduled to take place over the weekend.

In discussion with the other generals, Chief-of-Staff Gur was still not convinced that the now rapidly evolving plan was feasible. However he agreed to withhold judgment until some details were drilled both on the ground and in the air. Thus, as dawn broke on Friday, 2 July, all the preparations were being made for an operation that had not yet been approved by the Chief-of-Staff - or the Government of Israel. Shortly after midnight, Dan Shomron had a brief session with the Prime Minister, but the basis was still "let's wait and see..."

At 08:00 on Friday, 2 July, an "Orders Group" took place for the officers of the units assigned to "Thunderball." At 08:30, while three Hercules aircraft were landing at the base, to serve as stage props for the rehearsals of the operation, the Air Force team was presenting its detailed planning to Lt. Gen. Motta Gur. The pilots were assuming a flight plan that would bring them to Entebbe in a time slot between one scheduled commercial airliner taking off and another landing. It was highly unlikely that the control tower would bother to turn off the runway lights for a short period; in any case, Entebbe was, for the next few days, the "duty airport" for emergencies over East Africa. However, the C-o-S was concerned about the dangers of landing in the dark, so it was agreed that he should fly with Lt. Col. S., the command pilot, in a night exercise to prove that a Hercules could be landed safely without runway lights. For the time being, the assumption was that the aircraft would be refueled at Entebbe, from the airport's own tanks - though Nairobi, in Kenya, was suggested as a possible alternative.

At 10:00 hours, Yoni Netanyahu, Muki and their officers started to run through all the possible variants of an assault on the Old Terminal, while the other units mapped out their roles in securing the rest of the airport, including the New Terminal, control tower and refueling area.

Elsewhere, Air Force groundcrews were hard at work on "routine maintenance plus" of seven aircraft: four Hercules would be needed (there had been a suggestion to take many more - but Muki had argued vigorously and effectively against too large a force); one extra Hercules would be held in reserve; two Boeing 707s were included in the plan - though they would not be landing at Entebbe. Brig. Gen. Dan Michaeli's staff in the IDF Medical Corps were assembling the equipment that would be needed to convert one Boeing into a flying medical facility. Brig. Gen. Yisrael Zamir, the Chief Communications Officer, was working with his team on equipping the other as a communications link.

At 12:00 noon, the unit commanders presented their detailed plans for approval by Chief Paratroop and Infantry Officer Shomron. Two hours later, Yoni Netanyahu convened his own officers for a final "Orders Group" before the rehearsals on the model. There was some concern over how to achieve maximal surprise: the assault team would have to cover quite a distance by road to the Old Terminal, since taxiing the aircraft too close to the building was bound to alert the terrorists and the Ugandans. Muki suddenly had a brainwave. He grabbed a phone and told a startled staff officer in Tel

Aviv that they must have a Mercedes limousine immediately. Putting down the receiver, he explained that all senior Ugandan officers, including Amin himself, always traveled by black Mercedes. A limousine, escorted by Landrovers, would be a normal enough sight not to arouse undue interest until it was too late.

As the light was fading, at 17:00 hours, the assigned aircrews gathered for a briefing on the drills that were to take place after dark. Immediately after the briefing, Lt. Col. S. settled down at the controls of a Hercules, with Lt. Gen. Gur and Maj. Gen. Peled at his shoulder. Motta Gur had already told the pilots that it made no difference to the ground combat teams where they had to perform; it was the pilots' job to bring them safely to their destination. Lt. Col. S. now had to convince Motta that the pilots could indeed make a blind landing - if they needed to. The plane took off and flew south to Ophir, at the southern tip of Sinai. There it landed on a dark runway, but once was not enough for the C-o-S, so Lt. Col. S. took off again and repeated the maneuver. Coming in to Ophir airfield, the plane was a hundred yards off line, but there was ample time to correct - and the landing was again satisfactory. The Air Force had made its point.

Meanwhile, Yoni's paratroops were exercising, time and again, the drive to the model and the assault and elimination of the terrorists, while their CO held a stopwatch, urging them to clip more seconds until he was satisfied. A Mercedes limousine had indeed arrived, borrowed from a car dealer who specialized in used taxicabs, but - to Muki's horror - it was white! Never mind! That problem could be dealt with later. At 22:45 hours, after Lt. Col. S. had brought his load of top brass back from Ophir, the paratroops performed once again. This time, with a Hercules, and with the Chief-of-Staff watching.

At 01:00 hours, on the morning of Saturday, 3 July, Motta Gur phoned Shimon Peres and reported that the men were ready - and the operation could be staged. The news throughout the day had not been promising: the Embassy in Paris was relaying messages that indicated no progress, and no obvious desire for progress, on the diplomatic front. Now there was at least a ray of light.

Throughout the night, army mechanics labored on the engine of the aging Mercedes. As they finished, two soldiers began to slap black paint on the white bodywork. In the very early hours of morning, a dazed garage owner in Jaffa would climb back into bed, wondering why on earth would the Military Police need a set of new tires for a Mercedes taxi - on Saturday of all days! Yoni and Muki spent the remaining hours of darkness reviewing every aspect of the assault and devising answers to all foreseeable eventualities. Air Force headquarters drafted detailed operational orders and, at 05:00, issued them to the transport squadron. Briefing of the aircrews was set for 08:45 hours. Shortly after dawn, the combat units loaded their equipment, and drove on deserted roads to a nearby airbase, where ground crews stood ready to lash their vehicles securely in the bellies of the waiting aircraft. Alongside a runway, Dan Michaeli's doctors and medical orderlies made a last check of the equipment to be loaded on board the "hospital" Boeing. The IDF Medical Corps had quietly called in reservist doctors, that same morning, with no explanations offered for the unusual summons.

It was a sunny Saturday morning in Israel, though the plight of the Entebbe hostages overshadowed the normal Sabbath joys. There were no indications of progress in the negotiations for their release, and indeed it seemed that the terrorists were only interested in forcing Israel to its knees in a humiliating capitulation. Via France, Israel had insisted that the exchange must take place at a neutral venue preferably Paris, but the answer had been an outright refusal. There was little certainty in anybody's mind that trading convicted terrorists would save the lives of the 105 men, women and children in Entebbe Old Terminal.

Shortly after 11:00, the small ministerial team convened, for the last time, in the Prime Minister's Tel Aviv office. They listened in silence to General Gur's detailed presentation of Operation Thunderball. It was not a total surprise, since Shimon Peres had already told three of the ministers that a military option had opened up. Perhaps to retain a sense of the gravity of the situation, Yitzhak Rabin reviewed the risks involved and the implications of failure. The meeting concluded with a question to Motta Gur: "When do the planes have to go?" The answer was: "Shortly after 1 p.m. from central Israel."

Most of the ministers who gathered for the full Cabinet session, immediately after the team meeting, were expecting the agenda to contain just one item: a decision to accede to the hijackers' demands before tomorrow's deadline. Despite the holiness of the Sabbath, all the Cabinet members were present; one religious minister who lived in Jerusalem had received a hint from his colleague, Transport Minister Yaakobi - at midday on Friday - that he would not regret taking his family to Tel Aviv for the weekend.

The gloomy atmosphere and long faces gave way to growing astonishment as the Chief-of-Staff spread maps, sketches and photos across the table, and began yet another detailed briefing. While Gen. Gur was speaking, the heavy doors of five Hercules aircraft slammed shut, and the planes began to gather speed on the runway. At 13:20, they were airborne and southbound for Ophir in Sinai. The flight plan envisaged a last staging point as far south as possible, for reasons of both timing and range. But normal flightpaths would have taken the aircraft westward over crowded Tel Aviv beaches, before making the turn south. And there was no way that so many aircraft in the Sabbath skies could have passed overhead without arousing speculation. So each of the five planes took a separate route across the heartland of Israel. Over the Negev and Sinai deserts, the upcurrents of hot air made it a very rough flight. The soldiers on board the transports had been issued airsickness pills, but the turbulence was so bad that they were glad to set foot on solid ground at Ophir.

In the Cabinet Room in Tel Aviv, Motta Gur concluded his briefing, and the ministers were asking questions. Time was now short, but no attempt was made to stop the discussion: the decision was too important to rush the Government of Israel into it. At Ophir, four heavily laden transports (their payloads as much as 20,000 pounds over normal rated capacity) lumbered through the thin desert air and, after using up the whole length of the runway, were airborne. Watching them go were a very airsick paratrooper - and a very frustrated pilot of the reserve Hercules. The prevailing winds and weather forced the four planes to take off northwards, then bank slowly - five degrees at a time - back to their southerly course, making part of their turn over the empty desert wastes of Saudi Arabia.

A note passed across the Cabinet table from Yitzhak Rabin to Shimon Peres suggesting that the planes should go: they could always be recalled. From Peres' smile, the Prime Minister could understand that "Operation Thunderball" was already on its way. As if they had all the time in the world, Rabin summed up the debate, then called for a vote. It was unanimous: the IDF was going to Entebbe.

Fifteen minutes after the last Hercules was airborne out of Ophir, the second Boeing was on its way south from central Israel. It would also land at Ophir, then follow the transports - three hours behind to allow for its higher speed. On board were Maj. Gen. Kuti Adam, another senior officer, and a communications team.

In the cockpits of the four transport planes, which were now flying low over the Gulf of Suez, beneath the height of hostile radar surveillance, the pilots were studying a batch of aerial photographs of Entebbe Airport. Taken by an amateur, at an angle, from Kenyan airspace over Lake Victoria, and shoved into the pilots' hands seconds before takeoff - they held the answers to the remaining questions. In the bellies of the aircraft, the soldiers of the assault teams, and the doctors and medical corpsmen who were to land with them, sprawled alongside their vehicles getting whatever sleep they could. Some of the officers were studying their maps and orders again, making sure that everything was committed to memory.

Yitzhak Rabin and Shimon Peres went home for a few hours to try and relax before the long night ahead. Peres was expecting dinner guests, and there was no way to postpone without arousing speculation. Rabin had spent the last few minutes before leaving his office on the phone to France, doing his best to invent plausible reasons for delaying the negotiations, yet unable to tell General Zeevi in Paris what was actually happening.

Around the dinner table in Peres' home, the talk quite naturally turned to the plight of the Entebbe hostages. In the hope of keeping up pretenses before his American VIP guest of honor, the Minister of Defense turned to another of his guests, the publisher of a Tel Aviv daily who was known for his dovish attitudes, and asked him what he would do under the circumstances. Fully expecting an ardent plea for unconditional capitulation to the terrorists' demands, Shimon Peres was astonished by the publisher's answer: "Send the IDF!" Fortunately, Maj. Gen. Gazit, the Head of Intelligence Branch, was able to help his host explain just how impossible that idea was.

Motta Gur, who was spending every available hour that he could with his family - his wife's father had died earlier in the week - returned to his headquarters to chair a meeting of the General Staff. The generals, like the cabinet ministers that same morning, were convinced that they had been summoned to hear details of an exchange of convicted terrorists for hostages, and were surprised at the conspicuous absence of Kuti Adam and Benny Peled - until Gur began to speak!

Turning westward, the four Hercules headed into the African continent over Ethiopia. The weather was stormy, forcing the pilots to divert northwards close to the Sudanese frontier. However, there were no fears of detection. Firstly, it was doubtful that any alert radar operators would be able to identify the planes as Israeli and, secondly, the storm would wreak havoc with incoming signals on the screens. On the approaches to Lake Victoria, they hit storm clouds towering in a solid mass from ground level to 40,000 feet. There was no time to go around, and no way to go above - so they ploughed on through. Conditions were so bad that the cockpit windows were blue with the flashes of static electricity. Lt. Col. S. held the lead plane straight on course; his cargo of 86 officers and men and Dan Shomron's forward command post with their vehicles and equipment had to be on the ground according to a precise timetable. The other pilots had no choice but to circle inside the storm for a few extra minutes.

Yitzhak Rabin, with some of the other ministers and generals, joined Shimon Peres in his office, and waited tensely for a sign of life from the radio link-up on his desk. Shortly before 23:00 hours, they heard a terse "over Jordan" from Kuti Adam, confirming that the planes had reached Lake Victoria.

Lt. Col. S. held course southward, then banked sharply to line up on Entebbe main runway from the southwest. In the distance he could see that the runway lights were on. Behind him, in the cargo compartment, Yoni Netanyahu's men were piling into the Mercedes and the two Landrovers. The car engines were already running, and members of the aircrew were standing by to release the restraining cables. At 23:01 hours, only 30 seconds behind the preplanned schedule, Lt. Col. S. brought the aircraft in to touch down at Entebbe. The rear ramp of the plane was already open, and the vehicles were on the ground and moving away before the Hercules rolled to a stop. A handful of paratroops had already dropped off the plane to place emergency beacons next to the runway lights, in case the control tower shut them down. Lt. Col. S. switched on his radio for a second: "I am on Shoshana."

The Mercedes, and its escorts moved down the connecting road to Old Terminal as fast as they could, consistent with the appearance of a senior officer's entourage. On the approaches to the tarmac apron in front of the building, two Ugandan sentries faced the oncoming vehicles, aimed their carbines, and shouted an order to stop. There was no choice, and no time to argue. The first shots from the Mercedes were from pistols. One Ugandan fell and the other ran in the direction of the old control tower. The Ugandan on the ground was groping for his carbine. A paratrooper responded immediately with a burst. Muki and his team jumped from the car and ran the last 40 yards to the walkway in front of the building. The first entrance had been blocked off; without a second's pause, the paratroopers raced on to the second door.

After a searching debate with Yoni, Muki had decided to break a cardinal rule of the IDF. Junior officers usually lead the first wave on an assault, but Muki felt it important to be up front, in case there was need to make quick decisions about changes in plan. Tearing along the walkway, he was fired on by a Ugandan.

Muki responded, killing him. A terrorist stepped out the main door of Old Terminal to see what the fuss was about, and rapidly returned the way he had come.Muki then discovered that the magazine of his carbine was empty. The normal procedure would have been to step aside and let someone else take the lead. He decided against, and groped to change magazines on the run. The young officer behind him, realizing what was happening, came up alongside. The two of them, and one other trooper, reached the doorway together - Amnon, the young lieutenant, on the left, Muki in the center, and the trooper to the right. The terrorist who had ventured out was now standing to the left of the door. Amnon fired, followed by Muki. Across the room, a terrorist rose to his feet and fired at the hostages sprawled around him, most of whom had been trying to sleep. Muki took care of him with two shots. Over to the right, a fourth member of the hijackers' team managed to loose off a burst at the intruders, but his bullets were high, hitting a window and showering glass into the room. The trooper aimed and fired. Meanwhile Amnon identified the girl terrorist to the left of the doorway and fired. In the background, a bullhorn was booming in Hebrew and English: "This is the IDF! Stay down!" From a nearby mattress, a young man launched himself at the trio in the doorway, and was cut down by a carbine burst. The man was a bewildered hostage. Muki's troopers fanned out through the room and into the corridor to the washroom beyond - but all resistance was over.

The second assault team had meanwhile raced through another doorway into a hall where the off-duty terrorists spent their spare time. Two men in civilian clothes walked calmly towards them. Assuming that these could be hostages, the soldiers held their fire. Suddenly, one of the men raised his hand and threw a grenade. The troopers dropped to the ground. A machinegun burst eliminated their adversaries. The grenade exploded harmlessly. Yoni's third team from the Landrovers moved to silence any opposition from the Ugandan soldiers, one of whom was fast on the trigger. The troopers killed them.

While his men circulated through the hall, calming the shocked hostages and tending the wounded, Muki was called out to the tarmac. There he found a doctor kneeling over Lt. Col. Yoni Netanyahu. Yoni had remained outside the building to supervise all three assault teams. A bullet from the top of the old control tower had hit him in the back. While the troopers silenced the fire from above, Yoni was dragged into the shelter of the overhanging wall by the walkway.

The assault on Old Terminal was completed within three minutes after the lead plane landed. Now, in rapid succession, its three companions came in to touch down at Entebbe. By 23:08 hours, all of Thunderball Force was on the ground. The runway lights shut down as the third plane came in to land, but it didn't matter - the beacons did the job well enough. With clockwork precision, armored personnel carriers roared off the ramp of the second transport to take up position to the front and rear of Old Terminal, while infantrymen from the first and third plane ran to secure all access roads to the airport and to take over New Terminal and its control tower; the tower was vital for safe evacuation of the hostages and their rescuers. In a brief clash at the New Terminal, Sergeant Hershko Surin, who was due for demobilization from the army in twelve hours time, fell wounded. The fourth plane taxied to a holding position near Old Terminal, ready to take on the hostages. All the engines were left running. A team of Air Force technicians were already hard at work offloading heavy fuel pumps - hastily acquired by an inspired quartermaster one day earlier - and setting up to transfer

Idi Amin's precious aviation fluid into the thirsty tanks of the lead transport - a process that would take well over an hour.

In Peres' crowded room in Tel Aviv, Kuti Adam's terse "everything's okay" only served to heighten the tension. Motta Gur decided to contact Dan Shomron directly, but was little more enlightened by a laconic: "It's okay - I'm busy right now!"

The Medical Corps' Boeing had landed at Nairobi, in Kenya, at 22:25. Gen. Peled was now able to tell Lt. Col. S. that it was possible to refuel at Nairobi. Unable, for the moment, to raise Shomron on the operational radio, and uncomfortable with the situation on the ground - the Ugandans were firing tracers at random, while the aircraft with engines running were vulnerable at the fuel tanks - Lt. Col. S. decided to take up the option now available.

Muki radioed Dan Shomron to report that the building and surroundings were secure - and to inform him that Yoni had been hit. Though they were ahead of schedule, there was no point in waiting (possibly allowing the Ugandans to bring up reinforcements), particularly since Shomron now knew that refueling the aircraft in Nairobi was possible. The fourth Hercules was ordered to move up closer to Old Terminal. Muki's men and the other soldiers around the building formed two lines from the doorway to the ramp of the plane; no chances would be taken that a bewildered hostage could wander off into the night - or blunder into the aircraft's engines. As the hostages straggled out, heads of families were stopped at the ramp and asked to check that all their kin were present. Captain Bacos was quietly requested to perform the same task for his family - the crew of Air France 139. Behind them, Old Terminal was empty but for the bodies of six terrorists, among them a young European girl and a blond-haired German called Wilfried Boese.

It took seven minutes to load the precious cargo of humanity, while a pick-up truck - brought 2200 miles specially for this purpose - ferried out the dead and wounded, including Yoni. The paratroops made a last check of the building, then signaled the aircrew to close up and go. At 23:52 hours, the craft was airborne and on its way to Nairobi, while doctors worked over seven wounded hostages, and the aircrew distributed sheets of aluminum foil to make up for an inadequate supply of blankets. It was cold, and the hostages were exhausted, still in shock at the rapid change in their fortunes - and dimly aware that two of their number were dead, and that they were leaving behind an old lady, Mrs. Dora Bloch. She had been taken to a hospital in Kampala where she was subsequently murdered on Amin's orders.

At the other end of the airfield, an infantry team fired machinegun bursts into seven Ugandan Air Force MiGs. The decision to destroy the planes had just been relayed from Kuti Adam's Boeing. There was no point in tempting Ugandan pilots into pursuit.

The paratroops reloaded their vehicles and equipment. Their job done, they were airborne at 00:12 hours on Sunday, 4 July. Behind them, their comrades completed their tasks and checked that nothing was left behind - except the fuel pumps which were too much trouble to manhandle back on board a Hercules. The intention had been to leave the pick-up truck as a present for Idi Amin, but the soldier who had signed for it convinced one of the pilots to load that too. At 00:40, the last of Thunderball Force left Entebbe. Thirty minutes later, the second Boeing and the first Hercules landed at Nairobi, and taxied to the fuel tanks in a quiet corner of the airport.

Though the pilots could not know it, Prime Minister Rabin had made a decision, on Friday morning, not to inform the Government of Kenya. Firstly there was security to consider and, secondly, he did not want to embarrass the Kenyans, who had enough troubles of their own with Idi Amin. Without any fuss, fuel tankers moved into position by the planes and began the refueling, while the drivers presented the paperwork to the pilots for signature - just as they would to any commercial flight. No questions were asked and no information volunteered. Sergeant Hershko, who was seriously wounded, was transferred to the hospital Boeing. Two hostages whose wounds needed immediate care in a fully equipped hospital, were loaded into a waiting station wagon and taken into Nairobi, where one of them later died. At 02:04 on Sunday morning, the remaining passengers and aircrew of Air France 139 were airborne on the last leg of their long journey home.

Long after midnight, the Spokesman of the Defense Ministry made a phone call to a sleeping household in Tel Aviv. The relatives of the hostages had elected a committee to pressure the government; the committee in turn had chosen a chairman who had met throughout the week with Rabin, Peres, Yaakobi and anyone else who would listen. This time, it was the chairman who was listening - though it took some moments for the news to jolt him awake.

The flight home was long, easy and uneventful - except for one nasty jolt! At 03:00 hours, a Hercules pilot was twiddling the controls of a radio, hoping for some music, when he heard the Israel Army Network announce: "IDF forces tonight rescued..." Why would they announce it before the planes reached home? He could not know that the Agence France Presse in Kampala had filed a wire story of shots heard in Entebbe, and it was already a headline on Paris radio and the BBC. And, because of radio silence, he could not tell his colleagues in the other planes.

There was no mood of celebration on the transports. The hostages, huddled together against the cold, and aware now that their rescue had cost the life of a soldier, were thankful to be among their own again, but in no mood to join in the singsong that someone half-heartedly tried to start. They still needed time to absorb it all - to shake off the nightmare of Entebbe. In Lt. Col. S.'s plane, the paratroops were sunk in their own private thoughts. Despite all the efforts of the doctors, Yoni was dead. The mission would later be renamed "Operation Jonathan" in his memory.

Early in the morning of Sunday, 4 July 1976 - by chance the day that Americans were celebrating their Bicentennial - the lead Hercules flew low over Eilat, at the southern tip of Israel. The tired airmen in the cockpit were astonished to see people in the streets below waving and clapping. The plane landed at an Air Force base in central Israel. The hostages were fed and given a chance to shake off the trauma. The wounded were taken off to hospital, and psychologists circulated among the others, giving help where it was needed.

In a remote corner of the same airfield, the three combat teams offloaded their vehicles and equipment. They would return to their own bases, hardly aware of the excitement in Israel, and throughout the free world, over what they had done this night.

It was mid-morning when a Hercules transport of the Israel Air Force touched down at Ben Gurion International Airport, rolled to a stop and opened its rear ramp to release its cargo of men, women and children into the outstretched arms of their relatives and friends and a crowd of thousands. The ordeal was over.

PAGES
FROM THE
DIARY OF A
PARATROOPER

Although many armies, including the IDF, still use the terminology "paratroops," it would be more accurate to refer to them as airborne troops who are, among other things, trained and qualified in the use of parachutes. The paratrooper, as a soldier descending into battle suspended from a nylon canopy, was one of the shortest lived innovations in military history. Development of the military transport plane, in the late 1930s, opened the possibility of transporting large bodies of highly trained soldiers over great distances, and dropping them where they were needed, in conditions of maximal surprise for the enemy. The concept was put to good use by the Wehrmacht in 1940, and by the Allied armies later in World War II. However, the growing sophistication of anti-aircraft systems in the years since that war has added to the vulnerability of slow moving planes, flying at the heights necessary for parachute drops. Conversely, the rapid development of the helicopter has afforded the option of transporting those same troops, with greater accuracy, while evading many of the battlefield threats. The diary entries that follow will reflect the image of the paratrooper as a highly trained soldier, able to function in airborne operations, but by no means restricted to the parachute, or helicopter, as his means of transport.

Parachutes are still an important item in the military inventory - in the appropriate circumstances. Parachute training contributes to the shaping of character and self confidence in soldiers. Indeed, IDF combat officers in all arms of the service are encouraged to qualify for their wings - and the option is open to units other than the paratroops. Furthermore, while most mere mortals cannot grasp why anyone would want to jump out of a perfectly good aircraft, the experience breeds a special brotherhood among those who do. Airborne veterans, of all ages, cross the world for the chance to jump with other members of the brotherhood - and the IDF Parachute School regularly hosts missions of such veterans.

The IDF Parachute School is operated by the paratroop brigades, but is open to all IDF personnel who need or want to qualify for their wings. As the central facility for parachute training and use, the School is also responsible for air drop of supplies, heavy weapons and vehicles - and for drop zone marking. Its parachute packing facility is unique in the world, in that the work is done by women soldiers. The parachute packers - all conscripts doing their two year service - enjoy the privilege of taking the jump course and earning their wings - if they so desire. A course at the School lasts three weeks, including intensive training on the ground and a number of jumps. All paratroops return to the school periodically to make the jumps they need in order to retain their wings.

1948-1956
The IDF's first paratroop unit was formed in the summer of 1948. Its commander was a veteran parachutist, member of a group of Palestinian volunteers who had jumped into Nazi-occupied Europe in an attempt to save Jews. His task was hopeless. There was no equipment with which to train, and the only available parachutes were rejects sold by the British to a silk shirt manufacturer. The first volunteers were a mixed bunch of idealists and adventurers. Although a couple of missions behind enemy lines were proposed, both were rejected by the General Staff - and the War of Independence ended without the paratroops having seen action. After the war, all but 12 members of the unit were weeded out. With that nucleus, the paratroops were transferred to a proper training facility and began to play a part in IDF field exercises. However, their role in border clashes was minimal, largely because the unit commanders were not enthusiastic about actions that did not involve jumping.

In 1953, as a direct result of deterioration in the IDF fighting capability (see Chapter: Golani Brigade), the General Staff created a small (45 man) volunteer unit, 101, to stage retaliation actions against terrorists - and set standards of performance for the entire army to emulate. This "long-range penetration group" only functioned until December 1953, when it was dissolved by the new Chief of Staff, Moshe Dayan. Its members were merged with the existing paratroop battalion, and its commander - Arik Sharon - took over the new merger. A couple of border actions during 1954 led to a completely new training program, which in turn gave the paratroops their first strong sense of esprit de corps. By 1955, they had won virtual exclusivity in dealing with the fedayeen and their Egyptian controllers. The fighting spirit of the unit, and its officers' concept of "Follow me!" had permeated the whole of the IDF. And

the paratroops were no longer a single battalion; the unit had grown into 202 Brigade.

Despite earlier hopes that the 1952 military coup in Egypt would herald a change, terror raids - which had claimed 489 Israeli lives between 1952-54 - reached a new peak of 258 in 1955. The IDF took action against terrorist bases, but communities as far north as the outskirts of Tel Aviv still had to be constantly on the watch against the raiders, and those few adventurous souls who used the roads southwards after dark did so only if they were armed.

On 12 September 1955, Nasser intensified the Egyptian blockade of the Tiran Straits at the entrance to the Gulf of Eilat. The Suez Canal was already closed to Israeli ships and cargoes. Now Nasser was closing off the country's trade routes with East Africa and Asia. The IDF began to plan a campaign to open the Straits, based on a two battalion parachute drop and a cross-country trek of two more battalions, coordinated with strikes against Egyptian airfields to maintain air supremacy over the ground troops. This plan was shelved in December: Prime Minister Ben Gurion felt that the international climate was not yet right.

Nasser - annoyed by the Baghdad Pact which united Turkey, Iraq, Iran, Pakistan and Great Britain against Soviet Russia and threatened his own aspirations as the leader of Pan-Arabism - turned to the Eastern Bloc for arms. On 27 September, he announced a massive arms deal with Czechoslovakia, in proportions never before available to the Middle East. The Soviet Union was making its first overt bids for influence in the Arab world. On 17 October, Egypt and Syria signed a military pact, followed immediately by a renewal of Syrian attacks on fishing boats in the Sea of Galilee.

On 3 December 1955, under the terms of an agreement concluded in October 1954, the British handed over Fayid airbase on the Suez Canal to the Egyptians. Previously, Egyptian Vampire jets on penetration missions over Israel had to be deployed at el Arish in northern Sinai. Fayid and the new Soviet planes would now enable the Egyptian Air Force to strike without betraying its intentions by redeploying in Sinai. Within a year - allowing for absorption of the Soviet-Czech equipment - Egypt would hold air supremacy over southern Israel.

Not content with causing grave alarm to Israel, Nasser had annoyed France by aiding the Algerian rebels, and then the United

Kingdom - on 26 July 1956 - by nationalizing the British-owned Suez Canal. France and Britain considered that move a threat both to world peace and to their oil supply routes. In early August, the British began planning a military operation to occupy the Canal Zone, and the French sent liaison officers to sit with the British team. A deadline for diplomatic resolution of the crisis was set for early September. Meanwhile, the planners were ordered to prepare for the first weeks of September, as a reserve option. There were now three partners sharing a common interest in reducing Col. Nasser to size.

On 29 September, Foreign Minister Golda Meir, Transport Minister Carmel, C-o-S Moshe Dayan and Defense Ministry Director General Shimon Peres paid a secret visit to Paris to lay the groundwork for Franco-Israeli cooperation. They returned to Israel on 2 October, bringing with them a high level French military delegation. In the two days that followed, details were worked out for the supply of logistic services to French squadrons if they needed Israeli airfields: Paris was having doubts about British determination to go through with a Suez invasion from bases in Cyprus, and was seeking its own options.

On 5 October, IDF Operations Branch ordered, on a strict "need to know" basis, the detailed planning of "Kadesh I" which envisaged the dropping of a paratroop battalion at el Arish, the ultimate forming of a defense line facing the Canal, and an attack on Egyptian airfields to guarantee air supremacy. The planning deadline was three weeks. While "Kadesh I" was still on the drawing board, Prime Minister David Ben Gurion, accompanied by Dayan and Peres, paid a secret visit, on 22-24 October, to Sevres near Paris, to meet with the French Prime Minister, Ministers of Foreign Affairs and Defense and the British Foreign Secretary. Both sides had matters to discuss. Ben Gurion was concerned about possible Egyptian bombing of civilian targets. The French and British needed a plausible reason for their intervention. This was the obvious time for a trade-off. On 24 October, Ben Gurion having been promised French squadrons and pilots to protect Israeli airspace, signed an agreement whereby the IDF would supply a "tangible threat" to the Canal Zone. This, in turn, would allow the other partners to issue an ultimatum calling for withdrawal of both Israel and Egypt to ten miles from the Canal. The stage was set for the Mitla Pass.

Sinai Campaign

On 25 October 1956, Syria, Egypt and Jordan announced that the latter was joining the military alliance against Israel, and that an Egyptian general had been appointed to overall command. Dayan ordered a secret mobilization of the IDF along the Jordanian frontier - just noisy enough for the media to pick up rumors that Israel was "quietly mobilizing for a raid on Jordan in retaliation for terrorist activity on that frontier." Alert notices to the IAF in fact stressed the possibility of Iraqi troops moving into Jordan. Meanwhile, IDF Operations Branch cut the orders, in only 12 copies, for "Kadesh II," deadlined 29 October, under which a paratroop force would be dropped at the Mitla Pass and other paratroop units would cross Sinai to link up with their comrades. In the following stages, three IDF columns would break through Egyptian lines and head for the Suez Canal and the Tiran Straits. The IAF was instructed to plan strikes on Egyptian airfields, but these orders were amended on 26 October: the Air Force was to provide aerial cover and support, and leave the airfields to a promised British and French raid - scheduled for 31 October. The IDF plans, prepared in such secrecy that senior officers not in the know were excluded from meetings when the subject came up, were deliberately modular. Ben Gurion, concerned that the British might postpone their aerial participation, wanted an operation that could be described as a raid and withdrawn after successful completion of the first stage: the Mitla Pass.

The timing could not have been better. The USSR was putting down revolutions in Poland and Hungary, the United States was a week away from a presidential election, a planeload of senior Egyptian officers had crashed a few days before and, by pure chance, the Egyptian C-o-S was visiting Jordan and Syria.

On the afternoon of Friday, 26 October, the senior officers of 202 Paratroop Brigade, commanded by Lt. Col. Ariel Sharon, submitted their plan: 890 Battalion was to drop at the western end of the Mitla Pass and take up defensive positions, while the rest of the Brigade was to race westwards across Sinai to link up with their comrades and block the pass at both entrances - the eastern and western. Approval was given, and Sharon briefed his force commanders that same evening. At 20:00 on 28 October, Maj. Gen. Dan Tolkowsky, GOC Israel Air Force, convened a briefing for his wing and squadron commanders, at which the officers were told for the first time about the plans for the paratroop drop and the war that was to begin less than a day later. During the night, a flight of 16 Nord transports brought in 400 French airmen to prepare the groundwork for the promised squadrons which would arrive the next day.

Meanwhile, a photo reconnaissance, flown in the early afternoon of 28 October, showed that a camp - previously assumed to be roadworkers - at the western end of the Mitla Pass had grown from 11 tents at the beginning of the month to 29. The only possible cautious assumption could be that an Egyptian company strength unit now occupied the drop area. The plan was quickly revised. Maj. Raphael Eitan's 890 Battalion would now be dropped near the road fork at the eastern entrance to the Pass. Two aircraft were detailed to take a closer look the following morning. They returned with conclusive evidence that the camp was indeed a road repair gang, but their report was only available three hours before takeoff. Eitan decided that it was too late to revert to the previous plan.

At 14:00 on 29 October, four IAF Mustangs flew low over the paratroops of 890 Battalion sitting next to their transports, and headed into Sinai. Their mission was to cut Egyptian phone lines, and this they did with their wings and propellers. At 15:00 the first Dakota transports were airborne. Within five minutes, all 16 planes with their loads of paratroopers were headed south from central Israel to the Negev. The pilots stayed 100 feet above ground to avoid Jordanian radar, making use of the dry desert gullies and maintaining visual contact between each flight of four. At 15:33, two Meteor jets took off and flew a more northern route across Sinai to the Canal to distract Egyptian attention. The Egyptian Air Force did not react. At 16:00, ten Meteors, followed a half-hour later by six Ouragans, took position high over the Dakotas in case the Egyptians interfered.

At 16:30, the Dakotas changed course westwards and crossed the frontier into Sinai. Twelve Mysteres were airborne shortly afterwards. Their mission was to patrol over the Egyptian airbase at Kabrit and prevent the MiGs from taking off. The Dakotas gained height and began dropping the paratroopers, each flight of four dropping 100 men at a time. By 16:59, as daylight faded, all 395 men of the battalion were on the ground. Fifteen of the Dakotas turned for home. One remained to maintain radio contact between the paratroopers and their rear headquarters until they completed their deployment on the ground.

At the drop zone, Eitan and his operations officer, Lt. Moshe Levy, calculated that they were 4000 yards east of the planned point. The paratroops moved out on a two hour march to the road fork at the entrance to Mitla. They met no opposition. Deploying around the road junction, they dug in and settled to await their comrades. The night was uneventful, except for air support operations. At 21:00, IAF Dakotas parachuted two 120 mm mortars. The next air drop brought crews for 106 mm recoilless rifles - men who had been trained in the use of the weapon that same afternoon by a French instructor. By 02:00 on 30 October, airdrop operations were complete. The paratroopers now had eight jeeps, four 106 mm anti-tank rifles and a supply of food and ammunition. Eleven Piper Cubs had been assigned to the Brigade - eight for medivac missions and three for reconnaissance - and the pilots were so far reporting that all was quiet between Mitla and the Canal. One pilot made a forced landing in enemy territory, but was able to take off in the morning and get back to Israeli lines.

The other battalions of 202 Brigade crossed the frontier while their comrades were dropping at the Mitla Pass. The Egyptian positions at Kuntilla were unoccupied. At dawn on 30 October, under heavy but ineffective artillery and machinegun fire, they took the fortifications at Thamed, and moved on, leaving a company to hold the position and the road. The resistance at Nakhal was weaker: it was taken easily by Mordechai Gur's 88 Battalion. A reserve paratroop battalion remained while the main force pushed on to rendezvous with the forward battalion at 18:00 on 30 October. The going was not easy. Road conditions were bad and the Brigade was slowed down by lack of four-wheel drive vehicles and the inability of fuel trucks to keep up.

At 03:15 hours on 30 October, two scout Pipers landed on a quickly-cleared strip at Mitla and reported to Eitan (whose radio had been damaged in the drop) on the position of the Brigade - en route between Thamed and Nakhal. At dawn, units of 890 Battalion moved up to the Parker Monument at the entrance to the Pass, established lookout posts and positioned their heavy support weapons. Three pairs of Mysteres, which had begun aerial patrols up to the Canal at 05:45, reported enemy truck movements eastwards, but declined

Eitan's request to strafe the convoy. The pilots had been instructed to operate solely against enemy aircraft until the French and the British completed their bombing mission.

The oncoming force comprised two battalions (the 5th and 6th) of the Egyptian 2nd Brigade, which had been ordered across the Canal to take position at both ends of Mitla. By 05:00, the point company was three miles west of the Parker Monument. At 10:00, the battalions were digging in on the slopes and in the caves of the Pass, and zeroing in heavy mortars on the crossroads. Two Egyptian platoons moved forward to take the positions at the Monument, but were routed by the paratroops' mortars. Then the Egyptian Air Force made its first appearance. At 09:00, MiGs strafed the positions at Mitla and at Thamed, causing some casualties and destroying a Piper Cub on the ground. Eitan dispatched a small flanking force to eliminate the Egyptian mortars. However, shortly after 10:30, the Chief-of-Staff amended the orders to the Air Force; the pilots were now free to take action against ground targets. From midday to dusk the IAF flew 37 sorties, destroying the Egyptian mortars, all the trucks of the 5th Battalion and causing serious damage to the brigade transport that lined the road west. However, few casualties were inflicted on the men of the 5th Battalion, who were in caves out of sight of the Israeli pilots. At the end of the day, Eitan was able to report that the air support had considerably lessened the pressure on his battalion.

On the night of 30 October, the commander of 202 Brigade, Lt. Col. Sharon, inspected the positions occupied by 890 Battalion and their newly-arrived comrades, and decided that the Brigade would have to move forward into the Mitla Pass. The crossroads were on a flat area, exposed to north and east, and there were already reports that the Egyptian General Staff armored reserve had been ordered south to the same crossroads. In addition, the 7th Armored Brigade was scheduled to begin its attack on Abu Agheila the following morning and, in all probability, the route of retreat of the Egyptian armor would be Mitla. Positions within the Pass would offer the paratroopers a much better defense. Ariel Sharon briefed his force commanders accordingly, and notified Operations Branch of his intention to move out at 04:30 on 31 October, with a request for air support at 06:30, when the Brigade would begin its advance into the Pass. At 02:00 he was informed that air support would not be forthcoming. Nevertheless, he decided that his men could not remain on flat, exposed ground.

At 04:30, 202 Brigade was starting to move. Within minutes, Sharon received an order not to enter Mitla. He quickly ordered dispersal of the convoy against the possibility of aerial attack. Indeed, at 06:00 four Vampire jets appeared overhead. The Brigade air liaison officer radioed for assistance, and two Israeli Mysteres promptly appeared and shot down all four Egyptian aircraft. The reversal of Sharon's move had nothing to do with the Mitla Pass. According to plan, the 9th Infantry Brigade was to make the overland trek to the Tiran Straits - along a route scouted a year earlier - but could not move until the other partners had carried out their raid on Egyptian airfields. By early morning of 31 October, it was clear that the French and British operation to destroy the Egyptian Air Force would be delayed. Consequently, C-o-S Dayan was considering sending 202 Brigade south to take Tiran in place of the 9th Brigade.

In daylight, Sharon completed another inspection tour and was convinced that the Brigade could not defend itself against enemy armor on the low ground around the crossroads. This was now a matter of some urgency, because the GOC Southern Command, kept unaware of Ben Gurion's modular reasoning regarding the British effort in Suez, had committed the 7th Armored and other brigades to the attack on Abu Agheila ahead of plan. The General was convinced that the Egyptian presence at Kuseima and Abu Agheila threatened 202 Brigade's line of supply or retreat, as the case may be. For Sharon, this meant that the retreating Egyptian armor could overrun his positions at any moment. At 11:00, a Piper Cub brought Col. Rehavam Zeevi, the Southern Command chief of staff, to Mitla. In a brief consultation, Sharon and Zeevi agreed that a company strength patrol should penetrate the Pass, with strict orders to stop short if it met the enemy. Sharon passed an order on to Mordechai "Motta" Gur to this effect.

Sharon's patrol was more a battalion than a company. Under Gur's command, it included the brigade reconnaissance group, two Airborne Nahal companies, three AMX13 tanks, a battery of 120 mm mortars and supply vehicles. At the last moment, Deputy Brigade Commander Yitzhak Hofi joined the column. When they moved out, at 12:30, they had no idea that the Egyptians had laid a well-planned ambush. The pilots reported no enemy soldiers on the ground, and burning vehicles along the roadside confirmed this impression. The entrance to Mitla was a thousand yards west of Parker Monument. From this point, the crescent-shaped eastern section of the Pass - the Heitan Defile - was four miles long and 50 yards wide. Five Egyptian infantry companies had dug in along its steep sides, supported by 14 medium machineguns, twelve 75 mm anti-tank guns and 40 recoilless rifles.

At 13:00, two miles into the Pass, light arms fire was opened on the leading two halftracks, which were 150 yards ahead of the main patrol. Convinced that resistance was light, Gur ordered the halftracks to continue. Within minutes the fire intensified and the whole column was pinned down by bazookas, machineguns, anti-tank guns and a hail of small arms. Gur faced a difficult choice. He could back out, but that meant abandoning the men in the lead vehicles. Or, he could attempt to push on through the fireswept field, regroup, and take the Egyptians from the rear. He opted for the second choice. While Lt. Col. Davidi attempted to position the support company on top of the Pass to fire on the concealed Egyptians, Gur took the lead and raced on, pulling the column after him. The enemy fire on the vehicles was murderous, but it was impossible to shoot back. The Egyptians had the high ground and were invisible.

Passing a burning Egyptian vehicle, Gur's half-track landed in a ditch. He and his crew found cover 150 yards away while the column raced on past him. He ordered his three tanks to fire on the hillsides, but Egyptian fire was so heavy that the radio aerials of two of the tanks had been shot away; they moved on unaware. By 13:15, the force was split into four: Hofi with a company and a half, and the two runaway tanks, was west of the inferno; Gur, with one tank and a handful of soldiers, was pinned down; 150 yards to the east were a number of damaged halftracks; and Davidi's force at the eastern entrance, bringing fire to bear on the assumed positions of the Egyptians. Gur, knowing there were wounded soldiers in the nearby vehicles, radioed for assistance to clear the Egyptians from the northern slope. But Davidi's mortar fire was ineffective and dangerous to the paratroopers below, and Hofi's force could not be raised on Gur's radio. He sent his one remaining tank with a message to Hofi.

At 14:00, Davidi dispatched the reconnaissance group to outflank the north ridge above the force pinned down in the Pass. They made progress until they, in turn, found themselves pinned down by heavy fire from the south ridge. The commander reported to Davidi that he would have to wait for dark. Meanwhile, Davidi needed better target definition for his mortars. The Egyptians had turned the Pass into a solid wall of flying lead, but the support company could not tell where it was coming from, and a rescue force would need the same data for its night assault operations. Posting officers as "spotters," Davidi asked for volunteers to drive a jeep through the Pass to Gur, deliberately drawing fire on the way. A number of officers, including Eitan and Levy, stepped forward, but Davidi chose his own reservist driver. Pvt. Yehuda Ken Dror jammed his foot down on the accelerator, and raced through the Pass. Meanwhile, Davidi radioed all units to cease fire, so there would be no confusion for the spotters. Ken Dror bypassed Egyptian and Israeli vehicles, under heavy fire until the jeep was hit and he was thrown clear. Severely wounded and given up for dead, Yehuda crawled back under cover of dark to Davidi's lines. Meanwhile his comrades had the vital information.

At 15:50, Eitan's battalion moved up; one company joined the reconnaissance group on the north ridge, while the other two took position against the walls of the Pass. Shortly thereafter, the paratroopers came under attack from six Egyptian MiGs and sustained seven dead and 20 wounded. A flight of Ouragans was strafing Egyptian transport west of Mitla, but could not be raised on the force's radio. Meanwhile, the Brigade had asked for air support for Gur's force but, at 15:55, the Air Force responded that the paratroopers were unable to transmit accurate target coordinates, and in any case they were too close to the Egyptians who had to be hit.

At 16:30, with the light fading, two assault groups began to move along the north and south ridges, clearing the Egyptians from one dugout (or cave) at a time - as quietly as possible, to avoid interference from other enemy units. At 15:00, Hofi had brought his force back from the west, and his tanks were ordered to fire on the south ridge to lessen the pressure on the reconnaissance company pinned down on the north face. Hofi's force also split in two to move along the ridges eastward. Although the resistance was fierce, the paratroopers now had the advantage of darkness as nearby Egyptians could not fire on unseen targets within their own positions. By 20:00 the battle for the Mitla Pass was over.

By 17:30, the paratroopers had brought out 100 wounded to the brigade aid station at the eastern entrance. While the battle was still raging, an airstrip had been prepared for Dakotas, but an IAF engineer brought in by Piper ruled that the ground was too soft and sandy. At 18:10, Dakota and Nord aircraft began another supply drop - one which had been included in the pre-operation plan. Operations Branch and IAF Headquarters were not yet aware of the situation on the ground, and the pilots had been instructed not to land. But the Brigade commander radioed repeatedly that he had wounded who needed immediate evacuation. The transports circling overhead passed the message back and asked for the needed permission. Within minutes they had it. On the ground, the Dakotas were quickly stripped of their cargo racks and converted into "flying ambulances." In the hours that followed they evacuated 120 wounded and 38 dead. In the eight-hour battle the Egyptians had lost 260 soldiers.

On the morning of 1 November, the exhausted paratroopers, who had spent a tense and busy night following the battle, were relieved by the 4th Infantry Brigade. Gur's 88 Battalion returned to base, while 890 Battalion pushed on westwards.

Lt. Gen. Dayan, though furious with the paratroopers for converting a "patrol" into the conquest of Mitla, recorded in his battle diary: "The only course open to the paratroopers was to scramble up to the hillside caves of the Egyptians and in hand-to-hand fighting, capture one position after another. This was their sole course - not only to put an end to the battle as victors, but also to make possible the extrication of the scores of wounded and dead who lay at the side of the track among the burning vehicles. This then, is precisely what they did. I doubt whether there is another unit in our army which could have managed in these conditions to get the better of the enemy."

Six Day War

In 1964, the Arab League - prodded by Nasser - decided to divert the headwaters of the Jordan, to prevent Israel from using the Sea of Galilee for the National Water Network (80% of the country's water

comes from this source). The Syrians started to construct a 45-mile canal to channel the waters of the Hazbani and the Banias away from the Jordan. Each time work began, there were peaks in the ever-present tension along the Syrian frontier. On 7 April 1967, heavy long-range artillery fire was opened on all the Israeli communities along the border. The IAF was ordered to silence the fire, and Syrian planes scrambled to meet the Israelis. In a dogfight over central Golan, six Syrian MiGs were shot down. The Syrians responded by feeding President Nasser rumors that the IDF was mobilizing in Upper Galilee to strike at the Golan Heights. Nasser, who had been talking war for years, was not ready for it - but was caught in a trap of his own making. He began a series of actions, the consequences of which were no longer under his control.

On 15 May 1967, Nasser ordered his army into Sinai. The other Arabs promptly began to mock him: his army was in Sinai, but separated from the IDF by the United Nations Emergency Force. In response to Arab suggestions that he demand withdrawal of UNEF to the Straits of Tiran, Nasser approached U Thant with a request - presumably expecting the Secretary General to take the matter to the Security Council, where decision would be delayed and eventually vetoed. Instead, on his own authority, U Thant ordered withdrawal - not only from the frontier, but from the whole of Sinai. The Arab chorus promptly began to prod Nasser to blockade the Tiran Straits, which he did. All Israel's oil was coming through the southern waterway, as were vital supplies for the southern Negev and all the country's trade with East Africa and Asia. For ten days, an effort was made to raise an international naval squadron to break the blockade, but it failed and Israel was left with no choice but to go to war.

On the morning of 5 June 1967, IDF ground forces, that had been waiting like a coiled spring for three weeks, raced into Sinai. While Col. Raphael Eitan's paratroop brigade was heading in its armored personnel carriers to smash through the Egyptian 7th Division positions at Rafiah, and Col. Dani Mat's reserve paratroop brigade were preparing for their helicopter-borne assault on another division at Um Katef - 55 Reserve Parachute Brigade was assembling for a jump mission at el Arish. At 10:45, totally unexpectedly, Jordanian guns opened up on Jerusalem. Within minutes, an Arab Legion force occupied Government House - the UN headquarters in the demilitarized zone of Israeli Jerusalem - and threatened to move on into the western city. A battalion of 16 (Jerusalem Reserve) Brigade pushed the Jordanians back and thrust on to cut the Jerusalem-Hebron road at Zur Baher, an Arab village near Government House. With the defense of Jerusalem resting in the hands of the one reserve infantry brigade, the 10th Mechanized Infantry (Reserve) Brigade was ordered to move up the northern ridge above the Jerusalem-Tel Aviv highway - and 55 Brigade was recalled from the south to reinforce 16 Brigade in the city.

With the main highway under heavy shellfire, it was early evening before Col. Mordechai Gur's 55 Brigade was in position in the northern sector of the city. With Jordanian artillery fire intensifying along the frontier, including Tel Aviv and Ramat David airbase, Maj. Gen. Uzi Narkis - OC Central Command - had been given General Staff permission to take offensive action. Gur's mission was to clear the heavily fortified Jordanian positions at the Police School and Ammunition Hill, and to sweep through Shekh Jarrah Quarter and across the Jerusalem-Ramallah road to link up with the beleaguered 120 man garrison in the Mount Scopus enclave (two miles outside Israel, the enclave was held by Israelis under the 1949 armistice agreements).

Preceded by an artillery bombardment, at 02:15 on 6 June, 66 Battalion started to move across the minefields and barbedwire fences of "no man's land" facing the Police School. The fences had to be dealt with by Bangalore torpedoes, and the squads assigned the task were exposed to withering artillery, mortar and recoilless rifle fire. After a slow progress across the minefields, the lead company assaulted the heavily defended Jordanian positions of the Police School and Ammunition Hill. Under fire from every direction, the paratroopers had to clear, laboriously, bunkers, cellars and communicating trenches. In places the only solution was to advance along the trenches and on the pathways above them simultaneously. Casualties mounted, and the combat engineering company of the battalion labored to blaze a road for tanks to come up in support and for the evacuation of wounded. The battle on Ammunition Hill lasted four hours against stubborn resistance, and amid many acts of heroism on both sides.

In parallel, 71 Battalion was doggedly pushing through the fortifications of Shekh Jarrah Quarter, south of Ammunition Hill and

facing the north wall of the Old City. Though progress measured in yards was faster than at the Police School, the fighting was just as bitter since the Arab Legion had every open space covered by crossfire from concrete bunkers. Just before dawn, Gur committed 28 Battalion, on the right flank of 71 Battalion, to forge a way through to Rockefeller Museum - facing the northeast corner of the Old City wall. Though Jordanian troops on the wall continued to fire down on the area around the museum, the way was opened by mid morning to link up with the garrison on Mount Scopus. With 10 Brigade already on the Jerusalem-Ramallah road and 16 Brigade clearing the Jordanian strongpoints on the southern perimeter, the pressures on Israeli west Jerusalem were evaporating. To the east of the city, on the Jerusalem-Jericho road, IAF aircraft were dealing with Jordanian relief columns attempting to move up to the city.

The battalions of 55 Brigade were free to regroup in the area between Mount Scopus and the north of the Old City. Casualties had been heavy - 97 dead and hundreds of wounded - and some companies were reduced to platoon strength. But there was work still to be done. At 08:30 on June 7, 66 and 71 Battalions began a two prong assault on the Jordanian positions at Augusta Victoria - a high point on the ridge to the east of the city, dominating the Old City to the west, Mount Scopus to the north and the Mount of Olives to the south. At 08:04, Maj. Gen. Narkis informed Col. Gur that the General Staff had agreed to a move into the walled Old City. While part of 71 Battalion set up a roadblock on the Jerusalem-Jericho road, 28 Battalion began to move around the northern face of the city wall, from the Rockefeller Museum south to the Lions' Gate. Meanwhile, the Jordanian Governor of Jerusalem, concerned about vast stockpiles of ammunition and explosives in the area of the two mosques on Mount Moriah - the Temple Mount - had spent part of the night arguing against any defense of the Old City that might detonate this time bomb and endanger the holy sites. The Jordanian commander, aware that his relief columns had been stopped by the IAF, withdrew the last of his soldiers under cover of darkness.

At 10:00 on June 7, Gur led a column through the Lions' Gate. He was met by the Governor and the Mayor, with an assurance that the Old City would not be defended. Within minutes, while 16 Brigade moved in through the Dung Gate to the south, the paratroopers reached the Temple Mount and the narrow alleyway in front of the Western Wall - the sole remaining wall of the Second Temple. The battle for Jerusalem was over.

Attrition

The Six Day War was over. The IDF lines were now more convenient for defense and much further from civilian population centers. However, though a major defeat had been inflicted on three Arab armies, the engagement had not been decisive. Syria, Jordan and Egypt were neither prepared to concede nor ready to start talking. The first indication of that came on 1 July 1967, when an IDF patrol encountered Egyptian commandos on the causeway leading to Port Fuad. The clash, in marshland, afforded neither side advantages of maneuver. It lasted through days of sporadic battles, shellfire and aerial activity, at the end of which the commandos were uprooted, though left in possession of one solitary strongpoint east of the Canal at Port Fuad.

Between July and October 1967, there were a number of artillery duels, and even one bombing sortie on IDF positions near Qantara which employed almost all the remaining strength of the Egyptian Air Force. In September 1967, the Arab heads of state resolved at Khartoum that there would be no recognition of, or negotiation with Israel. Then, on 21 October 1967, Egyptian missile boats from the cover of Port Said harbor, fired at and sank the INS Eilat - a destroyer on routine patrol along the Sinai shore. The IDF reacted with an artillery bombardment of the Suez oil refineries. The message was understood: firing across the Canal diminished to acceptable proportions.

On 8 September 1968, the lull came to an abrupt end. Egyptian artillery rained down some 10,000 shells from 150 batteries on IDF positions along the Canal, claiming ten lives and wounding 18. The IDF responded against Egyptian targets on the west bank, including Suez and Ismaila. On 14 September, Gamal Abdel Nasser proclaimed that the first stage of his new war on Israel, the "Period of Defiance," was now at an end. The "Period of Active Deterrence" was about to begin, as prelude to the liberation of the "conquered lands."

This time the lull was much shorter. On 26 October, Egyptian artillery again opened a barrage of a few hours' duration, claiming 15

Israeli lives. The response was totally different: on 31 October, an IDF paratroop force struck simultaneously at three targets in Upper Egypt - a transformer station and small dam at Naj Hammadi, and the Nile bridge at Qena. Nasser was meant to grasp that provocation on the Canal would be counter-productive while the Egyptian hinterland was vulnerable. Whether the message was understood or not, full scale bombardments did cease for a few more months.

The escalating situation called for an IDF General Staff decision on whether to dig in on the waterline or, alternatively, to prepare for mobile warfare waged from positions deeper in Sinai. The debate was resolved in favor of a ramp along the Canal, with strongpoints placed to permit good observation down the length of the line. The IDF would maintain control over the shoreline while the small garrisons in each position would be better protected against incoming shellfire. Working against the clock, under harassing fire from snipers and artillery, the fortifications were completed during the winter of 1968-69. However, the General Staff was in no hurry to play the game by Nasser's rules. Static defense, never a part of IDF doctrine, would concede the field to Egypt's obvious numerical superiority in manpower and firepower - particularly in view of massive Soviet rearmament. Any attempt to match the Egyptians would necessitate mobilizing vast numbers of reservists, bringing Israel's economy to a standstill. Nasser obviously wanted to inflict painful casualties and paralyze the country economically. So the General Staff resolved to man the line with the standing army, and maintain mobility to keep Egypt off balance.

On 8 March 1969, Nasser's war moved to its next stage - the "Period of Attrition." The Egyptian campaign for the next 17 months, up to August 1970, was to be based on the assumption that superior firepower would destroy the Israeli positions and sap IDF morale, while Egypt would be protected against massive reprisal by the water barrier and the threat of Soviet intervention. Egyptian commentators explained that seven Israeli dead each day would be enough to bring the country to its knees. The massive barrage of 8 March did not go unanswered. In an artillery duel on 9 March, the Egyptian C-o-S was killed and damage was inflicted on Egyptian shipping and shore targets. For the next 80 days and nights, the Egyptian barrage was almost incessant. In the third week of April, the Egyptians attempted commando raids on the east bank, but were beaten back by the defenders.

On 20 July 1969, the Israel Air Force joined the fray over the Suez Canal. In the months that followed, the IAF would keep up its pressure on the Egyptians along the Canal and deeper into Egypt. In parallel, IDF raiding parties sank naval craft in their harbors along the Gulf of Suez, and struck at strategic targets deeper inland, including one foray that placed an armored task force on the west bank of the Gulf for a tour that lasted ten hours.

Under the pressure of events that he had precipitated, Nasser turned to the USSR to step up Egypt's air defenses. Among other measures, the Soviets provided additional advanced P-12 mobile radars, with special capabilities against low flying aircraft - equipment which threatened to restrict IAF freedom of action. So, on 24 October 1969, the Air Force bombed the radar station at Ras Gharib on the Suez Gulf coast. But reports of a radar of this type still operating in the area continued to reach IAF intelligence, suggesting that the Ras Gharib station had been a dummy. Under the daily pressures of the War of Attrition, the enigma of the phantom radar became a secondary preoccupation, though it continued to intrigue Air Intelligence.

At midday on 22 December 1969, an IAF Vautour flew a photo reconnaissance mission over the Suez Gulf coast in the sector of Port Safaga. The mission was a routine follow-up for damage assessment after a previous operation. The film arrived at an IAF photo analysis lab late at night, and, since there was no priority demand for its contents, the interpretation was held over to the morning of 23 December.

The Suez Gulf sector was not the photo analysis team's top priority. However, as they worked methodically through the strips of film, some professional instinct led a young sergeant to focus on a seemingly innocent feature. At first glance, it looked like a couple of Bedouin tents in the desert but - there was a shadow! Sgt. Rami took the photo to Lt. Y., the young officer in charge of his team, who compared it with the radar photos in his archive. Both were convinced that despite exceptionally good camouflage, they had found a real, functioning radar station. While they checked their results again and again, Rami - on the spur of the moment - suggested that, since there seemed to be no close ground or air protection for the station, why not just go and take it? Lt. Y. had been thinking along the same lines and was ready to stick his neck out.

That same afternoon, armed with enlargements of the photo, Lt. Y. reported to Col. S., the head of IAF Intelligence, and Col. Ivry, Assistant Head of Operations. He was complimented on his findings and instructed to prepare the necessary target designation paper for air attack. The young lieutenant stood his ground: "Why attack? We could take... It's not protected." The two senior officers needed no convincing. Col. S. picked up the photos and went to see the OC Air Force, Maj. Gen. Mordechai Hod. On Wednesday, 24 December, the OC IAF handed the findings to planning teams and to the C-o-S, Lt. Gen. Haim Bar Lev, and orders were issued to plan the removal of the radar - if indeed the suspicious object was the P-12.

The target radar was six miles away from the dummy that the Air Force had bombed, and 44 miles from Abu Rodeis on the Sinai coast. Perhaps because of the ingenious camouflage, there were no ground or air defenses around it, and no signs of personnel or traffic. A goat track led from the site to an Egyptian battalion position some four miles to the north. Three miles to the east, there were six large tents, probably for 40 or 50 men, and 14 vehicles equipped with anti-aircraft and machine guns. Air Intelligence estimated that there would be 30-40 men at the radar station.

There were gaps in information and problems to be solved. The initial problems were how to take the radar intact with minimal casualties, and to find the best method for bringing it home. The initial planning envisaged transport by "sky-hook" under Sikorsky helicopters - but no one knew the exact weight of the two caravans (or "shelters" in military parlance) that comprised the station, or whether the choppers could cope. This was a question that was to remain unanswered until the event.

During the morning of 24 December, the Senior Paratroop and Infantry Officer, Brig. Gen. Raphael Eitan, assigned to Col. Haim Nadel, OC of an airborne brigade, the implementation of the operation. The Colonel summoned a Nahal battalion commander, Lt. Col. A., and gave him the direct command. The two officers settled down with enlarged aerial photos to learn the terrain and plan the raid. At 11:00 hours, they were joined by an IAF squadron commander, Lt. Col. P., who arrived thinking that he had been

summoned to study the results of a previous raid. The pilot was quickly brought up to date.

The initial plan envisaged landing paratroops from three helicopters, and assigning one squad, armed with mortars, to create a diversionary attack while the main force headed for the radar. At the same time, another force of paratroops would land 25 miles to the north, to attack an Egyptian guard post and add to the confusion. At 20:00, Brig. Eitan ruled that both diversions were unnecessary. Instead, 66 paratroopers would be landed from three Super-Frelon helicopters three miles west of target, would make their way on foot to the radar, overcome any opposition and prepare the two caravans for airlift by the Sikorskys. The assault team would be picked up by three Super-Frelons.

At 18:00 on Thursday, 25 December 1969, the force commanders presented their detailed plans to Lt. Gen. Bar-Lev. In the words of one participant in the meeting: "The whole thing seemed too fantastic to be ready for implementation on the next night." The C-o-S and the officers were satisfied with the plan and Lt. Gen. Bar-Lev gave his approval.

The hardest decision of all was the selection of the raiding party. The problem started at the highest level with a demand from the C-o-S that a select commando team be assigned, and Brig. Eitan's retort that there were no commandos - the paratroops of Lt. Col. A's battalion would do the job! Within the brigade, everyone wanted to go. One company commander, having put together the team to take and secure the actual site, was told that his assignment was to be shared with another team; he had the thankless task of telling some of his men that they would be left behind. At the last minute, a TV cameraman reported in with all the necessary accreditation, and someone else had to be dropped. The sacrifice, a veteran sergeant, protested all the way up to the battalion commander - but to no avail.

Throughout Thursday, preparations proceeded at a feverish pace. The paratroops were learning to separate radar caravans from Russian Zil trucks, while their comrades of the assault team exercised time and again on a model of the site. Meanwhile, the pilots and loadmasters of the IDF's Parachute School were running through the procedures for marking the area and attaching the loads to the Sikorskys' sky hooks. In the early evening hours of Thursday, a

Sikorsky - still a very new aircraft in the IAF's hands - lifted a similar caravan and carried it twice around the airbase. The trial went well enough, though the pilot said that flying with it was no great joy. Rehearsals continued into the early hours of Friday, as the teams were augmented by an IAF electronics technician familiar with Russian-type radars: his job would be to supervise the dismantling and loading, and - if anything went wrong - he would select which components to extract.

At 13:00 on Friday, the pilots received their briefing at their squadron base. By 15:00, the helicopters were airborne en route to Abu Rodeis. During the early evening, they would join the whole force in a final briefing from Col. Nadel. In the presence of Lt. Gen. Bar-Lev, Nadel stressed the importance of silence, speed and a minimal stay on the ground. He concluded his briefing at 20:00.

The raiding force had taken off at 14:45 from central Israel, and flown through bad weather and near zero visibility. They sat through their colonel's briefing with mixed feelings; elation at the enterprise - and heavy premonitions about cancellation due to weather. Their fears were groundless: at 21:15 the force was airborne. Behind them in Israel, Lt. Y. agonized over the thought that all this was based on his and Rami's instinct: what if the target really was two innocent Bedouin tents...

Aircraft were already attacking targets at Ras Zafarana, 37 miles north of the target, while IAF helicopters were making sure that enough activity would show on Egyptian radar screens to cover the raiding party far to the south. Lt. Col. P. led the three Super-Frelons across the Gulf without difficulty. On the west bank, however, the terrain was too featureless for identification of easy navigational aids. His co-pilot peered at the ground below, seeking any dip or rise that would match his maps and photos. Despite the difficulty, the three craft arrived precisely on target. Here the alikeness of the desert terrain caused the pilots to feel uneasy: instead of landing in formation of three on the first attempt, they circled and came in to land on their third approach.

On the ground, the paratroops formed up in two columns and M., the commander of the brigade reconnaissance group, took the point. Three hundred yards from the landing site, they moved into a sandy wadi. At first the going was rough, but after 120 yards they found a hard-packed dirt track running along the southern edge. An oil derrick, north of the radar station, served as landmark. At a point 1300 yards from target M.'s column split into two - one to surprise any approaching enemy, and the other to pin them down. The "surprise force," though hampered by the terrain, began to place landmines along the track from the radar station northward. They were interrupted by the approach of two vehicles which suddenly halted, for no apparent reason, two thousand yards from M.'s position. While the battalion commander prodded the paratroops to arm the mines as quickly as possible, the Egyptian drivers began flashing their headlamps on and off as though signaling. The paratroops of M.'s roadblock remained wide awake and ready for anything, but the Egyptian vehicles came no nearer and no other menace materialized.

Once M. was in position, the main force passed on toward the radar station. At a distance of 500 yards from target, the column split into three teams. Their final approach would be as quiet as possible to obtain maximum surprise - even though, under a full moon, their progress had to be at a snail's pace. At the 200 yard mark they could see the target clearly in a small crater. A pair of sentries were strolling casually, chatting between themselves. Lt. Col. A. ordered the team assigned to cover the assault to a position on a hummock 50 yards from the radar, then called his team leaders. He instructed Nehemia to crawl with his team to the radar itself. Moti was to take his paratroopers, also at a crawl, to a nearby bunker. Yisrael was to take position behind them and assault a tent - which had to be the living quarters of the radar crew and guards - when so ordered. The battalion commander chose to remain with the covering party where he could see all that happened and react accordingly. While he watched, the teams crawled under the very nose of a sentry to within feet of their respective targets. One sentry finally noticed something and started to run - yelling at the top of his voice.

Despite the bright moonlight reflecting off the sands, the surprise was absolute. At a range of a few feet, the paratroopers opened fire on the sentries. The Egyptians did not know what had hit them. Within moments the site was secured and the paratroops were holding four prisoners: two Egyptians had been killed, and three others had escaped. Silence fell again on the desert, except for the occasional thump of bombs dropped a long way away in the night. In the distance, a fuel depot was blazing, adding eerie flames to the moonlight.

While the rest of the force secured the area, the team assigned to dismantling the radar went to work. The two trucks had been sunk 15 feet into pits in the desert, with no exit and protective walls of sandbags, all covered by desert-camouflage nets. The only protusion above ground was the 36 foot aerial. It took an hour of hard work to separate the radar caravans from the trucks. The problem was the antenna, and it was only overcome by a number of paratroopers shinning to the top and tipping it over by brute force.

Meanwhile, the diversionary attacks by the Air Force had switched to sporadic raids on the Egyptian strongpoint to the east, and on the battalion redoubt six miles to the north.

At 02:43, the battalion commander reported that the caravans were ready. Twelve minutes later, the first Sikorsky made contact with the raiding party and started its approach. Visibility was perfect, and the pilot could clearly see his objective. His only anxiety came at the moment of lift. But with a slight jerk the caravan swung loose, while the pilot's instruments recorded an added weight of 4.1 tons. Far away across the Gulf of Suez, his terse radio report elicited spontaneous cheers from the senior officers anxiously awaiting news. Then, as the helicopter's motion switched to horizontal flight, a red light flickered on, indicating that one of the craft's two hydraulic systems was failing. Normal operating procedures called for the chopper to land, even if unloaded. The pilot announced that: "Number two system has packed up..." In the command bunker, Lt. Gen. Bar-Lev turned to the helicopter squadron leader for an explanation. The latter quickly assured the C-o-S: "He'll apparently try to keep going..." The decision was the pilot's. He decided to take a calculated risk and fly on, but by a longer and safer route. Maintaining a height of 300 feet, he set course to the south of Ras abu-Bakr and toward Ras Sharatib on the opposite coast of the Gulf. Once across the water, he set down as fast as possible.

The other Sikorsky had no trouble at all in lifting the antenna caravan, which weighed 2.5 tons. Its flight home was uneventful but for a couple of shots from the ground that did no damage. The pilot offloaded the antenna caravan, and was ordered to pick up the operations caravan from his partner at Ras Sharatib and bring it to Abu Rodeis. No sooner was the helicopter rising from the ground than the pilot began to feel that both his craft and the load were swaying dangerously. For a few moments he thought about dumping the load, then finally decided to continue. The chopper flew on, low and slow, while the pilot agonized over every mile. On the ground at Abu Rodeis, it would become clear that a ventilation door on the caravan was flapping open, and it was this that had caused the instability.

On the ground, the paratroopers prepared all the remaining equipment - the trucks, generators and bunker - for demolition, then withdrew to the pick-up zone a short distance away. They lit flares in a wadi to guide in the three Super-Frelons and settled back to wait. The wadi made the pilots' task more difficult, because they could not spot the flares until they were immediately overhead. Nevertheless, at 04:00 the three craft set down next to the raiding party. At 04:35 the force was on the ground at Abu Rodeis, after an uneventful crossing. They had brought their prize home with no casualties.

The seizure of the P-12 was to have ramifications far beyond its actual value to the IAF. Though the IDF Spokesman issued a communique at 08:30 on 27 December 1969, and the senior Russian advisor on the sector reported the loss to the Egyptian C-o-S at 10:00, it was hours before the General Staff overcame their embarrassment and anxiety enough to inform Egyptian President Nasser, who was on a visit to Libya.

According to Egyptian sources, a military mission to Moscow on 9 January 1970, met with a Soviet refusal to supply more sophisticated, advanced and expensive military hardware. President Nasser hurried personally to Moscow on 22 January, but could not budge the Soviet Union from its resolve to supply him nothing more than routine and unsophisticated weapon systems - and that (according to Egyptian sources) only because Nasser threatened to turn to the West.

THE
MEN ARE
THE STEEL

The first armored vehicles were busses, trucks and tenders, clad in sandwiches of wooden sheets between two layers of iron plate. They were not meant to be fighting vehicles in the normal sense. From late November 1947, all interurban road transport was running a gauntlet of fire, roadblocks and improvised landmines. If people and supplies were to continue getting through to outlying communities, or traveling between the big cities, busses and trucks had to be protected, convoyed and escorted. The home-made armor was not an ideal solution. As fast as the workshops came up with designs that allowed Hagana escorts to perform their tasks effectively, the Arabs came up with new techniques for harassing and preventing passage. But with limited resources, and the British impeding overt defense, it was the best that could be done.

On 24 February 1948, with the "War of the Roads" exacting a heavy price in lost vehicles and supplies, the Hagana High Command decided to establish an Armored Car Service. On 11 April, the Command ordered the construction of armored cars to ACS specifications. With invasion inevitable when the British pulled out in mid-May, it was obvious that infantry alone could not hope to face regular armies equipped with tanks and other armored vehicles. And the War of the Roads, which had cost 72 lives in March alone, would have to be resolved by more forceful measures. At the end of May, the ACS was dissolved and all the IDF's armored vehicles were transferred to a new brigade - the 8th. Command of the 8th was given to the ACS commander, Yitzhak Sadeh.

Sadeh was a legend in the IDF. In 1941, he had been the man entrusted with the creation and training of the Palmach - the Hagana's only regular force - and he had built it up to four battalions within a year. From 1945 until the summer of 1947, he had been Chief of Staff in Hagana headquarters. In November 1947, Sadeh had set up the Hagana's "Armor School" in Tel Aviv. Though there were no tanks, the School had begun to teach the tactics of armored warfare. In June 1948, when the IDF first instituted formal ranks, Sadeh was made a major general (the rank of brigadier was only instituted much later; in 1948 there were only two ranks for

general officers - lieutenant general, restricted to the C-o-S alone, and major general).

The 8th, and other units that possessed armored vehicles, were not in a position to use tanks according to any traditional conception of a mobile steel fist. The entire "armored corps" inventory amounted to ten two-man Hotchkiss tanks, two Cromwells (complete with crews who had failed to report on the British evacuation day), four Shermans, miscellaneous armored cars - either home made, or acquired during the war from the invading armies - and a handful of the "sandwich" trucks and tenders. Nevertheless, small armored units did take part in some of the battles of the War of Independence. There were tanks on the northern front, in the columns that assaulted Lydda and Ramle and in the campaigns to clear the Egyptian Army out of the Negev. After the war, 8 Brigade's one tank formation - 82 Battalion - was transferred to 7 Brigade. The 7th was to remain as the standing army's only armored brigade; the 8th bceame a reserve infantry unit.

Early in 1950, Chief of Staff Yaakov Dori appointed an "Establishment Team," to produce a blueprint for IDF organization and tactical doctrine. The army that had fought the war was hastily organized in battle, and its tactical conceptions were largely dependent on the origins and previous training of the officers in each brigade. The team was expected to achieve unification of doctrine and provide a frame into which the standing army and the newly conceived reserve brigades could integrate harmoniously. One immediate recommendation was the creation of an "Armored Corps" to serve as a massed steel fist with which to achieve rapid victory on any future battlefield. Though the idea obviously appealed to officers of the newly created "Senior Armored Officer's Headquarters," prevailing General Staff thinking in the early 1950s was that the spearhead had to be infantry - with clear preference to the paratroops; armor was a support echelon for infantry. Since 7 Brigade was stationed in the Negev, it found itself involved more and more in border actions against infiltrators, sharing in what was basically an infantry function.

In mid-1952, the IDF established its first reserve armored brigade, the 27th, staffed by reservists who had served in the 7th as conscripts. Since some of the officers had not benefited from serious armor training, the brigade commander decided that all his staff,

himself included, should attend IDF Armor School to acquire a "common language" before they began to train the brigade.

Late in 1953, a new Senior Armor Officer was appointed and, in February 1954, he was given command of an entirely new headquarters - Armored Corps HQ. Col. Pundak, a graduate of the French Army's armor school, brought with him different conceptions. Firstly, he wanted to see tanks operating at battalion level; previously, operational training and exercises had been up to company level. Secondly, he was thinking in terms of combined "combat teams" of tank and mechanized infantry battalions, in proportions as dictated by specific missions. The combat teams were constructed by breaking up 7 Brigade into task-oriented groups. Combat Team A, which began intensive exercises in order to develop tactics for all situations, was based on the standing army crews of the 7th. Teams B and C were used mostly to train reservists. The Armored Corps could afford to contemplate such notions because the IDF was now acquiring Sherman M1s from US Army surplus. Since there was no experience in what Pundak wanted to do, he ordered his officers to study all available material on foreign armies - particularly the French and American - and submit written proposals for training and exercise routines.

In 1955, the Armored Corps took part in a large scale IDF exercise in the Negev. Since the Sherman tanks assigned to 27 Brigade were neither new, nor in a good state of repair, when they arrived in Israel - the results were disappointing. The General Staff, which had been in no hurry to accept the Establishment Team's concept of armor, was reinforced in its belief that the paratroops were the spearhead. And this belief was to surface in the initial planning of the 1956 Sinai Campaign. Meanwhile, the French were showing willingness to sell the IDF their new AMX13 tank - reputedly the most modern tank in the world. A number of tanks were brought to Israel for testing, as a result of which the IDF team submitted a report requesting some 90 changes. The French experts who had come with the tanks confirmed the Israeli assessment, and the deal was signed.

On 24 July 1956, Maj. Gen. Haim Laskov was appointed OC Armored Corps. Laskov had been a major in the British Army in World War II. In 1947, he had been appointed "Training Officer" of the Hagana. After the War of Independence, with the rank of major general, he had commanded IDF Training Branch and the Israel Air Force. From 1955 up to this latest assignment - and following a two year break in the UK for advanced studies in economics, political science and philosophy - Laskov had been Deputy Chief of Staff and Head of Operations Branch. He was bringing power and status to the position, but - most significant of all - he had commanded the first armored battalion of the IDF, and later 7 Brigade, in the War of Independence, and was a member of the 1950 Establishment Team. In the few months between his appointment and 29 October 1956 - the beginning of the Sinai Campaign - Laskov succeeded in changing the role of armor into that of an independent arm capable of spearheading an assault, rather than a support echelon for the infantry. He also had the task of absorbing the French AMX13s that began to be offloaded, in secrecy and by night, in September.

Laskov's concepts, though shared by his officers, were not yet acceptable to the General Staff. In one planning debate that preceded the war, in the presence of Prime Minister Ben Gurion, C-o-S Moshe Dayan argued that small detachments of tanks should follow the mechanized infantry, loaded on transporters - to be used as mobile gun platforms where necessary. The protestations of the armor commanders that the tanks should be used in company formations were of no avail. In the event, the Sinai Campaign was fought the way the armor officers had foreseen - and the Chief of Staff would later admit that they had been right.

For the first time, the IDF was operating in "ugda" formations. The Ugda - only roughly comparable to a division in other armies - is a task force, constituted according to the needs of its mission and combining infantry, armor, artillery and combat engineers. The plan for the Sinai Campaign envisaged a paratroop drop at the Mitla Pass and a fast thrust by 202 Paratroop Brigade overland to link up with the battalion at Mitla. An infantry brigade, the 9th, would penetrate through the supposedly impassable terrain of eastern Sinai, to take the vital positions at the Straits of Tiran. The central Sinai task force, 38 Ugda, was to advance from Nitzana, northwest of 202 Brigade, and smash the main Egyptian fortifications at Um Katef and Abu Agheila; 38 Ugda included 4 and 10 Infantry Brigades, 7 Armored, an artillery regiment and an engineer battalion. The northernmost force, 77 Ugda commanded by Laskov, comprised Golani Infantry Brigade and 27 Armored Brigade; its objectives were the Egyptian 3rd Division positions at Rafiah and el Arish. The 11th Infantry Brigade, with an armored combat team from 37 Armored, stood poised to attack the 17 fortified positions in the Gaza Strip.

All the other operations were timed to develop after the paratroop drop; the Prime Minister's instructions were to maintain the option of a raid in depth, that could be withdrawn if the French and British did not deliver on their promises. However, 4 Infantry Brigade ran into problems in its advance to Kuseima. Like most reserve units at the time, their transport was mostly mobilized civilian trucks without four-wheel drive, and their supply columns were held up by the desert terrain. Unaware of Ben Gurion's reservations, and concerned about alternative routes of supply or retreat for the paratroops at Mitla, Maj. Gen. Simhoni, GOC Southern Command, committed the 7th to the battle at Kuseima in the early morning of 30 October. By the time 7 Brigade arrived at Kuseima, the 4th had done their job - so the armor moved on to tackle the Um Katef-Abu Agheila concentration.

The Abu Agheila complex had been built to control three roads westwards across Sinai. It consisted of three layers of fortified positions, surrounded by minefields and a triple ring of barbed wire apron fences. All approaches were covered for miles by artillery and anti-tank fire. The route of 7 Brigade brought it upon the complex from the south, where the fortifications were virtually impenetrable. While 10 Infantry Brigade attacked Um Katef from the east - the shortest route from the frontier - the 7th moved westward, constantly probing to the north for an easier access route. Scouts of 7 Armored found a narrow path, negotiable only by tracked vehicles, in the Daika Defile. The reconnaissance unit pushed on through and found themselves, by evening on 30 October, on the Abu Agheila-el Arish road, effectively cutting the Egyptian complex off from supplies and reinforcements.

While other units set up blocks against Egyptian columns reported advancing from the west, a combat team of Shermans from 82 Battalion and mechanized infantry, commanded by Lt. Col. Avraham "Bren" Adan, traversed the defile and emerged, at 05:00 on October 31, 2000 yards south of the Ruefa Dam and Abu Agheila. The Egyptians were expecting the move; the approaches were covered by heavy artillery fire. While the tanks supplied covering fire against both Egyptian positions, mechanized infantry moved on Abu

Agheila. The position fell within an hour. But now the combat team faced the threat of the Egyptian 1st Armored Brigade moving in from the north. Supported by IAF aircraft, another 7 Brigade combat team intercepted the Egyptian column and pushed it back to Bir Gafgafa and on to the Suez Canal.

In the evening of 31 October, Adan was ordered to take the Ruefa Dam, which was defended by more than 20 anti-tank guns and field artillery. The fire was so heavy that every single tank of the assault company was hit. Nevertheless, the force persisted. Running short of main gun and machine-gun ammunition, some of the crews rolled through the Egyptian positions throwing handgrenades out of their turrets, while others jumped from their tanks and continued as infantrymen. With the Ruefa Dam in their hands, the exhausted crews had barely enough time to repair their damaged vehicles and refuel and rearm before they had to face a counterattack from Um Katef. "A" Company of 82 Battalion became the first IDF unit ever to receive a "unit citation" for their performance at Ruefa.

The 10th Infantry had not been so successful at Um Katef. Their attempts at assault were thrown back. Eventually the position was secured when the Egyptians withdrew for fear of being cut off. At Rafiah, to the north, Golani infantry had spent five hours negotiating minefields, under Egyptian searchlights. Once across, they assaulted position after position, and then dug in while mechanized infantry and tanks of 27 Brigade, commanded by Col. Haim Bar Lev, swung around the complex from the north, eliminating 17 Egyptian anti-tank positions - and finally linking up with Golani at the Rafiah crossroads. The 27th, with a total strength of three companies of Sherman tanks, one company of the light AMX13s and a mechanized infantry battalion, then pushed on to el Arish. They stopped short of the town overnight to reorganize, only to find on the morning of 2 November that the Egyptian 4th Brigade and 1 Motorized Division had retreated during the night. All the roads to the Suez Canal were open.

The Sinai Campaign was a turning point. The blockade of the Tiran Straits had been removed. Israel was free of the shadow of the immense Czech arms deal that would have allowed Nasser the freedom of the country's skies - and the ability to invade whenever he chose. Southern Israel need no longer fear the incursions of fedayeen terrorists, sent by Egyptian Intelligence. Indeed, the

presence of the United Nations Emergency Force, that replaced the IDF as it withdrew to the international frontier, seemed to promise that none of those threats would be allowed to materialize again. At the operative level, it was also a turning point for the IDF. If the War of Independence had been something of an amateur war, fought under the force of circumstances with inadequate preparation and training, the Sinai Campaign had given the army a sense of professional self-confidence - which had been lacking through the early 1950s. In particular, the 100 hours of the Sinai Campaign had confirmed the Armored Corps' claim to predominance among the ground forces. Since the Arab force build up in years to come would be largely based on the most modern tanks in the Soviet arsenal, this early recognition was to be more important than the armor officers themselves could possibly foresee.

After the war, Maj. Gen. Laskov took over as GOC Southern Command; Assaf Simhoni, his predecessor, had been killed in a plane crash during a sandstorm on his way back from reviewing a parade of 9 Brigade at the Straits of Tiran. Laskov was replaced as OC Armored Corps by Col. Uri Ben Ari, who had commanded 7 Brigade during the Sinai Campaign. It fell to Ben Ari to draw the conclusions and lessons from the war for the Armored Corps, with implications that were to affect the entire IDF ground forces. In his report, dated 25 February 1957, he referred to the need for mobile garage units and rescue tanks in the companies, and stressed the importance of brigade medical teams capable of field surgery. Ben Ari recommended the introduction of self-propelled artillery, since the towed guns had proved unable to keep up with the armor in desert terrain, and the inclusion of APC-mounted heavy mortars in the mechanized infantry units. His report also dealt with the necessity for combat engineer companies, tank mounted bulldozers and mine flails in close support. For the Armored Corps itself, he recommended the restructuring of tank platoons and companies and the inclusion of a mechanized infantry company in each battalion.

Ben Ari's findings, for the most part, were now acceptable to the General Staff. In the few months that were left to him as OC Armored Corps, he laid the foundations for the new tactical doctrines and force structures that derived from the Corps' enhanced status. He retired from the IDF in July 1957, and it fell to his successor, Col. Haim Bar Lev - who had commanded 27 Brigade in the Sinai Campaign - to implement most of the changes. Foremost among these, obviously, was the physical growth of the Corps. Despite budgetary restrictions, and the priority given to the acquisition of aircraft, new tanks were becoming available: British-made Centurions, which had proved themselves in the Korean War and in NATO, and which were equipped with a 105 mm gun. The Shermans and AMX13s packed a lighter punch with their 75 mm main armament. In fact, the IDF Ordnance Corps workshops were hard at work up-grading new Sherman M50s to produce their own version - the M51 - with a more powerful diesel engine and French-made 105 mm guns.

By 1961, when Bar Lev took time out to study economics and management abroad before becoming Head of Operations Branch, the Armored Corps had grown both in its standing army strength and in the number of reserve brigades. He was replaced by his deputy, David Elazar. The new OC's background had been in infantry, both in the Palmach and in the IDF through both wars. In 1958, when he was appointed to command 7 Brigade, Elazar had removed his rank badges and taken the basic course at IDF Armor School together with the year's new recruits. He spent his three years as OC Armored Corps exercising the brigades in combined operations with the new self-propelled artillery and combat engineering echelons. With one eye on the Soviet doctrines that were being taught in the Egyptian and Syrian armies, Elazar instituted a "brigade commanders' forum" at which views were exchanged and new tactical conceptions took shape.

In late 1964, when Elazar - now a major general - was GOC Northern Command, he contended to Chief of Staff Rabin that tanks, employing flat trajectory fire, could deal with the Syrian positions and guns that were harassing farmers and the work on the National Water Carrier in Galilee. Yitzhak Rabin agreed to give the armor a chance to prove Elazar's thesis. But the first clash, on 3 November 1964, when Israeli Centurions replied to Syrian fire, was not exactly impressive. Maj. Gen. Yisrael Tal, who had taken over as OC Armored Corps only two days earlier, was shocked to find that 89 shells fired by the tank gunners had not eliminated a single Syrian tank. His conclusion was that the fault lay with the gunners - not the 105 mm gun. Convening all his officers from lieutenant colonel and upwards, he impressed on them that enemy tanks were the prime target. The message was clear and a crash program began to improve the sharpshooting of all the tank crews.

On 13 November, the Syrians opened fire again. Not quite trusting the Centurion gunners, Tal had ordered up an experienced Sherman platoon on the assumption that this tank had seen action already in the IDF. The Centurions were ordered to supply support only if needed. In the event, the Shermans took firing positions within three minutes of the opening of the Syrian barrage, but one of their number slid down a steep slope as its engine failed - and a Centurion platoon commander, Lt. Avigdor Kahalani, seized the opportunity, moved his tank into position and began firing. Every shot hit its target. The honor of the Centurions had been restored - and young Kahalani had earned the first of many pages in the annals of the Armored Corps. As far as the Corps was concerned, the two incidents - only ten days apart - had pointed to a major oversight: a great deal of attention had been paid to force building, tactical conceptions and doctrines, but too little effort had been expended on the professionalism of tank crew members. Maj. Gen. Tal set about establishing new norms for discipline and performance. He was also to take a close look at the IDF's future tank needs and would eventually become the father of the Merkava - the first main battle tank to be designed, developed and built with the specific requirements of the IDF Armored Corps in mind.

The Six Day War, in June 1967, had not been planned by either side. Although Israel's Arab neighbors had been building up their arsenals with the ultimate objective of going to war, President Nasser was not convinced that the time was ripe. He was maneuvered, primarily by Syria, into transferring an army of 100,000 men and 930 tanks into Sinai on 15 May 1967, while the United Nations Emergency Force still occupied a buffer zone along the Egyptian-Israeli frontier and the crucial bases at the Tiran Straits. Prodded by insinuations from other Arabs that he was hiding behind UN skirts, Nasser ordered his Chief of Staff to request withdrawal of UNEF from the border. To all accounts, the Egyptian President expected the UN Security Council to reject or veto the request. However, Secretary General U Thant responded with immediate instructions of his own for UNEF to withdraw from the whole of Sinai and the Gaza Strip. Caught in his own trap, on 22 May Nasser announced a renewed blockade of the Tiran Straits.

The waterway was even more vital to Israel than it had been in 1956. The bulk of Israel's oil supply came through the Straits to the pipeline terminal at Eilat. While fruitless international diplomatic efforts continued, in the hope of removing the blockade, the IDF had no choice but to prepare for a war that neither side really wanted.

The Egyptian plans for war in Sinai, drawn up in 1966, envisaged the massing of mobile forces in the center of the peninsula, with only a token defense of the frontier area. In the event, Nasser intervened to order redeployment far forward - at Rafiah, Abu Agheila, Um Katef and el Arish. His battle plan assumed that the IDF would attempt a strike in the rear - as the paratroops had done in 1956 - allowing Egyptian forces on the frontier to penetrate deep into the Negev. As the days passed with no offensive moves by the IDF, Egypt began to assume that Israel had given in to the blockade and was too powerless and panic-stricken to defend its own interests. The impression was further deepened when, on 2 June, Defense Minister Dayan ordered a partial demobilization of the reserve army.

Hard as it was to achieve surprise with two armies facing each other across the frontier, the first moves of 5 June - a pre-emptive air strike on Egyptian airfields, beginning at 07:45, and a breakthrough at Rafiah launched at 08:00 - were unexpected. So were the tactical moves. Ugda 84, commanded by Tal, was assigned the northern sector. With the Egyptians apparently expecting the main attack to come in a westerly direction across central Sinai, Tal struck in the north - towards the northwest. The 7th Armored Brigade crossed into the Gaza Strip at Khan Yunis, separating the Egyptian 20th Division in the Gaza Strip from the 7th Division at Rafiah and el Arish. Reinforced by a mixed battalion of Pattons and AMX13s, Col. Gonen, the commander of 7 Brigade, thrust at Khan Yunis, then - without stopping - swung southeast in two columns. His own battalion of Pattons headed along the coastal railway line to Rafiah, while the attached mixed battalion moved in parallel along the inland road. Gonen's Centurion battalion brought up the rear of the inland column, which headed straight for Rafiah crossroads just inside Sinai.

The Egyptian anti-tank positions at the crossroads found themselves caught in a pincer with the Patton battalion hitting at their rear and the other two battalions coming at them head on.

Both tank columns were coming from the least expected direction - the Egyptian held Gaza Strip. While 7 Brigade mopped up around the crossroads and turned southwest again, a paratroop brigade moved in on Rafiah itself. The town was defended by two brigades, with artillery support. But the paratroops made a wide sweep to the south, then attacked northwards over supposedly impassable sand dunes, again achieving tactical surprise.

At Shekh Zuweid, which was defended by an infantry brigade and a tank battalion, Gonen repeated his pincer approach. The Centurions assaulted from the expected direction, while the Pattons outflanked the complex and approached from north and south. Leaving behind a small force of Centurions to help the paratroops mop up at Shekh Zuweid, the 7th pressed on westward to the Jiradi - a heavily fortified position on the approaches to el Arish. The Jiradi positions, many of which were permanent reinforced concrete bunkers, were of vital importance since the road to el Arish passed between sand dunes; with supply columns unable to traverse the treacherous terrain, the tanks had to forge a way for them through the road block. The Centurions led the column, broke through and moved into el Arish to mop up. Meanwhile, the Egyptians - equally aware of the importance of the Jiradi and no longer suffering the initial trauma of surprise - retook the complex. The Pattons had to break through again, which they did though the Egyptian defenders remained in place. It was only in the early morning of 6 June, after bitter hand to hand fighting, that units of Tal's ugda finally cleaned out the Jiradi positions.

As 7 Brigade progressed along the northern axis, from Khan Yunis to el Arish, 60 Brigade - with two battalions of Shermans and one of AMX13s - was returned from the Southern Command tactical reserve to Tal's ugda. Tal committed the brigade, commanded by Col. Aviram, to an assault on the Egyptian positions south of Gonen's route through Shekh Zuweid. Penetrating between two strongpoints, Aviram's lead battalion found itself under heavy fire from all directions. Aviram's battle against the Egyptian division developed at such an intensity that Tal began to consider recalling one of 7 Brigade's battalions to come to the rescue of the surrounded battalion of 60 Brigade. But Aviram broke out of the trap, then turned on the strongpoints with two tank battalions and one of mechanized infantry.

Throughout 6 June, Tal's ugda continued to move from battle to battle in two prongs. The first, led by 7 Brigade, moved during the morning southward into an armored battle at el Arish airport, then along the road to Bir Lahfan and Jebel Libne to link up with 200 Brigade from Maj. Gen. Avraham Yoffe's 31 Reserve Ugda. At Bir Lahfan, Gonen employed a different tactic. In a stand off battle, he employed the tank guns to snipe at the Egyptian forward line. Then, when the line had been demolished, he moved in on the heart of the position with the Centurions advancing along the road while the Pattons swept around the east flank - across "impassable" sand dunes. The Egyptian position collapsed, and 7 Brigade turned southwest to join 200 Brigade.

Operating in a window between Tal and Sharon's ugda - which was advancing southwest through Abu Agheila - Yoffe's ugda had achieved total surprise by doing what the Egyptians thought to be completely impossible. Progressing 35 miles in nine hours, the ugda had moved from the frontier through soft sand in an area that had not been considered worth defending. By the evening of 6 June, 200 Reserve Brigade, with two battalions of Centurions and AMX13s, was lying in wait hull down around Bir Lahfan crossroads. The crack Egyptian 4th Division was reported to be moving up from Ismailia on the Canal along the Bir Lahfan road. The brigade did not have long to wait. In the early evening, an armored brigade and a mechanized infantry brigade materialized out of the darkness straight into 200 Brigade's ambush. In a fierce tank battle, the Egyptians were routed and the road west to Jebel Libne was open.

Tal's second prong, "Granite Force" composed of ten tanks, a jeep force with mounted recoilless rifles and a handful of armored personnel carriers, followed the coast road - between the sea and sand dunes - directly westward to the Suez Canal at Qantara. Granite Force would reach the Canal on the morning of 8 June. Meanwhile, on June 7, the battle had changed shape. Tal, Yoffe and Sharon were no longer fighting breakthrough actions in eastern Sinai. The armored brigades were flowing westward, fighting occasional actions against mobile Egyptian columns and blocking the retreat of routed units from Rafiah, el Arish, Bir Lafhan and Abu Agheila. Almost all the movement of both armies in Sinai was now parallel and westerly, as one raced to block the route of retreat of the other. By the fourth day, the whole of Sinai was in IDF hands, and the roads westward were littered with destroyed Egyptian armor.

On the frontier with Jordan, where every diplomatic effort had been made to avoid war, King Hussein had acted under pressure from Egypt and the frenzied atmosphere in the Arab world. Though he had shown signs of initial hesitation, a message from Egypt at 09:00 on the morning of 5 June - informing the king that most of Israel's air power had been destroyed - forced his hand. History would record that Nasser, when he sent the message, was unaware that his own air force no longer existed. Within a couple of hours Jordanian artillery was active along the entire frontier. In the north of the enclave known to the Jordanians as the "West Bank" (of the Jordan River), shells were falling on Ramat David airfield, and threatening to put the IAF's only operational base in the north out of commission. While IDF Central Command was dealing with the situation developing in and around Jerusalem, Northern Command was responsible for silencing the gunfire on the Jezreel Valley. The war that Northern Command faced was totally different from that being waged across the empty expanses of Sinai. This was an area of hills, valleys, rocks, villages and farmlands.

A reserve brigade, 45 Mechanized commanded by Lt. Col. Moshe Bar Cochba, was assigned the penetration of Dotan Valley to deal with the batteries of Long Toms and cut the town of Jenin off from Nablus to the south. Bar Cochba's mechanized infantry and one battalion of Sherman tanks had not seen action in the 1956 war. However, most of the men were from the northern towns and farming settlements, and Bar Cochba believed that their "family spirit" would compensate for the lack of combat experience. At 17:00 on 5 June, while a battalion of mechanized infantry, supported by a small tank force, turned westward to seek another access route, the main body of the brigade took the road from Megiddo crossroads straight through the frontier towards Jenin. Meeting heavy Jordanian fire, the mechanized infantry - under cover of smoke-screens laid by artillery - placed a roadblock then turned south to ascend the slopes. A mile behind them, the reduced tank battalion was also turning up the hillside. The task of both columns would be to seek routes down into the valley from the westward slopes under cover of night.

As the tank battalion passed a wooded slope, its commander spotted what appeared to be abandoned anti-tank gun positions. He radioed back to the end of the column and instructed his sergeant major to neutralize the guns. Taking with him seven military policemen armed with rifles, the sergeant major approached the position, only to find that the Jordanians had returned. The policemen charged and, after a short scuffle, found themselves in possession of three of the long range guns that had shelled the Jezreel Valley throughout the day. By sheer chance, the sergeant major had attained one of the brigade's major objectives.

After a couple of false starts down narrow paths through the terraced terrain, the two columns reached the Dotan Valley south of Jenin, effectively cutting the main north-south road that linked the town with Nablus. As the columns converged, the brigade commander ordered all round defense of a brigade base - and dispatched his reconnaissance group to take Kabatia crossroads to the south. During the night, a Jordanian armored force attempted to surround the brigade. But the Arab Legion's new Patton M48s were no match for the aging Shermans with their new 105 mm guns.

At 03:30 on 6 June, Bar Cochba's tank battalion turned to advance on Jenin. The terrain did not permit deployment, so the tanks advanced along the road, encountering anti-tank ambushes and small units of Jordanian Pattons - each of which had to be dealt with. While units of the brigade took position on the surrounding hills, the Shermans raced through the town, despite fierce resistance from infantry and Pattons placed in the side streets to create crossfire. Arriving at the police fortress on the western approaches of the town - from the "wrong" direction, the tanks opened fire. Seventeen hours after crossing the frontier, Bar Cochba's force left the mopping up of Jenin to an infantry brigade, and turned to meet Jordanian armor moving up from the Damia Bridge. Short of fuel and ammunition, and exhausted from a series of tough encounters, the brigade asked for and got air support to gain a much needed respite to refuel and rearm.

The fresh Jordanian reinforcements moving up from the Jordan Rift Valley had meanwhile surrounded the brigade reconnaissance group at Kabatia crossroads. Through the late afternoon of 6 June and into the night, a fierce battle raged around the crossroads, until a small armored force succeeded in punching a hole in the Jordanian

lines, allowing the reconnaissance group an exit to rejoin the brigade. The battle continued through the night. But, meanwhile, 37 Armored Brigade had crossed the frontier to the east of the 45th, had secured the road from the Damia Bridge over the Jordan and was climbing towards Nablus. Since the area seemed quiet, the commander of the 37th ordered a small detachment of tanks and mechanized infantry to enter Nablus during the early morning. They were amazed to find the streets of the town packed with cheering Arabs. Since they had entered from the east, the people of Nablus were convinced that this was an Iraqi Army relief column.

With 10 Brigade racing down the hills from Ramallah to the Jordan bridges and then north to link up with infantry coming down the Jordan Valley, and 16 (Jerusalem) Brigade occupying Bethlehem and Hebron, the Jordanians were ready for cease-fire by 20:00 on 7 June. With the bulk of the IDF committed against the Egyptian and Jordanian armies, the OC Northern Command, Maj. Gen. David Elazar, had been ordered to avoid action against the Syrians - even though their harassment of the northern Galilee valley and attempt to divert the Jordan River waters had led to Nasser's military moves in Sinai and blockade of the Tiran Straits. On 8 June, under pressure from the population of northern Israel, Minister of Defense Dayan and Chief of Staff Rabin ordered Elazar to initiate action against the Golan Heights. The Syrian deployment on the 45 mile long Heights consisted of eight brigades, each with a tank battalion, and four more in reserve between Kuneitra and Damascus. Quite apart from the tactical difficulties of assaulting heavily fortified high ground, with its chain of formidable fortresses and millions of landmines, the main problem was time. The war was already four days old, and two Arab armies had been beaten. It could only be a matter of hours before the Soviet Union moved to achieve a cease-fire resolution in the United Nations, particularly when the battlefield shifted to involve their own clients in Syria.

Elazar assigned the northern sector of Golan to an ugda commanded by reservist Brig. Gen. Dan Laner, who had under his command Golani Infantry Brigade, 8 Armored Brigade (which had already fought in Sinai) and a battalion of 37 Armored. The 37th had fought in Samaria, but one battalion had been assigned to the defense of Galilee, and had in fact already repulsed a Syrian armored probe against Kibbutz Dan on the first morning of the war. On 9

June, while Golani were assaulting the Syrian fortresses of Tel Aziziat and Tel Faher (see Chapter: Golani Brigade), 8 Armored commanded by Col. Albert Mendler ascended the steep slopes immediately south of the infantry, with the objective of taking the crest at Zaura. Mendler's brigade climbed under heavy artillery fire, led by combat engineers with bulldozers. The losses of the engineers and the lead battalion were heavy, but the column reached the crest and the battalion turned southeast to assault the Syrian position at Qala. With only two tanks still operational, the crews of the other tanks fought as infantry. The remainder of the brigade took Zaura, then returned to help the lead battalion at Qala. By the night of 9 June, Golani and 8 Armored were holding the first crest.

On the morning of 10 June, Bar Cochba's 45 Mechanized Brigade had arrived to follow through on Golani's success in the north, and 37 Armored had also moved up from Samaria to pass through two infantry brigades hat had attained the crest above the Daughters of Jacob Bridge on Central Golan. By mid morning, the armor had smashed through the Syrian line and was heading along three east-west roads to converge on Kuneitra. The Syrians were running, abandoning their tanks, some of which were in perfect working order. By 18:30 on 10 June, when a UN imposed cease-fire took effect, the IDF had established a perimeter along a line of volcanoes that extended north-south across Golan some 12 miles from the frontier. Now the IDF had the high ground looking down on the Syrians - and the villages and farms of Galilee could relax in the knowledge that their 19 year long nightmare was at an end.

Immediately after the war, the IDF began to examine the lessons of the three very different campaigns. This time, the task of coordination fell to Col. Yehuda Wallach, who was both a tank soldier and a historian. There were a number of immediate conclusions to be drawn about the role of the Armored Corps. The tanks had both set the pace and proven that the word "impassable" was not in their lexicon. Neither soft sand nor rocky hillsides had prevented the columns from rolling wherever they chose. The armor commanders had substituted speed for cautious moves with fully defended flanks. There was an implied risk - but the decision had paid off. Unquestionably, the aerial supremacy achieved by the IAF in the first hours of the war had been a vital component of this speed; the ability to bring up fuel, ammunition and other logistic supplies under clear skies had been the key.

By comparison with the tanks, the mechanized infantry of the combined task forces had reached less expression in battle. Clearly, keeping the tanks concentrated in large forces, rather than splitting them up as support for infantry, had proven to be the correct concept. The IDF's most advanced armor had been assigned to the campaign in the south - based on the recognition that Egypt was the greatest threat and, therefore, had to be the first to be dealt a decisive blow. However, the second-line armored vehicles assigned to Central and Northern Command had performed admirably, despite their qualitative and quantitative inferiority when matched against the enemy's arsenal.

The main factors in this success had been correct tactical use and professionalism of the crews - and the reservists had performed every bit as well as the standing army brigades. The highest marks had to go to the tank gunners, who had maintained a high hit rate, even when firing on the move. One factor that could not be ignored was that senior commanders were on the battlefield and led their men. The IDF paid a high price in officers on the casualty lists, but the control of developing situations was immensely enhanced by their presence up front.

Another basic conception confirmed by the Six Day War was that the IDF must always be prepared to carry war to the enemy. In other words, the proximity of population to the frontiers - unavoidable in a country the size of Israel, but not so prevalent across the borders - could not permit battles to be fought on Israel's own ground. However, the achievements of that war in the south forced a re-evaluation of strategic thinking, at least as far as Sinai was concerned. The process began with a recognition of the needs created by the dimensions of the desert between the Negev frontier and the Suez Canal. The force normally assigned to the south was augmented by another armored brigade. The ugda had been a formation created for the immediate needs of war, but it was now to become a regular feature of the IDF line up. An armored ugda, the first of its kind, was established for the routine defense of Sinai, and Maj. Gen. Tal's deputy as OC Armored Corps - Col. Bren. Adan - was given command with the rank of major general (the IDF had still not instituted the interim rank of brigadier general). The new ugda was to consist of two armored brigades and supporting echelons - and it would be attached to a newly created "Sinai Armored Headquarters," which would also be Adan's responsibility.

On 8 September 1967, the Egyptian Army broke the cease-fire with a heavy artillery bombardment that killed ten Israeli soldiers and wounded 18 more. On 26 October, a nine hour barrage claimed another 15 lives and injured 34. Clearly the IDF urgently needed to make some decisions about the nature of its defenses along the Canal. As the debate developed, two options emerged. Either the army could prepare a number of brigade strength infantry positions along the forward line, which would be manned by a skeleton force to be beefed up by reservists when necessary - or the principle of a massed and mobile defense could be preserved.

Adan was given an inter-service team of experts and assigned the task of recommending the preferred defensive system. There had to be a presence on the waterline to serve as forward observers and to deal with Egyptian incursions. However, Adan rejected the infantry brigade conception, on the grounds that the skeleton holding force would be too ineffectual to prevent any sudden Egyptian crossing for the purposes of grabbing a foothold - to be secured by a fast appeal for yet another UN cease-fire. His solution, which he submitted to Maj. Gen. Yeshayahu Gavish, the OC Southern Command, was to build fortifications at intervals along the Canal line, each manned by a small infantry force well protected against incoming artillery fire and able to observe any Egyptian moves. These "strongholds" were to be an "early warning line," while the actual defensive capability was to rest on mobile armor patrols between the strongholds, supported by armor and artillery deployed to the rear. Gavish accepted the plan and submitted it to the General Staff for approval. There was opposition: Maj. Gen. Tal and Maj. Gen. Sharon - the Head of Training Branch - favored a system entirely built on mobile armor, but the C-o-S, Lt. Gen. Haim Bar Lev, opted for Gavish's view that a physical presence on the Canal was vital.

The strongholds and the supporting roads - one for easy movement of artillery, and a second some 30 kilometers from the Canal for supply convoys and armored reserves - amounted to an engineering operation larger than any previously undertaken in Israel. Nevertheless, by March 1969 when Nasser initiated a full-scale "War of Attrition," the bulk of the construction work was

complete. In the same month, Bren Adan was appointed OC Armored Corps. Yisrael Tal had moved on to the Ministry of Defense, where he was responsible for the development of armored fighting vehicles and would become the creator of the Merkava Main Battle Tank. Adan was replaced as OC Sinai Armored Headquarters by Maj. Gen. Shlomo Lahat.

Adan now had the unenviable task of presiding over an Armored Corps that was deeply involved in a war of attrition on one front, was constantly called on to respond to PLO-inspired incidents on the Jordanian and Lebanese frontiers - and was preparing itself for a possible further round of total war. And all this, as usual, had to be done with minimal resources. The concept of the armored ugda was being extended from Sinai throughout the IDF. The Corps was in the process of doubling in size, with up-dated diesel powered Centurions, M60s and tanks acquired from the Arab armies in the Six Day War. All the tanks that had taken part in the 1967 war were being up-dated and standardized on the 105 mm main gun. A new armored personnel carrier, the M113, was becoming available to the mechanized infantry as a replacement for the vulnerable World War II half-tracks. New echelons had to be created, staffed and trained. Much of the training, by necessity, turned to simulation. Gunners were trained on the firing ranges with smaller caliber weapons, and only after acquiring marksmanship skills were initiated into the use of 105 mm shells. Field tactical exercises were carried out with token forces representing much larger echelons.

On the Sinai front, Adan instituted specialist teams to examine, in real time, the lessons to be drawn from each and every action of the War of Attrition. In parallel, he resisted pressures to increase the number of armored brigades involved in the mobile defense system. His argument was that, tempting though the idea might be, committing larger forces would result in wear and tear on engines and vehicles that must be in first rate condition against the eventuality of full scale war. In any case, the "attrition" was being carried to the Egyptians by the Israel Air Force and by ground forces raiding parties operating behind enemy lines. The tanks gave support where necessary, but not at the expense of preparedness for the future. And that preparedness also included the learning of new tactics and techniques - among others, the crossing and bridging of water obstacles.

Nasser's War of Attrition ended in August 1970, but not before it had strengthened in public minds - in Israel and Egypt - a basic misconception that the "Bar Lev Line" of strongholds was a Maginot-type defense, intended to prevent any crossing of the Suez Canal. The positions along the line had been built to maintain the presence of an observer force, protected against artillery fire - while the defense philosophy was based, as it always had been, on mobile armor supported by artillery and infantry. Indeed, Sinai Armored Headquarters was proceeding on that philosophy in preparing its contingency plans under which Sinai Ugda was building logistic back up and infrastructure for absorbing reinforcements in the event of war.

There were two basic plans: the first - codenamed "Dovecote" - was designed to deal with small scale Egyptian incursions, and based on the use of the regular Sinai force alone; the second - "Rock" - envisaged reinforcement by reservists, in the event of total war. Operation Rock included beefing up the size of the infantry garrisons in the forward strongpoints, the deployment of the regular armored ugda as the front line of defense, and the bringing up of infantry to protect vital areas in the rear and the passes through the mountain range that paralleled the Canal to the east. Within this conception, three armored brigades would each be responsible for a sector of the 100 mile long Canal line. Additional tank companies would be deployed 30 minutes away and ready to move to the support of the strongholds in prepared firing positions on an earthen ramp along the waterfront; the ramp was the result of decades of dredging operations in the Suez Canal, but had been given added elevation by IDF engineers. Twenty miles back from the Canal, tank battalions would be deployed along a lateral road as reserve, each for one of the forward brigades. A fourth armored brigade would be concentrated on the same road, ready to move against the main Egyptian thrust. The task of these forces would be to stabilize a line, while two more ugdot (the Hebrew plural of ugda) would move into Sinai for the counterattack phase. The entire conception of "Rock" was founded in the assumption that the IAF would control the skies.

That same concern with aerial supremacy, together with the recognition of the primacy of the tank in the ground battle, was now to permeate Egyptian planning - and IDF Intelligence conceptions that would contribute to the surprise of the Yom Kippur

War. Intelligence Branch, and Defense Minister Moshe Dayan, believed that the new Egyptian President - Anwar Sadat - wanted another war. However, he would not launch it until the Soviet re-supply built Egyptian air power to a level where it could strike at IAF bases, preventing raids in depth in Egypt. The Israeli analysts and most of the Egyptian generals shared the same belief that the Egyptian Air Force could not be ready before 1975.

Sadat, who was not prepared to wait that long, was convinced - together with his Minister of War, General Ismail Ali - that the problem could be solved by other means. Israeli air supremacy could be neutralized by a dense surface-to-air missile umbrella, the primacy of the IDF tank force could be reduced by massive use of infantry operated Sagger anti-tank missiles, and deep air strike capability could be replaced by surface-to-surface Scud rockets. All these tools could be supplied by the Soviet Union much earlier than the MiG 23 and other aircraft, on which the 1975 assumption was based. To make Sadat's concept workable, two more elements were needed. Firstly, Israel must be forced to fight a multi-front war simultaneously, a condition that had been absent from the 1967 confrontation, when the IDF had dealt with Egypt first, then with Syria at its leisure. This requirement was satisfied when Ismail, in a February 1973 visit to Damascus, achieved agreement with President Hafez el-Assad. Secondly, strategic and tactical surprise were vital, for otherwise Israel would have time to mobilize the reserve army and strengthen the Canal line defenses.

According to Sadat's memoirs, his decision to go to war was taken on 30 November 1972. From that point on, and despite the secrecy that hid his intentions from most of his own generals, Sadat invested major efforts in a misinformation campaign directed at achieving the necessary element of surprise. Leaks to the press confirmed the belief, in Israel and elsewhere, that the Egyptian Army was not ready and its equipment was in a sad state of disrepair. The Egyptian President was even prepared to face Arab mockery with his frequent statements of intent to go to war, which had begun with a declaration in 1971 that this was "the year of decision." By telling the simple truth, Sadat let the world believe that he was issuing empty threats.

Starting in November 1972, the Egyptian Army staged clearly visible maneuvers along the Canal, including crossing exercises, at

monthly intervals. Each time, the IDF moved to full alert, and then relaxed. Each time, the Egyptians apparently retired their troops to their barracks, but in fact left some echelons on the line. Sadat had originally intended to strike in May 1973, but postponed the operation to October - the next occasion on which the waters of the Suez Canal would be at their highest level. There only remained one point to resolve: the exact date. The choice fell on Yom Kippur, the Day of Atonement, on the assumption that the IDF guard would be down and Israel would have difficulty in mobilizing. In addition, Yom Kippur fell in the month of Ramadan, when IDF Intelligence would consider the Moslems preoccupied with their own fast and religious observances. As far as the Syrians were concerned, an aerial battle over the Mediterranean in mid-September, in which they lost aircraft, would make mobilization a seemingly natural defensive move. In fact, the choice of Yom Kippur was a mistake; it happened to be the one day when the IDF could be sure of finding its men easily - and when the lack of vehicles on the roads would prevent the chaos that might impede heavy military traffic.

Late in September 1973, the constant Syrian build up on Golan was causing unease in IDF Northern Command. The C-o-S, Lt. Gen. David Elazar, had ordered a routine alert in the standing army units based in Sinai and on Golan, but neither he nor Defense Minister Dayan were inclined to mobilize reserves. On the one hand, there had been considerable criticism in May 1973 when mobilization, in the face of yet another Egyptian exercise on the Canal, had hampered the country's economy and made a dent in the defense budget. On the other hand, Intelligence Branch was still insisting that the probability of war was low. However, on 26 September, Dayan went to Golan to see for himself. In response to the insistence of Maj. Gen. Yitzhak Hofi, GOC Northern Command, that the Syrian artillery build up was hardly defensive in nature, Dayan agreed to transfer a battalion of 7 Brigade from the Negev. At that point, the Golan garrison consisted of Barak Brigade, with 70 tanks, and two infantry battalions - 50 Paratroop Battalion of Nahal Airborne and 17 Battalion of Golani - in the forward line strongpoints. While Barak mobilized its own reserve of 30 tanks, 77 Battalion from 7 Brigade moved up to Golan. The battalion, commanded by Lt. Col. Avi Kahalani, drew tanks and equipment from the stores of Barak Brigade.

With the smell of something in the air, the ugda on Golan began to take whatever measures it could, short of mobilization, to prepare for any eventuality. Combat engineers dug anti-tank ditches and laid minefields, Col. Yitzhak Ben Shoham's Barak Brigade manned its reserve mobilization centers and 7 Brigade - spurred on by the instincts of its commander, Col. Yanosh Ben Gal - rotated all its officers through 77 Battalion to ensure their thorough knowledge of the terrain. Ben Gal's instincts were soon justified. With the Syrian deployment steadily growing to 800 tanks and 108 artillery batteries by 2 October - and on to 900 and 140 respectively by Friday, 5 October - the remainder of 7 Brigade was ordered to Golan. Thus, by the morning of Yom Kippur, 6 October, the garrison had increased to 177 tanks. Facing them were the Syrian 5th, 7th and 9th Infantry Divisions, each with an infantry brigade, a mechanized infantry brigade and an armored brigade. Since the infantry and mechanized infantry brigades each included a tank battalion, the armor force on the first line mustered some 600 tanks. Behind them stood the Syrian 1st and 3rd Armored Divisions, with 250 tanks each, and some independent armored brigades, each of 120 tanks.

Intelligence Branch, which as late as Wednesday, 3 October, had reassured the General Staff and the Government that "the probability of war was low," were ready at 04:00 on Saturday to pass on hard information that war could be expected that same day, probably at 18:00. The information, coming from other sources, had still not convinced the Head of Intelligence Branch. Nevertheless, Lt. Gen. Elazar ordered the IAF to prepare a possible pre-emptive strike and instructed the General Staff to mobilize essential reservists. At 06:00 a meeting took place in the Minister's office, but the decision for total mobilization was delayed by Dayan for the consideration of Prime Minister Golda Meir at an 08:00 session of the Government. Golda Meir ruled against pre-emptive air action, but sided with Elazar in authorizing the mobilization of 100,000 reservists as opposed to the 50,000 that the Defense Minister considered sufficient. In the event, on his own authority, the C-o-S ordered a call for more reservists, and his deputy - Maj. Gen. Yisrael Tal - in executing the order, instructed the brigades to send battalions, companies and platoons to Sinai and Golan as soon as they were ready, without waiting for a 100% turn out. Runners from the reserve combat units began, at 10:00, to call men from

Yom Kippur prayer in the synagogues and from their homes. All over Israel, men were hurrying, some still in prayer shawls, to report to their reserve assembly points.

In Southern Command, assuming the 18:00 deadline, the OC Sinai Armored Headquarters - Maj. Gen. Albert Mendler - was instructed to deploy according to Plan Dovecote by 17:00. Mendler, who had at this point 280 tanks, protested that 17:00 would be too late and was authorized to move at 16:00. Meanwhile, the tanks would remain in their normal positions to avoid any indication of major preparations. On Golan, Brig. Gen. Raphael Eitan assigned sectors to his two armored brigades: Barak Brigade would deploy behind the line of extinct volcanoes from Kuneitra south to El Al (where the perimeter dropped into a steep and impassable ravine); 7 Brigade would take the sector from Kuneitra north to the slopes of Hermon; 74 Battalion of Barak Brigade would remain where it was on the northern sector. Each brigade now faced a full division, with the third Syrian division, the 9th, facing the seam where the two brigade sectors met. However, there were only four points along the perimeter where Syrian armor could easily cross the line of volcanoes - two in each brigade sector.

Close to 14:00, the war began with an air strike on Nafah - the Golan Ugda base camp. The hour defied all military logic, for the Syrians were attacking with the sun in their eyes. It would later become obvious that the time chosen was a compromise to suit the Egyptians - who were attacking eastwards. The immediate result was that the first containment battles had to be fought by the standing army alone; it was too early for reserve units to have arrived on Golan. For the first time in the history of the IDF, 18-19 year-old conscripts were about to embark on a major war by themselves. The 700 tank crewmen of the 7th and Barak were all that stood in the way of 30,000 Syrian troops and 600 tanks of the first wave. The air strike caught Maj. Gen Hofi, the OC Northern Command, circling in a small plane unable to land at Machanayim airfield in Upper Galilee - while Brig. Raphael Eitan waited helplessly on the ground to greet him. For the time being, Col. Ben Shoham was in charge on Golan.

Immediately after the air attack, the Syrians laid down a 45 minute artillery barrage from all 140 batteries. Nevertheless, Ben Shoham's 74 Battalion on the northern sector, and 53 Battalion in the south, were in position and ready to fire. The IDF Centurions occupied the high ground, looking down on the massed Syrian armor - and their prepared fire positions, behind earthen ramps on the slopes, gave the gunners an advantage of range over the Soviet-made tanks below them. As long as the Syrians remained immobile, the outnumbered IDF crews were scoring with their superior gunnery. Meanwhile, Lt. Col. Kahalani's 77 Battalion was ordered forward from Nafah. Detaching one company, under Capt. Meir "Tiger" Zamir, to positions immediately south of the Kuneitra Gap, Kahalani moved to the firing ramps on Booster Ridge between Kuneitra and a 2000 yard wide valley to the north. Lt. Col. Yair Nafshi's 74 Battalion had been strung out along a 13 mile perimeter, and one company was already at 15:00 engaged in the first direct clash - with 30 tanks of a Moroccan brigade. With Barak Brigade facing a major Syrian push on the southern sector, 74 Battalion was transferred to 7 Brigade command, to which Kahalani had been returned. To save unnecessary movements, 82 Battalion and part of 75 Battalion, both from the 7th, were placed under the command of Barak.

In the south, the Syrian 5th Division offensive was developing much faster than that of the 7th Division in the north. While the 7th, in the confusion of its advance, had allowed its tanks to reach the anti-tank ditch ahead of the engineers and their bridging equipment, the 5th with elements of the 9th was sweeping through Rafid crossroads and swinging north with 600 tanks: Some sixty tanks of Barak Brigade were desperately trying to hold back an attack that was developing simultaneously to the north, in the direction of Kuneitra, to the northwest along the oil pipeline road that crossed Golan diagonally, and to the west in the direction of the Sea of Galilee. As darkness fell on the Rafid-Kuneitra road, "Tiger" Zamir placed his seven Centurions at intervals alongside the road and waited till the southernmost reported that 40 Syrian tanks had passed on their way north. While a projector lit the Syrian column, Tiger ordered a broadside. Unable to pinpoint the source of fire, the Syrians turned tail, leaving behind more than 20 damaged tanks of the 43rd Mechanized Brigade. Tiger promptly backed off and moved south parallel with the road. Just before dawn, again from ambush positions, Zamir's company dealt with the remaining tanks of the 43rd and attacked a Syrian supply column. Having accounted for 40 enemy tanks, Tiger's force had not sustained a single scratch.

On the next north-south road to the west, the Tapline Oil Road, Lt. Zvika Greengold was performing a similar function. Zvika had been on leave, prior to taking a company commander's course. Alerted by the movements on the road, he left his kibbutz in Western Galilee and hitchhiked to Nafah. There, he persuaded the armorers to repair damaged tanks, and putting together two crews from stragglers like himself, he set out along the Tapline Road southwards. His first encounter was with a single Syrian tank four kilometers from Nafah. Setting it on fire, he moved on until shortly after 21:00 on 6 October, when he spotted a three-tank forward patrol of the Syrian 51st Tank Brigade. Destroying all three, each with a single shot, Zvika pulled off the road into a perfect ambush position. He did not have long to wait. Thirty tanks and a number of supply trucks materialized in an orderly column on the road. Zvika's tank fired at one, then moved and fired at another. By continually moving, Zvika left the Syrians confused as to the size of the ambushing force. He accounted for 10 tanks, bringing his score to 14. The Syrian battalion retreated while Zvika looked for another ambush site. The first eight tanks of the reserve army to arrive on Golan were sent to help Zvika Greengold. Most of them were destroyed. Zvika went on to fight through 12 or 13 encounters, the last of which was against a Syrian tank that was penetrating the fences of Nafah base.

Through 6 and 7 October, Barak Brigade fought a desperate action to stem the Syrian flow across southern Golan. The Brigade was almost completely wiped out, but - in actions like those of Tiger and Zvika - they had won the necessary hours. By nightfall on 7 October, after an infantry commander had organized the cooks and drivers to defend Nafah, a reserve armored brigade had begun to arrive and was being committed to battle, company by company. Further west, Maj. Gen. Dan Laner's reserve ugda was moving up from the Arik Bridge at the north of the Sea of Galilee. To the south, Brig. Moshe "Musa" Peled was moving his armored ugda up the slopes to counter the Syrian sweep towards the lake and the Jordan Valley. The battle was far from over but, by midnight on 7 October, the Syrian penetration was blocked. As their documents would reveal, they had expected to hold the whole of Golan by

midnight on 6 October. Although versions differ, the Egyptians were to claim that Assad had made overtures for a ceasefire on the first day.

On northern Golan, in 7 Brigade's sector, the situation was different. Facing the Syrian 7th Mechanized Division and elements of the 3rd Armored Division, the Brigade was holding fast, but at a price. During the night of 6 October, Kahalani's 77 Battalion deployed across the 2000 yard valley between the Hermonit and Booster Ridge. The oncoming Syrians were equipped with infrared headlamps and projectors, and Kahalani's tank crews - at a distinct disadvantage - used infrared scopes to pick out the intruders. During each lull, the Centurions shut down their engines in order to be able to hear the enemy vehicles. Here and there, Syrian tanks penetrated the thin line and were picked off by one tank aiming a searchlight while a second fired, sometimes at point blank range. By the morning of 7 October, the valley was littered with 80 or 90 burning Syrian hulks. At 08:00, the Syrian 78th Tank Brigade renewed the attack, this time making its main thrust through a deep wadi under the Hermonit. The 77th, reinforced by a company from 75 Battalion, held them off. In the afternoon, a company of the 77th destroyed 20 tanks of a Syrian force that was advancing on Kuneitra. At 22:00, the Syrian 3rd Division committed its 81st Brigade, equipped with new T62 tanks, to the battle for the valley.

By now, 7 Brigade was facing 500 Syrians. Behind the lines, armorers and mobile garage crews were laboring, under artillery fire, to repair each damaged Israeli tank and return it to action. The battle raged at ranges as low as 30 yards, as the Syrians infiltrated infantry with RPG rockets. At 01:00 on 8 October, the Syrians having sustained heavy losses again backed off, only to renew the offensive at 04:00. During the night, two battalions of Syrian infantry had launched an assault on the Golani infantry positions on the Hermonit - on the north edge of the valley - but were beaten back by the 20 defenders. In the first light of the new day, the crews of 7 Brigade could pick out the wreckage of 130 Syrian tanks and the bodies of dozens of infantrymen. To the south, at Kuneitra, Tiger Zamir with his seven tanks was holding the Kuneitra Gap, the Brigade's right flank and had destroyed another 20 Syrians. During the night, Tiger was ordered to take his force to Booster Ridge, where they encountered a company of tanks and a detachment of mechanized infantry - which they drove back onto the plain east of the valley. The Brigade, severely depleted - with 50 dead so far - and exhausted after three days and two nights of battle, was about to enter the third night.

At dawn on 9 October, after a relatively quiet night, 7 Brigade was hit by the heaviest artillery bombardment yet. As the rain of shells and Katyusha rockets reached its peak at 08:00, a fresh Syrian force of 100 tanks and infantry began yet another attempt to break through the thin line in the valley. The brigade commander, Yanosh Ben Gal, ordered his tanks to pull back 400 yards in an attempt to evade the worst of the artillery bombardment. At this point, 74 Battalion was down to six tanks, Tiger Zamir with his seven needed to withdraw to refuel and rearm, and 77 Battalion - now the Brigade reserve - could muster six tanks. Nevertheless, Ben Gal ordered a counterattack. Moving forward through the smoke and dust of the battlefield, Kahalani took position around the ravine at the north end of the valley and engaged two battalions of the Republican Guard's T62s. Firing down into the ravine, the six tanks of the 77th destroyed both battalions. By now, the Syrian tanks were all around and the Israeli crews were fighting a 360 degree battle. With virtually no ammunition left, Ben Gal reported to sector commander Raphael Eitan that he could not hold the tide any longer. Eitan asked for another half-hour.

Lt. Col. Yossi Ben Hanan, a Barak battalion commander, was on his honeymoon in Katmandu, Nepal, on Yom Kippur. Hearing that war had broken out, he had somehow contrived to get space on a plane home. En route, at a transit stop, he phoned his family to bring his uniform and kit to the airport. Arriving on Golan, he gathered the survivors of Barak, goaded them and the armorers into repairing 11 tanks - and was now on his way forward to join Kahalani. Arriving on the battlefield, he promptly destroyed 30 Syrian tanks. The 7th Brigade was down to seven tanks, but the Syrians had apparently had enough. Within minutes, a Golani forward position reported that the Syrian columns were turning and withdrawing. They left behind them 700 armored vehicles, including 260 tanks. The valley - thereafter named the "Vale of Tears" - had been the site of the most intense armored battle ever fought.

By the morning of 10 October, the Syrian forces had been beaten back to the ceasefire fire line of 1967. On the morning of 11

October, with Dan Laner and Musa Peled crossing the line to the south, 77 Battalion led the northern spearhead of a counterattack that was to bring them within artillery range of Damascus.

The course of the war against Egypt was different, though the end result was much the same. Mendler's tanks had moved, on 6 October, too late to take up their prepared positions on the Suez Canal. Few of them managed to get through to the Bar Lev Line positions that they were intended to reinforce. The first waves of Egyptian infantry, who had crossed the Canal in thousands, were armed with anti-tank missiles in quantities that staggered the imagination. Some of the Bar Lev positions held out for days against impossible odds. Some of the tank units fought actions that compared with Tiger Zamir and Zvika Greengold. But, by the morning of 7 October, only one-third of Mendler's starting force of 280 tanks were still operational. With the wisdom of hindsight, it is apparent that had the tanks been in position according to Plan Dovecote, they would have been unable to prevent the Canal crossing - and the initial losses would have been even heavier. With reserve forces pouring into Sinai piecemeal, the first problem was to stabilize a line. On 7 October, the OC Southern Command was given permission to evacuate those of the forward strongholds that were accessible, and make a tactical withdrawal to a more defensible line.

With a force of three ugdot in Sinai, and despite the priority given to the containment battle on Golan, the IDF was ready to attempt a counterattack on 8 October. Facing five Egyptian infantry divisions, each of which included 120 tanks, with three mechanized and two armored divisions in reserve - a force of 980 additional tanks - the counterattack was staged by three brigades. The plan was to sweep down the line of the Egyptian Second Army from the north. However, the lead brigade passed in front of the Egyptian line instead of from its flank, and the other two brigades were met by a massive ambush of anti-tank weapons - and were forced to withdraw. On 9 October, the IDF stabilized a line which the Egyptians were no longer able to break. Although Egyptian infantry and armor attacked repeatedly, the defenders had got the measure of the new weapons. In addition, a brigade and the reconnaissance group from Arik Sharon's ugda had discovered, on 10 October, that there was an open seam between the Egyptian Second and Third

Armies through which it was possible to reach the Canal and cross into Egypt. Plans were being drawn for that eventuality, but the C-o-S, Lt. Gen. Elazar, and the commander in the south, reserve Lt. Gen. Haim Bar Lev, preferred to wait for an expected Egyptian offensive that would probably draw their armored reserve across the Suez Canal.

On the morning of 14 October, the Egyptians launched an attack that was to become the largest armored battle in history, involving 2000 tanks. In the north, the 18th Infantry Division, supported by a T62 tank brigade attempted to reach Rumani. In the center, the 21st Armored Division and a brigade from the 23rd Mechanized pushed east from Ismailia. In the south, three brigades attempted to sweep down the Gulf of Suez coast. There were six Egyptian thrusts, and all were thrown back with heavy losses. By the end of the battle, 260 Egyptian tanks were left on the field. The cost to the IDF was ten tanks. Lt. Gen. Elazar was ready to order the Canal crossing for the same night. Sharon's ugda was to lead the way and seize a bridgehead on the west bank, allowing Maj. Gen. Adan's ugda to pass through, followed by Brig. Kalman Magen's ugda. Initially, the paratroops would hold the bridgehead while a floating bridge was constructed to allow the tanks to cross. Sharon's force reached the Canal and crossed unheeded by the Egyptians. The others had to fight their way through the corridor and cross under heavy bombardment. Despite heavy opposition, the force on the west bank of Suez completed the encirclement of both Egyptian army groups and were holding a sizable bridgehead by 24 October, when a ceasefire ended the Yom Kippur War.

The lessons of the war had to be drawn in a turbulent atmosphere. The nation was mourning more than 2500 dead - among them 600 officers - and tending 7500 wounded. In a country as small as Israel, this meant that almost every family had been touched by the war. Public indignation was growing over the failure of intelligence and the politicians responsible for security to foresee the war. And, in the background, military experts in Israel and worldwide were debating the proposition that the advent of massed missiles on the battlefield rang a death knoll for the tank and combat aircraft.

The IDF analysts, led by Maj. Gen. Musa Peled - who became OC Armored Corps in April 1974 - were more interested in what had actually happened than they were in the academic arguments. And the facts were conclusive. On two fronts, a numerically inferior IDF force had contained, and eventually turned back, armies that had fielded some 3200 tanks. On the Golan Heights, the enemy offensive had been held and turned in four days, even though the Syrians had committed five divisions with 1500 tanks. In Sinai, with the opening priorities given to the Syrian front, the IDF was successfully counterattacking by the eleventh day. In the absence of adequate initial air support, since the IAF had to contend with its own missile problems, the containment battles had been fought primarily by the tank brigades. Without exception, the tank crews - both regular and reservist - had displayed professionalism, exceptional gunnery, dedication to mission and motivation. And they had done so in many cases with makeshift crews that had never operated together, as the survivors from tanks that had sustained dead and wounded were regrouped and returned to battle. Often operating without senior officers, the young sergeants, lieutenants and captains had exhibited tenacity and superb tactical judgment. Above all, they had proved that the tank was still the best answer to other tanks.

Peled faced a number of tough decisions, the first of which was a choice between maintaining a high quality small force or building a larger armored corps quickly. With Israel's Arab neighbors obviously able to replace lost equipment easily, and showing every intention of increasing beyond their pre-October 1973 strength, the IDF could not risk impossible force ratios - so Peled opted for the second choice on the assumption that hard work could achieve quality later. New crews were trained in shortened courses and sent in double time to reconstitute the standing army's tank brigades. Patton M60 A3s were arriving from the United States, and the Ordnance Corps armorers and garages were working feverishly to repair and overhaul the vehicles damaged in the war. The Armored Corps was also thinking ahead to the acceptance, in 1979, of its first Merkava tanks, which were being built to entirely new conceptions and to meet the precise specifications of the IDF. Modern munitions, such as those that had appeared on the Yom Kippur battlefield, were influencing thinking about the survivability of tanks and, first and foremost, the crews. The designers of the Merkava had already assigned top priority to survivability. It now remained to find

solutions for the older generation tanks. Work done on the Merkava had also opened up, within Israeli industry, the entire field of computerization of gunnery - and the Centurions and Pattons were not being ignored.

One of the most important lessons of the war related to inter-arm cooperation and coordination. There had been situations on the battlefield where infantry were needed but not available, or where artillery could not supply sufficient support immediately. Consideration also needed to be given to the emerging weapon systems - anti-tank missiles, helicopter-borne rockets, etc. The answer lay in creating new training bases for inter-arm operations of armor, infantry, artillery, combat engineers and air support. Eventually, a new command, Ground Forces Headquarters, was established to deal with the development of, and training in coordinated tactical doctrines. There were conclusions to be drawn about the mobilization of the reserve army on Yom Kippur. Problems had arisen around equipment that was not ready for battle, and the logistics involved in transporting large forces over considerable distances before they could become effective. The findings of Maj. Gen. Peled and other commanders resulted in a restructuring of the reserve emergency stores, both for improved ongoing maintenance and readiness and for closer proximity to potential battle areas. Simply put, it would be easier to move men over long distances to their vehicles than to transport long and slow convoys of heavy equipment in an emergency.

The war had forged an even stronger esprit de corps in the armored brigades. A resolute resistance among the survivors of Barak Brigade caused reversal of a decision to write the echelon off from the IDF's order of battle. In the years that followed Yom Kippur 1973, as many as 48% of new recruits were stating a wish to join the Armored Corps as their first preference, and over 90% were listing the Corps in their top three choices. As far as the armored vehicles were concerned, the outward appearance of tanks might have remained the same as it had been in World War II, but there the similarity ended. As a result of the Merkava project, and of the lessons of the 1973 war, the IDF Armored Corps was moving ahead with equipment that must rank among the best in the world. The days of improvised wood and iron sandwich armor were no more than a quaint memory.

MERKAVA -
A NATIONAL
ENTERPRISE

The IDF has rarely been able to acquire exactly what it needs with the same ease with which modern military hardware has been made available to Israel's Arab neighbors. Indeed, in the first two decades of Israel's existence, the supply of weapon systems was dependent on sources that tended to withhold critical parts and ammunition precisely at the moment that the hardware needed to be used. In recent years, the relationship with the United States has offered a more stable flow - but, even here, there has been a need to make frequent modifications and additions in order to fit the precise requirements of the arena and its terrain, and of an army firmly committed to having the best possible tools to do the job on hand.

One obvious result of the necessity to face enemies, and potential enemies, that have relatively free access to the best on offer from both East and West has been the rapid development of a capacity to design and manufacture military equipment in Israel. Perhaps the best example of the country's ability to marshal this capacity is the Merkava Main Battle Tank (MBT) - and the national enterprise that made it possible.

Pre-History

Prior to the mid-1970s, the only tanks available to the IDF were second-hand vehicles - Shermans, Centurions, M-48s, etc. - that needed to be reconditioned, modified and up-graded to make them fit for service on a battlefield which was constantly keeping pace with the latest technologies. What seemed to be the first major breakthrough into new tanks came in the mid-1960s, when Israel was offered British-made Chieftains. A number of these tanks were brought to Israel and put through their paces, on a trial basis, with an eye to eventual production under license in Israel. With a number of modifications, which were passed on to the British manufacturers, the tank was found suitable. However, prolonged negotiations were fruitless because of Arab pressures brought to bear on the British suppliers.

The 1967 war had strengthened the claim of the tank to the title of "king of the battlefield," yet it left some misgivings in the minds of armor experts - and foremost among them, Major General Yisrael

Tal - as to areas in which the tank was somewhat less than perfect, and where the imperfections could only become more obvious as a result of the developments in ballistics, electronics and other fields that were accompanying the East-West arms race. Clearly, after the Chieftain fiasco, the IDF could no longer afford to wait for a miracle. The answer had to be an Israeli-made tank - a seemingly unattainable ambition. True, the IDF Ordnance Corps, the Israel Military Industries and a handful of local suppliers had acquired some experience and expertise in the production of replacement parts, minor modifications, small arms and ammunition, but no one in Israel had yet attempted to build a complete armored fighting vehicle, let alone design a main battle tank.

Nevertheless, General Tal, who is generally regarded as a world leader in the field of armored warfare, was determined that the IDF should not be left behind in the race, even if it meant creating an entirely new industry to produce an entirely new MBT. In August 1970, the Merkava project was born. Under General Tal's command, two teams started to work, one team on the development of the tank, and the other on the preparation of the industrial infrastructure that would be necessary to reduce the theory to practice.

The Underlying Conception

The design of a tank must answer not only the demands of the mission that it is to perform, but also the user's preferred mix of three component elements any one of which might only be improved at the expense of the others. Thus, General Tal and his team had to determine their priorities for: 1. protection (survivability) - not only is a crippled tank worse than useless, but a direct hit implies a high risk of burns, serious injuries and fatalities among crewmen; 2. mobility - which must take into account an assumption of the terrain on which the tank will operate (whether, for instance, road speed or negotiation of the rocky Golan Heights is to be the more important factor); 3. firepower - not just in terms of quantity and rate of delivery, but also accuracy, since it is an axiom of armored warfare that the first shell fired discloses the tank's location, thereby increasing its vulnerability.

These three elements of survivability, mobility and firepower are basic, but provision had to be made for a fourth, which was vital to

the IDF - easy repair, maintenance and re-arming, to add to the tank's active service time on a battlefied where the IDF could expect to face vastly superior forces, and where every available and serviceable weapon platform could be critical to the outcome.

In keeping with the IDF tradition that places high value on the lives and wellbeing of its men, General Tal opted for survivability as the prime element in design, while using the most advanced technologies in order not to compromise mobility and firepower.

Survivability

The experience of previous wars taught that most direct hits on tanks are frontal and on the turret, and the majority of casualties are caused, or aggravated by, exploding ammunition or flammable materials. The first priority in survivability was to offer the smallest posssible target to enemy fire. Thus, the Merkava was designed to present in firing position a frontal silhouette smaller than that of any other modern MBT. The frontal turret area of the Merkava in firing position - the actual target visible to an opponent - is 0.76 square meters as against 0.90 for the Soviet-made T-62 and T-72, 1.7 for the US Army's M1, 1.19 for the German Leopard and 1.55 square meters for the American M60.

In a departure from traditional tank design, the engine of the Merkava was front mounted, thereby giving the crew additional protection against direct hits. The entire surface area of the tank was designed for spaced armor - i.e., at least two layers of ballistic steel between the crew and the enemy on any side - and shaped to present sharp angles to incoming fire, so that any projectile would have to penetrate a greater thickess of steel than it would at 90 degrees head-on. Within the ballistic steel casing, all the systems and sub-systems that make up a modern armored fighting vehicle were positioned wherever possible around the crew compartment on the outside, in order to provide added protection. Thus, for example, the highly combustible hydraulic system, was in the outer casing, and those pipes that carry hydraulic fluid into the compartment could be shut down quickly. Fuel tanks, the battery compartment and machinegun ammunition storage were situated between the armor layers for the same purpose.

The main suspension system and shock absorbers, constructed of ballistic steel, were to be installed in their entirety on the outside of the hull. The tank tracks were composed of dry pin metal segments which, apart from giving high performance in rough terrain, added yet another layer of protection. Fully 70% of the tank's weight served as all round protection for the crew, as opposed to 50%, the accepted norm in most MBTs.

Survivability considerations did not stop with the outer casing of the Merkava. The main gun ammunition, unlike other tanks, was all stored below the turret ring, in the least exposed area of the tank, and stowed in heat-proof containers. Tank ammunition can explode at 170 degrees Centigrade, while a direct hit can raise temperatures inside the crew compartment as high as 800-1200 degrees. The containers would withstand such temperatures, certainly for as long as it takes to douse fires, or alternatively to get the crew out. The crew compartment could also be fully pressurized for protection against NBC (nuclear, biological, chemical) hazards of the modern battlefield, to allow a Merkava crew to function without having to use masks, as is the case in most other MBTs.

In another radical departure from conventional tank design - one made possible by the front mounting of the engine - the Merkava was equipped with a rear hatch to allow access and exit by a route other than the exposed turret or upper deck. Not only did the hatch enable safe evacuation, but it also permitted re-arming of the tank easily in the shelter of the vehicle's bulk. Since the containerized ammunition could be removed quickly, the rear area of the Merkava and the hatch made it eminently suitable as a command vehicle, battlefield ambulance and, if necessary, a troop transport; there was ample space for four stretchers or for a fully equipped infantry squad.

Mobility

The design team was faced with a choice between fast road travel - which, for example, is paramount in armored vehicles intended for use in European conditions - or good cross-country capabilities, or perhaps a rather unsatisfactory compromise between the two. They opted for a package that would perform well in the kind of off-the-road terrain that usually confronts the IDF. The Merkava's 900 h.p. air-cooled diesel, which was specially designed for the tank, could deliver cross-country speeds in the range of 40 kph and rapid acceleration from a standing start to 32 kph in 13 seconds. The tank was also designed to ascend 60 percent gradients, climb meter-high obstacles, cross three-meter trenches and negotiate water obstacles. Particular attention was paid to the center of gravity and the suspension system: all the above qualities would be meaningless if they entailed too great a physical punishment for the crew - and Merkava crews would later claim that they could drink coffee in comfort while moving across country at speed. An additional factor in all round mobility was the equipping of the driver with a passive light (SLS) scope to ensure no drop in performance at night.

Firepower

The Merkava's main armament was to be a 105 mm gun capable of firing five standard ammunition types. The gun's accuracy was to be assured by a combination of means. Firstly, the turret was gyrostabilized, allowing fire on the move. Target acquisition was handled by a ballistic computer, coupled to the gunner and commander's sights, that took into account all the necessary data, including environmental conditions and ammunition type. However, this alone would still leave one major problem of all heavy guns - the influence of weather and other factors on the straightness of the barrel; sun or rainfall can affect the temperature above and below a gun barrel sufficiently to cause unequal contraction and expansion. Although the distortion in the barrel may only be fractions of an inch, this is sufficient to cause an error of several meters in delivery of shells to target. The problem was not unknown, but there was insufficient data on the causes, and the solutions used on other tanks were not really good enough. So the team called in outside specialists in stress analysis to pin down the precise parameters of the problem and then to supply a satisfactory solution in the form of a unique thermal sleeve, which equalizes the heat factor over top and bottom of the gun barrel, virtually removing the distortion as a critical factor in tank gunnery.

Other armament was to include two MAG 7.62 machine-guns, though this was later upped to three - partly as a result of lessons of the 1982 war - 60 mm mortar and the usual small arms issued to tank crewmen. An optional feature was an 0.5 Browning mounted above the main gun. The objective of the armament package was to give the Merkava all-purpose weaponry, while emphasizing its first-hit capability, thereby reducing vulnerability to answering fire. But, in addition, the load of ammunition for the main gun was to be slightly larger than in other MBTs, and the rear hatch was to enable much faster and safer re-arming of the tank.

Maintenance and Modification

In keeping with the IDF requirement for quick turn round of disabled equipment, wherever feasible the component elements of the Merkava were designed to be supplied in easily assembled kits. The target was to enable as much as possible of the routine maintenance and repair - including in combat conditions - to be done in the field units themselves, or at forward garages and workshops, thereby cutting the time and effort required to return tanks to service. The engine was designed to permit a complete replacement in the field in a matter of minutes. An eye to modular structure of systems would also make it comparatively easy to retrofit tanks already in service with the latest modifications as they became available. Thus, there would be virtually no question of a mix of more advanced or improved models together with first generation tanks; the earlier tanks would be up-graded to keep pace with the new ones rolling off the assembly lines. In this respect, the Merkava was to differ from the "frozen" specifications so typical of some MBTs until the new "Mark" goes into production.

Decision and Organization

The initial findings and recommendations had to be presented for approval - which had to come primarily from Minister of Finance Pinhas Sapir, since the Merkava project had to be viable economically, and since the Ministry of Finance would have to foot the bill. The approval was given based on three major considerations: 1. the project was economically viable and would in the long run save public funds, while upgrading Israeli industry to a level where it could compete abroad on spillover projects; 2. the project would significantly reduce Israel's dependence on sometimes shaky outside sources for essential defense equipment; 3. the Merkava, for the first time, offered the opportunity to provide the IDF ground forces with a major weapons system tailor-made to IDF specifications - in other words, no need to make expensive modifications on somebody else's worn-out surplus.

Two major decisions needed to be taken: which production route to take, and how and under what auspices to organize the entire project. The first involved a choice between the conservative mode of prototype building and testing till everyone was satisfied with all aspects of the tank, then gearing up for production - or a "telescoped development" in which the stages of production would proceed in parallel with the various trials, perhaps a riskier route to take, but one that offered immense benefits if it succeeded. The choice fell on the latter, and perhaps the best measure of its success was that the first Merkava went into service nine years from commencement of the project, as opposed to 13 years for the American XM1, 13 for the Leopard and ten years for the Chieftain. Even these figures are misleading, because the Americans, Germans and British respectively all started with an existing and experienced industry, while the production capacity for the Merkava had to be created from scratch.

The second decision was straightforward and pragmatic. A "Tank Program Management" was set up, to serve as the prime contractor, as a department of the civilian Ministry of Defense, though staffed by army personnel. The first commander, or Program Manager, was General Tal himself. Budgetary responsibilities were to be handled by the finance division of the Ministry, which set up a special sub-unit for the Merkava. The legal work on contracts would be handled by the Ministry's lawyers. Ministry of Defense Purchasing Missions abroad would be co-opted to deal with overseas suppliers. The Ordnance Corps would accept responsibility for engineering and logistic coordination, for quality control and inspection. And, of course, the Armored Corps would keep a friendly eye on the entire proceedings and share in the field testing. All the above, together with the civilian industries involved, would operate as informally as possible, as one big family under the guidance of the Program Management.

Industrial Infrastructure

As the organizational and design details fell into place, the limelight naturally shifted to the findings of the team that surveyed industrial infrastructure. There was little question, in August 1970, that Israeli industry was not ready to take on the production of a Main Battle Tank. There were far too many technological and organizational gaps for that. Furthermore, it would take years and a massive investment to build, from the ground up, an industry capable of fitting the role of prime contractor. The task, then, was to sub-divide the industrial effort involved into categories. Firstly, the main categories of what, in ideal conditions, should be produced in Israel - and of those items which, in any event, would be best procured from abroad. The second category would include, for example, the main tank engine, where the IDF could order from existing manufacturers and specify the necessary modifications; conversely, the effort required to design and produce in an as yet non-existent Israeli plant would not be justified in terms of the number of engines that would eventually be needed - even if it was possible in the available time.

The first category - component parts and systems best made in Israel - would sub-divide yet again into: items where the industry exists, but has to be assigned the specific design and production problem; components for which potential manufacturers did exist, but where they needed to be guided, coerced or assisted in acquiring the necessary technological know-how to meet the stringent requirements of an MBT; fields where the basic know-how did exist, but where the Merkava project would be channeling that know-how into new avenues and new production lines; and, lastly, the logistic coordination, stocking and assembly of all the components.

Thus, for example, in the first sub-category, a sophisticated computer manufacturer could be assigned the development and production of the ballistic computer. In technological upgrading, a local foundry was to acquire know-how from abroad to enable it to expand into a completely new plant for casting of ballistic steel. An electro-optical instruments plant, with experience in producing gunsights would move on to produce the optical systems for the Merkava, in coordination with the ballistic computer, thereby substantially increasing their production capacity - an example of sub-category three. The logistic coordination and assembly, including the welding and machining of the ballistic steel tank hull, would be undertaken by the IDF's own Maintenance and Rebuilding Depot, directly attached to the General Staff Logistics Command; its workshops were not only the obvious choice, because of their experience in armored vehicle maintenance and modification - but, in fact, the only possible choice.

All in all, 200 different enterprises were to be involved in the production of 30,000 components. Without exception, the Merkava project presented challenges and resulted in upgraded technology and enlarged production capacity capable of conforming to the very tight tolerances of military specifications. For most of the companies concerned, the Merkava project would open the door to new export markets. Throughout all this effort, as the plants themselves willingly testify, the IDF - whether the Program Manager, the design engineers, the Tank Development Authority, the Ordnance Corps of the Depot - would maintain a day-to-day working relationship on every aspect of design and production; this was to be a partnership in which the army would demand high standards of performance, but would willingly help in every way possible.

With little time to waste, improvisation served to close gaps until solutions were available from regular production. Thus, for example, while waiting for final hull specifications, the first prototype was constructed using a Centurion hull that was cut in half and then widened. As each component part or system was produced, tested, modified if necessary, the final configuration of the Merkava took shape so rapidly that the first production models rolled off the line into service in April 1979. In order to save training time, the Armored Corps crews that carried out the field trials went on to become the first operational Merkava unit.

Throughout the production saga, the Merkava was maintained as a flexible conception; in other words, any addition or modification that made sense was incorporated into production models and, in parallel, retrofitted to tanks that were already in service.

The success of the production effort in Israel is best measured by the results of the first 13 years of the Merkava project. Of a total cost per tank of $1.5 million, 82.3% is local input, 38.8% of that coming from civilian industries while the IDF workshops' own direct share is 15%. In technical terms, the Merkava is composed of 124 "kits" - both for production purposes and for easy maintenance. Of these, 100 are totally locally produced, 12 include imported parts but are completed in Israel with local input, two are built in Israel from imported parts and only ten are imported in their entirety. Much of the production effort was colored by a uniquely Israeli factor. Among the engineers, technicians, machine operators and assembly line workers employed in the production process, there are men who have served in the Armored Corps, who still do as part of their reserve service, or whose sons now do - and the result has been a direct contact between "producer" and "customer" unparalleled in similar endeavors elsewhere in the world. This has contributed to the flow of suggested improvements, and has enhanced the already-present motivation to produce only the best for the IDF's tank crews.

Operation Peace for Galilee

No amount of field testing can completely satisfy the designers of a weapon system as to the performance of their brainchild in battle conditions, with all the stresses and strains that these bring to bear on men and machines. The 1982 war, therefore, was the first real opportunity to evaluate the Merkava in the situations for which it was built. And the results were better than the most optimistic expectations. All the tank's systems functioned perfectly. Above all, the survivability elements were proven to have been correct in every detail. The Merkava armor protected the lives of crew members and burn cases were practically unknown. In the few cases where suspension units were damaged, the external installation allowed easy removal and replacement in the field.

The quantity of ammunition carried (larger than in other MBTs) enabled the Merkava to remain on the firing line for longer periods of time. And the immense effort devoted to human engineering paid off in the comfort and satisfaction of the tank crews. Perhaps the ultimate, if unexpected, combat test came on three separate occasions when Merkava tanks clashed with T-72s, the ultra-modern and heavily-armed first line Soviet-made MBT - and beat them. According to foreign publications, Merkava tanks destroyed a half of the total T-72s accounted for in the war (the remainder were hit by anti-tank missiles).

Tank Development Authority teams were in the field with the Merkava crews from the second day of the war, examining and evaluating, interrogating crewmen and commanders, checking on maintenance and repair and compiling copious notes. Their findings, where they called for changes or modifications, were incorporated immediately in the production facilities and retrofitted to tanks in the field. Thus, built-up area and roadside situations, with frequent confrontations with soft-skinned vehicles and so on, indicated a need for a third MAG machinegun; within days, the gun was supplied and installed on the tanks for use by the radio-operator/loader.

The Road Ahead

The constant evolution of the Merkava has already led to production of a Mark III. Meanwhile, the Merkava has satisfied its designers and users on all counts. It is the only Western main battle tank to have been tried in combat, and to have coped with the best that the Soviet arsenal can offer. It has relieved Israel of one area of external dependence to the point where the IDF no longer purchases tanks abroad. And, perhaps above all, it has proven that an army and an industry that are determined enough can meet any technological challenge and overcome any obstacle.

THE ARTILLERY
CORPS - 1948
TO THE
PRESENT

The heavy gun made its debut on the battlefield with the advent of gunpowder in 14th century Europe. Early developments were aimed at enlarging payloads and barrel diameters but, even with 300 kg weight projectiles, the artillery piece was limited to sieges and static campaigns because of its immobility. Charles VIII of France was the first to employ mobile cannons, but the biggest breakthrough of the 15th century belonged to an Italian ruler, who began his battles with a barrage on the enemy while his own troops remained comfortably out of range. In the mid-17th century, King Gustav Adolph of Sweden achieved the hitherto impossible by reducing the weight and barrel length of his guns so that armies could easily move their artillery alongside the other troops; the loss of accuracy of shorter barrels was balanced by new munitions that could shower a wide area. For the first time, generals could integrate artillery, infantry and cavalry at the tactical level.

In the late 18th century, a British officer, Shrapnel, gave his name to a new shell that could fragment above ground and wreak havoc among enemy troops. Meanwhile, a Frenchman named De Borsa was changing organizational concepts with the introduction of army divisions that obviously included artillery. Then, in the 19th century, Napoleon - himself an artillery officer - used massed guns to control decisive points. Meanwhile, the rifled barrel and other improvements by Krupp in Germany and Rodman in the United States were turning heavy guns into much more accurate weapons. The Prussian army, under Moltke, used its artillery so effectively against French infantry that no close encounters were necessary.

In World War I, the main battlefields were static, so the cannon's relative lack of mobility was unimportant. Railroads and internal combustion engines made it easier for both sides to keep their guns supplied with heavy ammunition. Ranges were greater than in the past - Big Bertha achieved a range of 122 km - and tanks and aircraft were still too unsophisticated to rival a heavy barrage laid down from well behind the lines.

World War II added new dimensions of mobile warfare. Tanks had improved in the years between the world wars, and strategists like

De Gaulle and Liddell Hart had influenced doctrines in the direction of fast moving campaigns based on direct fire from heavy guns mounted on tanks, sometimes led or backed by airpower. Guderian, Zhukov and others had ample opportunity to prove the effectiveness of the armored vehicle with heavy firepower. Thus, artillery - probably the most powerful weapon on the World War I battlefield - now had to keep up with a shifting battlefield; guns were towed behind trucks, necessitating time to prepare for firing and imposing some limits on the size of guns.

Since World War II, the battle environment has developed out of all recognition in terms of technology and firepower, and artillery has moved to self-propulsion, combined with better target location and control and precision munitions. Artillery shares with airpower the inability to take and hold terrain. In the constant competition for the role of ground support to assault and defensive forces, the advent of smart munitions has noticeably revolutionized the use of planes and helicopters; modern artillery is not lagging behind, even though the gunners rarely bask in the limelight enjoyed by their aerial competitors.

Artillery in the IDF

The IDF Artillery Corps first took the field on 20 May 1948, when two antique mountain guns, which had only arrived in the country a few days earlier, were hastily brought up to the western ridge above the Sea of Galilee to aid in the defense of the twin kibbutzim of Degania A and B. The Syrians, who had begun a combined assault of tanks, infantry and artillery on these settlements early that morning, were so surprised by the sudden appearance of artillery on the Israeli side that they abandoned the assault and withdrew. They were totally unaware of the fact that the two guns lacked sights and rangefinding equipment; the gunners had lobbed their first shells into the lake to get some idea of range.

The first steps towards creation of the IDF Artillery Corps had been taken in January 1948, when veteran gunners of the World War II Jewish Brigade were invited to a reunion in a Tel Aviv theatre. Most of them had already been recruited as infantrymen in Hagana units. The organizers of the reunion had different ideas: posting guards on the doors, they declared that all those present now constituted the "Hagana Artillery Corps." It was an optimistic gesture. Unlike some other units of the army that was taking shape, there was no immediate shortage of skilled artillery officers and gunners - but there were no weapons. On May 15, 1948, months after the reunion, despite desperate procurement efforts, the total available artillery in the IDF amounted to 24 Hispano-Suiza 20mm anti-aircraft guns, five 65mm mountain guns and two small caliber guns mounted on armored cars.

The Jewish Brigade veterans brought with them a British-based combat doctrine - which was to remain with the Corps until the 1956 Sinai Campaign. Their operations during the War of Independence were complicated by a makeshift order of battle. By the end of the war, the gunners were using an unwieldy assortment of 19 different British, French, German, Mexican, American, Swiss, Italian and Israeli cannons - variously acquired by procurement of World War II surplus and scrap, as spoils taken from the enemy and some from local manufacture. The shortage of weapons forced the army to transfer guns from one front to another according to the campaign needs. Nevertheless, the Corps succeeded in supplying support despite the logistic headaches of shifting guns, mortars and some 60,000 rounds of 13 different calibers of ammunition across a country at war.

Perhaps the most outlandish piece of equipment available in the War of Independence was the Davidka, a locally designed and fabricated mortar, which fired a 44 kilogram projectile over a distance of four kilometers. Though it only used 222 shells through the whole war, and was sometimes considered more dangerous to the crew than to the enemy, the Davidka was decisive in a number of battles because of the psychological impact of the noise that it made. In at least one clash - the relief of the siege of Safad - the enemy abandoned his positions under the impression that the attacking force was using nuclear weapons.

In the post-war period, the gunners had to face a new reality. All the units of the IDF were reorganizing and seeking the unified combat doctrine that had eluded an army born in battle from men and women of different background and experience, speaking different languages and relying on the drills and tactics learnt in different armies. But the artillerymen had additional problems that were very much their own.

It was clear, at least in some quarters, that the art - or science -

of gunnery was progressing in the outside world far beyond World War II knowhow. Officers sent for courses abroad were made to realize that they would have to bear the burden of making the necessary changes. And they faced objective problems. Inter-arm exercises were showing the gunners that their colleagues in the armored and paratroop echelons were impatient and fast moving men - unwilling to grasp that moving artillery, unhitching the guns and preparing to fire was a time consuming process. In addition, the role of artillery in these exercises was misleading. The tanks, infantry and combat engineers could play out their game according to the rules. But the rolling barrages - so much a part of war situations - were reduced to symbolic participation in the exercises.

The disdain for artillery generated by the exercises would only fade away when the heavy guns began to play an important role in the retaliation actions against terrorist incursions that plagued Israel in the 1950s. Indeed the first real recognition only came in a major action on the Jordanian frontier in early October 1956, although the gunners had already participated in operations at least a year before.

The Corps had made strides towards improving its inventory, organization, operational abilities and training. The number of gun models in service was reduced to the 75mm Krupp, the British 25-pounder, the 105mm howitzer and 120mm mortar - both from France. By 1956, the Corps had not only acquired 105mm towed cannons, as well as various anti-aircraft guns, from France - but was also taking its first steps towards self-propulsion by purchasing its first battery of 105mm guns mounted on AMX tank hulls. Artillery units had been reorganized in battalion frames - that had already been exercised - and the artillery school was an established fact.

The October 1956 Sinai Campaign was altogether a sad experience for the artillerymen, but one that was to pay future dividends. Infantry commanders were only dimly aware of what artillery could do for them; in one classic case - the overland trek of the 9th Brigade from Eilat to Sharm e-Shekh - the commander only realized that he had artillery with him when the gunners, on their own initiative, fired a few rounds in the final assault. At the Mitla Pass, where mortars had dropped with the paratroops and 25 pounders caught up with them overland, the artillerymen played a minor role because they were neither asked for support nor supplied with the data they needed. Indeed, the paratroop approach, espoused by their brigade commander, was that the use of barrages was contrary to the concept of surprise assaults.

On all fronts in Sinai, the artillery had problems in keeping up with the tanks in sandy terrain. In many cases the gunners had to push the vehicles and guns to keep them moving. The outstanding exceptions, and probably the ones that were to determine the future, were the batteries that moved with the 7th and 27th Brigades through Abu Agheila and Rafiah. The 7th Brigade action started badly for the artillerymen. At the Rueifa Dam, which was a magnificent success for the armor, a battalion commander, asked by a gunnery officer why he wasn't asking for support, responded that in the heat of battle he had forgotten that the brigade had artillery. Later, however, the guns with both brigades were assigned solos against oncoming columns of tanks, and succeeded in repelling the Egyptians.

The Sinai Campaign changed some high level thinking in the IDF. After the war, the Chief of Staff went on record with the belief that the emphasis had moved - and must continue moving - from infantry to tanks operating together with highly mobile artillery. In other words, the Artillery Corps must be based on self-propelled guns, of which there had been only one battery in the Campaign. The consequent re-evaluation of the Corps' combat doctrine led it away from its British and French origins towards an original Israeli approach. Emphasis was placed on self-propulsion and updated techniques, that would enable the artillery to provide constant, accurate and rapid support for armored and infantry formations. The Corps had deployed in divisional support groups for the first time during the Sinai Campaign. After the war, it began to integrate a divisional artillery concept into its doctrine. Meanwhile, the anti-tank function, which already included wire-guided missiles, was transferred from the artillery to the infantry.

By 1967 the Corps had acquired various mobile weapons, including additional 155mm and 105mm guns from France, and 105mm "Priest" self-propelled guns of American manufacture. In 1965 the French M-50 was mounted on a Sherman hull and added to the arsenal. The Soltam factory in Israel also began producing a 120mm mortar for mounting on armored personnel carriers.

Between the War of Independence and the Sinai Campaign, the

Corps' primary operational concern had been retaliatory measures in response to terrorist attacks. Following the Sinai Campaign, the role of artillery was to expand. In accordance with an Arab League decision to deny Israel the source waters of the Jordan River - and, thereby, the 80% of its water that was to come from the Sea of Galilee - Syria began diversionary works along the length of the Golan Heights. IDF artillery had already been active in silencing Syrian fire on fishing boats and the communities along the frontier. Now the gunners were to act, together with tanks and aircraft, in preventing the earthmoving works on the Syrian diversionary canal.

The first major actions were spearheaded by tanks firing high trajectory anti-tank shells, but the artillerymen were able - not without argument - to convince their comrades that the heavy guns could cover areas far more effectively, and could do more damage to the earthmoving equipment. In addition, even though the Air Force could do a good job, artillery was limited neither by weather nor poor visibility. The point had been made and the General Staff was ready, finally, to allot the Artillery Corps the priorities that were to make it effective in the Six Day War.

The Artillery Corps that went to war on the morning of 5 June 1967 was accorded a vastly different role to the one it had played in the Sinai Campaign. At Um Katef, where they had been almost ignored in 1956, the artillerymen opened the IDF assault on a fortification that was known to contain 66 tanks and 160 heavy guns. An entire artillery regiment laid down an opening barrage, then continued to support the advancing assault teams with rolling fire ahead of them in the trenches. More than 5000 shells were fired in this one action. In two other unconventional incidents in Sinai, an artillery unit waged its own battle, in direct trajectory fire, against Egyptian tanks 500 yards away - and, in the dark at the Mitla Pass, the guns were used to separate a mixed column of Egyptians and Israelis, with an artillery officer issuing instructions: "The first vehicle is ours, the second is theirs..." The first unit to reach the Suez Canal was an artillery battalion.

In the battle for Jerusalem, the gunners provided close support for each of the three brigades engaging the Jordanians, while paying exceptional care to an accuracy that avoided the holy sites of any of the three religions in the city. In the opening battle for Golan, a young artillery lieutenant, who had been transferred from the

Egyptian front, was assigned as gunnery liaison to a tank battalion. He was soon to find himself, not only directing the fire of four artillery battalions, but also commanding the armor to which he had been attached. All along the Heights the gunners supplied close artillery support to infantry and armor on a massive scale, while themselves under fire from Syrian artillery positioned on higher ground with a better view.

Following the Six Day War, the Corps was busy incorporating captured artillery (122mm long and short barrel guns, and 240mm Katyusha rocket launchers), much of it Soviet-made. In parallel, local industry was encouraged to expand its production of guns, including a mobile 160mm mortar. But the updating and training progressed under pressure. Though the Six Day War ended in June 1967, there were artillery duels across the Suez Canal in July, and they continued until October 1967. On 21 October, Egyptian missile boats fired at and sank an Israeli destroyer, the INS Eilat, on routine patrol off the Sinai shores. The artillery were ordered to retaliate with a shelling of the Suez oil refineries. The message was well received and the Egyptian bombardments across the Canal dropped in intensity.

Then, on 8 September 1968, the Egyptian batteries opened what was to become the War of Attrition. An exceptionally heavy barrage of 10,000 shells, from 150 batteries, rained down on IDF positions, killing ten Israeli soldiers and wounding 18. The IDF again responded in kind, by shelling targets on the west bank of Suez. The next serious artillery violation of the ceasefire was on 26 October, but this time the IDF response was with deep penetration raids in Upper Egypt.

In the months that followed, work began on providing the forward units with adequate shelter against bombardments. The construction was completed, under sporadic sniper fire, in the early spring of 1969 - and not a moment too soon. On 8 March 1969, the Egyptians began an artillery barrage that was to last, day and night, for 80 days. The first IDF soldiers to take action against the Egyptian initiative were the artillerymen. On 9 March, the Egyptian Chief of Staff was himself killed by shellfire answering the barrage he had ordered. Apart from the repulse of occasional commando raids across the water, the gunners were to have a virtual monopoly until the Air Force joined the fray on 20 July 1969. The War of Attrition lasted 17 months, and spread to the other frontiers. IDF artillery was in action almost every day, reminding President Nasser that attrition could not bring the IDF and Israel to their knees.

Under the pressures of the War of Attrition, the Corps further updated and expanded its arsenal with 155mm self-propelled M-109 guns. Towards the end of that war, mobile 175mm guns, which could be converted to 203mm, were also added to the line up. After the war, in 1971, an Israeli-made 155mm gun, the L-33, was mounted on a Sherman tank chassis - in keeping with the philosophy of self-propulsion. The efforts towards modernization and mobility were a reflection of steadily changing IDF attitudes to artillery, which would propel the Corps into the high-tech revolution of later years.

Like the entire IDF, the Corps was taken by surprise by the Yom Kippur War. Though vastly outnumbered on both fronts, artillery was called on to combat the effects of hand-held anti-tank missiles fired from ranges beyond the reach of the tanks' own guns. It also had to replace the Air Force in the first few days, since the planes could offer little support to ground forces operating under the enemy's missile umbrella. All in all, the Corps fired 350,000 shells, and proved itself in difficult conditions on both the Syrian and Egyptian fronts. It participated, among others, in the decisive battle over the Chinese Farm, the assault on Mount Hermon, and the epic armor clash of the Vale of Tears. In an operation that was more reminiscent of commandos than artillery, two 155mm cannons were helicoptered to the top of Jebel Ataqa, deep behind enemy lines and only a few hundred yards above Egyptian army camps; for 50 minutes the guns shelled convoys moving up on the Cairo-Suez road and were then helicoptered home. On Golan at one point IDF artillery pounded the outskirts of Damascus and its airport. But, for the first time, the Corps suffered very heavy casualties - 191 gunners fell in battle.

After the war, the operational emphasis moved to the north. The Syrians continued to wage a campaign of attrition for some months, and the PLO, which had been driven out of Jordan in 1970, began to operate from across the Lebanese frontier. The artillery was active in neutralizing terrorist fire, and in covering the 1978 Litani and 1982 Peace for Galilee Operations; indeed, in 1982, the gunners' role was greater than ever before.

Routine Tasks of the Artillery

Since the expulsion of the PLO from Jordan, in 1970, and the beginning of talks with Egypt, in 1974, the ongoing security focus has moved north. The Lebanese frontier and the security zone in southern Lebanon present the artillery with a three-fold mission: to respond to terrorist artillery and rocket fire aimed at Galilee and the security zone, to provide rapid and effective support for Israeli units in action against Shi'ite extremists and Palestinian terrorists, and to support the South Lebanese Army (SLA). With these tasks in mind, batteries are deployed along the frontier, and sometimes within the security zone itself; the choice of location is not only operational - but also in order that the guns' noise should not disturb local residents.

The Corps makes a point of thoroughly training every outpost and patrol commander, so that even NCOs can request and receive artillery support when under attack. Their requests can be directed straight to the artillery battery without the loss of time which accompanies a long chain of command. Thus, the job of artillery officers in each infantry and tank battalion is to make sure that each junior commander receives adequate briefing - rather than to act as forward observers for the batteries. The result is a growing reliance on artillery fire in preference to direct contact, wherever possible. Bearing in mind the nature of the area of operations, strict orders forbid fire near any UNIFIL post or civilian concentration. The versatility of modern, self-propelled guns enables the artillery to intervene before combat helicopters - whose pilots need to be briefed before take off, and even before infantry.

The IDF artillery presence on the Golan Heights, in the zones that were delineated by the 1974 Separation of Forces Agreement with Syria, is primarily as a deterrent. The batteries must always be ready to fire or to move eastward and are, therefore, in a high state of readiness, difficult to maintain when the front is almost completely, if deceptively, calm. Frequent training exercises, often involving inter-arm cooperation, have paid off in other ways: within minutes after a recent night accident - when a civilian fell into a ravine - a battery was firing flares to aid the rescuers.

There are no illusions about the potential threat on Golan. In the words of a senior artillery officer on the sector: "The balance - of - forces is so much against us that numbers lose all significance.

The Syrian front can be measured by artillery pieces per kilometer, not to mention the BM-21 'tank-breakers,' which effectively represent the equivalent of 40 guns per piece. Under these conditions, our tactics are to concentrate firepower on those elements of Syrian artillery which are the most troublesome for our forces, and to be as mobile as possible."

The Men, The Equipment and the Future

The central task of artillery is still to assist the ground forces in accomplishing their mission, but new technologies are reshaping doctrine: strategists now realize that the gunners will be able to pinpoint targets from great distances, allowing acceptance of missions previously beyond their capabilities. The artillery of the future will not only support other ground forces, but will also share in the battle itself, much as the air force does, by destroying point targets with great accuracy. The technology already exists.

In the past, artillery represented a statistical threat. Targeting areas of 200 or more square meters with intense fire, a certain percentage of hits could be expected. Given the means by which one or two shells will suffice to destroy a target, the problem becomes one of target acquisition and selection. For example, if hitting the command tank of a brigade or battalion paralyzes the entire force, then it is wasteful to expend thousands of shells to destroy the other tanks.

There has been a classic tendency amongst field officers in all armies to engage the forces immediately facing them, while the most serious threat may well be some 20 kilometers away. Using the new technologies to destroy targets which tanks could hit just as easily would not be utilizing artillery's qualitative advantage. The new doctrines - and the equipment to back them up - therefore presuppose that air strikes will attack targets at distances over 30 kilometers, artillery will engage those between 10 and 30 kilometers away, and armored divisions and infantry will take care of the rest.

The IDF Artillery Corps was the first echelon of the ground forces to introduce computerization for faster and more accurate responses. A second element of the technological revolution relates to the gunner's ability to "see" his target, well beyond the horizon, and correct his fire without dependency on observer officers alone. Transmission of signals of this sort on the modern battlefield is not enough: the signals need to be secure against electronic interference. A third aspect of the revolution is the artillery rocket, which is both maneuverable and able to employ a wide variety of payloads. The net result of these and other developments is that the modern artilleryman is no longer simply a man who shoves projectile and propellant into a gun breech. He needs to be conversant with electronics, computers, drones (remotely piloted vehicles) and the other paraphernalia of the late twentieth century.

More than three-quarters of the men serving in the Artillery Corps are volunteers. According to Corps' research, high school graduates are attracted by the technological sophistication, compared with other arms. NCOs and junior officers have to be able to combine tactical conceptions with sophisticated professional knowledge. Artillerymen can advance rapidly: a youngster can become a lieutenant 20-24 months after being drafted. But prior education is not necessarily the criterion. According to the Senior Artillery Officer: "There are youngsters who spend more time on Tel Aviv beaches than in school, and we often find in them an extraordinary natural leadership potential. We look after them and send them to NCO courses. Youngsters who did not succeed in the civilian educational system for all sorts of reasons - family or social problems, for example - can break out of the vicious circle of personal failure. In the Corps they learn self-confidence and realize their own value. Marginal characters can become full-fledged citizens. We also absorb hundreds of new immigrants."

In recruiting new men, emphasis is placed on the corps' sophistication and on the wide range of tasks an artillery officer must do in a relatively short time. Junior officers can serve in topography units where they use geodesics and trigonometry, in the battery itself and also as forward spotters in front units.

The attention paid to the individual soldier in the artillery is considered to be among the most thorough in the IDF. The familial atmosphere of a battery contributes greatly to gun crews' effective functioning.

The Artillery Corps became in the 1970s the first combat arm to use women instructors to train fighting soldiers. Though they do not have active combat roles, they can become officers and hold jobs in the Corps HQ, where they perform liaison functions. The Senior Artillery Officer testifies: "In most cases their performance is even better than their male counterparts. We have a policy of equal opportunity for instruction and staff positions, the only limitations being physical ones."

The Artillery Corps faced a hard uphill fight to establish its credentials as something more than a support arm for infantry and armor. Its own performance, enhanced by the new technologies, have won it a respected place in the order of battle of the IDF. Indeed, in 1983 the Artillery Corps became part of the Ground Forces Command, increasing the degree of cooperation and integration with various branches of the IDF. Combining effective utilization of high technology with a modern combat doctrine, the Corps will continue to provide the IDF with a powerful and efficient artillery capability.

CAPTAIN'S
LOG - ISRAEL
NAVY

Early in 1988, an IDF press release noted that a committee, appointed by the Chief-of-Staff and chaired by Major General Yisrael Tal, had recommended acceptance of the Israel Navy's proposals for procurement of its next generation ships. The communique confirmed that the decision related to reallotment of funds resulting from cancellation of the Lavi aircraft project. This press release was noteworthy because of its departure from past practice in two aspects. First, the IDF rarely announces future procurement plans, unless they are subject to contracts announced by foreign governments and legislatures. Second, the Navy was being singled out for the first open reference to major procurement plans emanating from the recently freed funds.

Marine needs had never before been high in the order of priorities. In pre-State days, agricultural settlement and its defense were foremost in the minds of the Jewish community in Palestine. The British mandatory authority - itself representative of the greatest maritime and naval power of its time - discouraged local Jewish shipping. And Jaffa Port was a virtual monopoly of Arab longshoremen. In 1926, a seafaring kibbutz motivated by a fierce desire to "conquer the sea" and develop fishing and merchant marine occupations, set up operations on a beach to the north of Tel Aviv. However, their achievements, in building fishing boats and sailing between Tel Aviv and Haifa, fell far short of the dream. But they did build a foundation on which youth and sports organizations could develop.

Then, in 1936, Arab riots and strikes shut down Jaffa Port. For months the Jewish community was without a vital lifeline for its supply from abroad. That problem was solved when, in a three month marathon, Tel Aviv built its own lighterage port to break the strike. But the sea was already providing another focus of national attention: since 1934, clandestine immigrant ships had been trickling through with refugees escaping the Nazi regime in Europe and evading the harsh limitations imposed by the British. This unlikely combination - of a port strike and illegal immigration - resulted in a new awareness of the sea, particularly among the youth. By World War II, the sports organizations had trained 1600 young seafarers,

ten percent of whom went to work in seagoing trades. In parallel, the Haifa Technion set up a school for marine officers.

World War II created its own demands at sea. Many of the graduates of the fledgling training courses found jobs in the Allied merchant marines. In April 1942, after prolonged negotiation between the Jewish Agency for Palestine and the British Ministry of War, the Royal Navy began to accept Palestinian Jews: 1400 volunteers served, mostly in support and technical functions, though a few were posted to shipboard duties. In late 1943, the Palmach established its own seagoing platoon. Palyam - "Strike Companies - Sea" - was primarily designed to give inshore assistance to the clandestine immigrant boats.

In 1945, after holding ten courses for boat commanders from 1943 onwards, the Palyam was upgraded to company status. In the same year, the Haifa Technion began a series of six more courses for deck officers. In the course of time, transport from ship to shore was not enough; the Palyam also developed skills in sabotaging the transfer of "illegals" from Haifa to the Cyprus detention camps. By late 1947, Palyam mustered 370 seamen, including 80 officers. Neither their training and experience nor the available resources were sufficient for more than coastal operations. The conflict that began in November 1947 was exclusively a land-based war, so most of the Palyam force was assigned to ground units or to the weapons procurement effort abroad. Indeed, in Hagana and Palmach thinking, the sea was important as a route for immigration and supply - but not as a naval theater of operations.

In December 1947, however, David Ben Gurion summoned Gershon Zack - a schoolteacher, Hagana veteran and member of the National Committee - and told him: "We have no ships hidden away. Find money, men and ships!" Ben Gurion was aware that the Egyptian Navy - with 42 ships (including four armed with 6-inch guns, eight minesweepers with 3-inch guns and 21 landing craft) - could constitute a major threat to the sea routes and coasts in the invasion that was now inevitable.

Zack could find men from among the Palyam and Royal Navy veterans, but there were no ships or weapons. The only available source was the rusting "shadow fleet" of illegal immigrant ships, seized by the British and now moored by the breakwater in Haifa Port. Under the noses of the British, Zack's first recruits smuggled

themselves aboard an old American icebreaker and began to recondition it. The ship, with a large "16" painted on the bows in the hope that the Egyptians would assume a large Israeli navy, put to sea on 21 May 1948. Armed with two 20 mm guns and a few machineguns, it was hardly a warship, but the thinking was that at least it could ram enemy vessels. The "Sea Service," created by the Hagana on 17 March, now had its first ship.

The A16, renamed "INS Eilat," was soon joined by other vessels from the reconditioned shadow fleet. Among them were the INS Hagana (K20) and the INS Wedgwood (K18) - two Canadian Flower-class corvettes, purchased as war surplus to carry immigrants. The two corvettes were armed with 65 mm French mountain guns lashed to their decks. These would be replaced by regular naval 4-inch guns only in December 1948. Work progressed on salvaging "naval vessels" from among the rusting immigrant fleet. The fourth, the INS Maoz (K24) - a river cruise boat - joined the active navy in September 1948 as a mother ship for small explosive laden boats; with not enough naval guns, other methods would have to do. These first four craft were to bear the ambitious name of "The Grand Fleet."

At first, the Egyptians were content to use their navy to transport supplies to the army in Gaza and for occasional patrols along the southern coast. But, on 2 June 1948, an Egyptian corvette put 20 3-inch shells into Kibbutz Sdot Yam - the Palyam's main base on the Caesarea shore. The kibbutz members replied with small arms fire. Neither side had done much damage. On 4 June, the Eilat was alerted by a message that a large Egyptian ship was moving north from Gaza. By the time A16 arrived on the scene, the "large ship" turned out to be a troop carrier, a large landing craft and a corvette. The out-gunned A16 was ordered to take evasive action until air support could be supplied. The planes materialized as the convoy reached the coast off Jaffa. Meanwhile, the Eilat had fought a minor battle with the corvette. The Egyptian's gunnery was inaccurate, though two shells did cause minor damage to the Eilat. The Israeli ship returned the fire, but its 20 mm shells fell far short. Six sorties by the three available aircraft were enough to make the Egyptians turn tail.

The time had come for the Sea Service to flex its muscles in more ambitious actions. On 17 July, despite engine trouble, faulty steering gear and a blocked field gun, the Eilat and the Wedgwood bombarded Tyre in Lebanon. The purpose was to discourage Lebanese participation in the war, and it did in fact compel them to divert effort to cover the vulnerability of their shores. Acting on information received from Italy, on 26 August, the Hagana and the Wedgwood intercepted, off Crete, a cargo ship carrying arms for the Egyptian Army. The 8000 rifles, eight million cartridges and explosives that were transferred to the two Israeli ships were a welcome addition to the IDF arsenal.

In October 1948, the navy was accorded its first opportunity to coordinate offensive actions with a ground forces operation. The IDF was engaged in Operation Yoav, to clear the Egyptian Army from the northern Negev. The Sea Service was to aid in the encirclement of Egyptian forces in the Gaza Strip, and prevent their resupply by ship. On 19 October, a patrol off the Gaza coast encountered a corvette, laden with fuel and supplies. The Israeli ships scored a few indecisive hits, but eventually their improvised naval guns blocked. Shortly thereafter, Egyptian Spitfires bombed and strafed the patrol, which retired with casualties - after shooting down one plane.

Three days later, on 22 October, two Egyptian ships were reported off Gaza. The Maoz detached itself from the patrol at sunset, and moved inshore. As it approached the Egyptians - their flagship, the Emir Farouk, and a minesweeper - the enemy vessels began to move slowly northwards. Rather than risk losing them (the top speed of the Maoz was 18 knots), the Israeli ship immediately lowered three explosive laden boats into the water - one for each Egyptian and a third in reserve. Under the cover of darkness, naval commandos steered directly for the two enemy vessels, set their charges and jumped into the water. The battle was over within minutes. A spout of water, flame and smoke shot a hundred and fifty feet into the air over the Emir Farouk. The enemy vessels opened up with all their guns, but the fire was random and the Farouk was already listing badly. Within four minutes the Egyptian flagship tilted up on its bows and slid under the waves. The minesweeper was badly damaged, but still afloat under a pall of smoke.

Intelligence had been filtering through about a fast (32 knot) yacht, originally owned by Adolf Hitler, which was being reconditioned and refitted in Beirut for use by the Egyptian Navy. There was little enthusiasm over the idea of a vessel that fast in the enemy service. On 29 November, a frogman penetrated Beirut Port and placed two limpet mines on the hull of the yacht. Apart from satisfaction at the successful achievement of the mission, the Sea Service derived considerable enjoyment from the wild Arab speculations as to how the ship had been sunk: these ran the whole gamut from mines spotted much earlier but ignored to private vendettas by secret societies that had been sending threatening letters to the previous owners.

There was only one more naval encounter during the war. Acting on a report that two Egyptian ships were interfering with merchant vessels bound for Israel, the Navy began a search. Meanwhile, on 1 January 1949, the two Egyptians took position off Tel Aviv. They fired some thirty shells at the city, but all fell short. After ten minutes of the bombardment, the two ships turned westward and beat a retreat, pursued by Israeli ships. Since the Egyptians had the advantage of speed, contact was lost and the encounter was indecisive.

For the remainder of the war, the Navy blockaded the Egyptian Army at Gaza. IDF ground forces were engaged in Operation Horev, designed to push the Egyptians back beyond the frontier. The naval blockade, and occasional bombardment of shore positions, denied the Egyptian Army the possibility of convenient resupply by sea. It also pinned down sizable enemy forces in protection of the coastline. The Navy's last action in the War of Independence took place on 8 March 1949. Although it was minor, uneventful and unopposed, it does deserve a place in history for its uniqueness. In a combined amphibious operation involving six vessels, naval crews transported an infantry force from Sdom to Ein Gedi on the banks of the Dead Sea - 2700 feet below sea level.

In November 1948, the Sea Service had officially become the Israel Navy. Its senior captain, Paul Shulman, a graduate of the US Naval Academy at Annapolis, was appointed OC Navy with the rank of Rear Admiral. For the next few months, he and Gershon Zack functioned together - Shulman as Officer Commanding and Zack in the role of "Secretary for the Navy." With the end of the War of Independence, in March 1949, these two men began the work of building a permanent navy, though it was only in October of the

same year that the status of the seagoing service was clarified. On
27 October, Defence Minister Ben Gurion ruled that the army, navy
and air forces would all be subject to the one General Staff of the
IDF. Neither Zak nor Shulman remained for long in the Israel Navy.
Late in 1949, the command passed to Major General Shlomo Shamir
- who came from the infantry, via the IDF's first armored brigade,
and later moved on to the Air Force.

Shamir, and his successor, Palyam veteran Rear Admiral
Mordechai Limon - who, at 26, was the youngest flag officer
appointed by the IDF - completed the task of establishing training
and organizational patterns. However, their task was not easy.
Though, at an intellectual level, nobody could question the need for
protecting Israel's coasts and sea lanes, the Navy came a low third
in the order of procurement priorities. The IDF General Staff was
thinking in terms of short wars, in which the Navy would have no
influence on the outcome. The few events at sea in the War of
Independence had done little to convince the soldiers and airmen
that the enemy had demonstrated a major naval threat.
Nevertheless, the Navy remained aware that its frontier, even if
shorter than the land borders, was not simply measured in linear
miles. Territorial waters needed to be patrolled. The Navy had to
have the capability to prevent harassment of the coastline by long
range gunnery. And heavy maritime traffic on the north-south
routes paralleling the Israeli shore - flowing from one Arab port to
another - made neither task simple. Furthermore, these missions did
not even begin to encompass the possible protection of inbound and
outbound Israeli shipping.

Since the available resources were inadequate, the Navy
could not avail itself of the normal patterns of procurement of
other, larger and better-heeled navies. Unlike tanks and aircraft,
ships are not off-the-shelf items. They are usually commissioned
according to specific needs, at considerable expense and with long
design and construction schedules. Moreover, most navies put to
sea with a mix of ships - aircraft carriers, minelayers and sweepers,
convoy escorts, heavy gun platforms, etc. - each designed for a
specific purpose. The Israel Navy could afford none of these luxuries.
Although Defense Minister Ben Gurion declared, in February 1950,
"Without rule over the sea, Israel will become a besieged city,"
nothing could alter the priority accorded to the land and air

forces. Ironically, while Israel was investing in a merchant marine capable of carrying all the country's needs, the Arab countries were devoting major effort to building their navies. The Israel Navy, unable to function effectively with converted illegal immigrant ships, acquired wherever it could a flotilla of World War II surplus frigates and corvettes - five in all - and motor torpedo boats for fast patrol duties.

The years immediately following the War of Independence were uneventful at sea. Consequently, the officers and crews were able to train, develop combat drills and doctrines and embark on voyages designed to gain experience of international naval customs and "show the flag." Thus, in 1951, a frigate and a corvette paid an official visit to New York and Boston, where they received a royal welcome. The crews had to pay a price for the trip: they spent days rehearsing for ceremonial parades through the two cities (marching drill is not regular routine anywhere in the IDF). On another excursion, on 12 August 1953, four ships of the flotilla were exercising north of Crete when they picked up a radio report of serious earthquake damage that threatened total destruction of three islands in the Aegean Sea. Abandoning their exercise schedule, the ships proceeded to the stricken islands. The crews cleared rubble to get at survivors, treated the wounded and evacuated hundreds of people to the Greek mainland.

The massive arms deal between Czechoslovakia and Egypt - first announced publicly on 28 September 1955 - threatened to throw the naval arena out of all semblance of balance. Apart from submarines, the Egyptians were to receive Soviet Skouri-class destroyers, for which the Israel Navy's aging, lightly-armed frigates were no match. The British decided to sell to Israel and to Egypt two Z-class World War II destroyers each, and the Royal Navy agreed to refit the Israeli ships with modern communications and fire control equipment - and train the crews. By March 1956, the refit was complete and Israeli crews began a series of exercises with a British squadron. The two ships, the INS Jaffa and the INS Eilat, sailed for home late in May. In fact, both crews had maintained constant readiness to sail earlier if the situation deteriorated. As they slipped their moorings and set course for Haifa, the sailors of the Jaffa and Eilat had the satisfaction of knowing that - amid growing tension between Nasser's Egypt and Great Britain - a couple of Royal Navy ships had dropped anchor alongside the Egyptian destroyers to prevent their departure.

The two 33-knot destroyers, with their radar and sonar, 4.5 inch and 40 mm guns, fire control systems and depth charge racks, offered a new dimension of professionalism in naval warfare. With war clouds gathering on the horizon, the Navy began intensive exercises, both to gain experience with the ships and to integrate them into the already existing flotillas. The order-of-battle of the Israel Navy now included three obsolete frigates, the two refitted destroyers, six torpedo boats, three tank landing craft, eight small landing craft (based in Eilat) and an armed "mother ship" for naval commandos.

The Sinai Campaign, which began on 29 October 1956, was coordinated with the joint Franco-British "Operation Musketeer" to occupy the Suez Canal Zone. With some 500 Royal Navy and French ships supposedly neutralizing the Egyptian Navy, the IDF General Staff did not allot the Israel Navy any clearly defined major missions in the Mediterranean theater. However, on the evening of 30 October, the Ibrahim el-Awal - an ex-Royal Navy Hunt-class destroyer - moved north from its station off Port Said for a hit and run attack on Haifa port and oil refineries. The waters off the Israeli shores were crawling with French, British and American warships. Threading its way through them, the Ibrahim el-Awal arrived six miles off Haifa at 03:40 hours on the morning of 31 October. Opening fire with its four 4-inch guns, the Egyptian destroyer rained 160 shells down on the port area - without doing any serious damage. After a 20 minute bombardment, a nearby French destroyer spotted the Ibrahim el-Awal and fired some 80 shells. The Egyptian turned north, keeping up the shellfire, then withdrew westwards.

The Eilat, Jaffa and Maznek - all three commanded by ex-immigrant ship captains - were on night patrol 50 miles west of Haifa. Alerted at 03:55 by a message that Haifa was under fire, the three Israeli ships turned to an intercept course and went to 30 knots. By 05:10 hours, assisted by precise information from the shore, the ships' radars had locked on their prey. As they approached the Egyptian, there were a few moments of trepidation. The screens revealed four fast ships, in battle formation, moving in from the west. The first thought on the bridges of the Israeli flotilla was that the Egyptians had laid a trap. Within minutes, the

oncoming destroyers were identified as belonging to the US Sixth Fleet. Warned that the Israeli destroyers were about to open fire on an enemy, the Americans turned clear and hovered in the background to watch the battle. At 05:32 hours, 40 miles northwest of Haifa and 9000 yards from target, the Israeli gunners fired their first salvo.

The Egyptian captain, obviously hoping for air support from Syria and Port Said - only 175 miles away - adopted evasive maneuvers in preference to a high speed run for a Lebanese port. His own gunnery was ineffective, water splashing up on either side of the Israelis but with no direct hits. All four captains were experiencing their first naval battle. By 06:37 hours, when IAF Ouragans appeared on the scene, the Ibrahim el-Awal was already taking on water from holes in the hull and its speed was down to 15 knots, as a result of a direct hit on the engine room. Its generators were no longer supplying electricity to the stricken ship. The aircraft scored a couple more hits with rockets. At 07:00 hours, the Egyptian captain ordered his crew to open the scuttlecocks and, at 07:10 - to the amazement of the Israeli crews - an Egyptian sailor scaled the mainmast and hung a white flag of surrender.

The commander of the flotilla faced some tough decisions. The Egyptian Air Force could appear at any moment, and any casualties that air attack would inflict would sour the taste of victory. A couple of well placed salvoes could finish off the Ibrahim el-Awal. On the other hand, the destroyer - which was listing slightly - would be a handsome prize. While the Jaffa picked up survivors from the water, the Eilat put a boarding party onto the Egyptian. Rounding up the crew members still on the destroyer, the Israeli sailors closed the scuttlecocks and assessed the damage. At 08:10 hours, the Eilat maneuvered into position and began to tow the Ibrahim el-Awal. Because of damage to its steering gear, the destroyer drifted alternately right and left of the tow cable and progress was slow. An Israeli damage crew labored to repair the gear and the Eilat slowly picked up speed to 10 knots. After four nervous hours, with all hands alert for possible air attack, the Eilat handed over the tow to two tugs from Haifa port. The repaired and refitted Ibrahim el-Awal entered service under its new name - the INS Haifa.

On the Red Sea, armed landing craft of the Navy provided supporting gunfire and seaborne supply for the 9th Brigade on its cross-desert trek from Eilat to the Straits of Tiran - but there was no additional naval action on the Mediterranean. Immediately after the Sinai Campaign, the Red Sea was invested with a new significance, political and naval. If the Straits of Tiran were to remain open to Israeli shipping, the Israel Navy needed a little more power than its small landing-craft. Three torpedo boats, that had been designed and built with the southern waters in mind, were transported overland from Haifa and down the desert tracks and passes of the Negev to Eilat. In parallel, two frigates made the 12,500 mile month-long voyage from Haifa through the Mediterranean, south along Africa and around the Cape of Good Hope.

Shortly after the Sinai Campaign, the Israel Navy was called on to stage an operation reminiscent of its pre-State origins. Operation Musketeer had failed, and the British and French were preparing to withdraw. The Jewish population of Port Said were terrified of the consequences of the withdrawal - and something had to be done urgently. While two Israeli agents and a radio operator smuggled themselves into Port Said to make contact with the community, naval crews prepared two 150-ton fishing boats with lifesaving and medical equipment and stores of food. The boats were chosen deliberately for their ability to slip through the chaos of the naval armada at Port Said without arousing undue interest.

On 15 November 1956, the boats left Haifa, hoisted Italian flags and headed south - escorted to within 15 miles of Port Said by a torpedo boat that would await their return. On the morning of 16 November, eight miles from the harbor, they were stopped - yet another familiar memory - by a British destroyer, curious to know what Italian fishing boats were doing in these waters. They were ordered to follow the destroyer to the port entrance and wait there overnight - with the British ship anchored alongside. According to a message from the shore, their human cargo would be at the evacuation point on the quayside.at dawn. Taking advantage of the heavy traffic in and out of the port, the two fishing boats slipped away from their hovering escort, attached themselves to an inbound French frigate and headed for the quay. With engines still running, the Israeli sailors helped their passengers aboard and turned back to the port exit.

As luck would have it, they were hailed yet again - this time by a

British landing craft. The commander of the operation chose to ignore the challenge. Making use of a strong wind, he swung the boats eastward, along a coast abounding in reefs and rusty wrecks. The Royal Navy vessel could not keep up. Apart from seasickness, the rest of the voyage was uneventful - though the passengers were treated to an unusual sight: at the Bardawil lagoon, as they sailed past, an Israel Navy crew were busy hoisting an Egyptian MiG out of the water and on board ship. As the boats neared the Israeli coast, the Italian flags were replaced by Israeli ensigns and machineguns were brought out of hiding for protection against possible air attack. At dawn on 18 November, the Jews of Port Said were put ashore safely in Haifa.

The main effort from 1958 to 1962 went into deepening the Navy's level of professionalism. The destroyer flotilla - the Jaffa, Eilat and Haifa - was constantly improving its ships and exercising the crews. The torpedo boat flotilla was shaping its own combat concepts and commissioning new, light and high speed vessels. The Navy also added to its order of battle two submarines, the Tanin and the Rahav, purchased - after overhaul - from the Royal Navy. Because of the needs of the ground army, the IDF allotted funds for landing craft, which were built to Israel Navy specifications in the Haifa shipyard. However, by 1962 there were clear indications that the nature of war at sea was undergoing drastic and dramatic changes. Apart from other conventional vessels, both the Egyptian and Syrian navies were acquiring fast missile boats from the Soviet Union.

The Navy obviously needed missile boats of its own. Work was being done in Israel on the development of a sea-to-sea missile - the Gabriel - but they needed an appropriate platform. Destroyers put too large crews in too few places at a time. Conversely, the Soviet concept was inapplicable: their missile boats were single-purpose vessels appropriate to navies that could afford a mix of platforms at sea. In the thinking of its own officers, the Israel Navy needed multi-purpose boats capable of offensive action, able to defend themselves against a variety of threats and appropriate for patrol duties. In other words, the next generation of ships needed to be fast-moving, small-crew weapons platforms, with a minimum of weight and space devoted to other factors. There was only one problem: the concept did not exist anywhere.

Late in 1962, with the promise of available funding, the Navy wrote up its specifications and started to work with West German naval architects on reducing the ideas to practice. For the first time, the Navy was commissioning sophisticated major warships according to its concepts, rather than acquiring hand-me-downs from other navies. There was an element of gamble, but the Israel Navy staff and captains were confident that the direction was right. By 1965, the designs were complete, but - under pressure from Arab interests - the West Germans were forced to back out from the construction contracts. At their recommendation, the plans were handed on to a French shipyard (see Chapter: The Cherbourg Boats).

At the outbreak of the Six Day War, in June 1967, the Navy was immersed in organization and preparation for its new craft - but they were not yet in service. As Rear Admiral Telem - who would command the Navy from 1972 to 1975 - later very aptly put it: "...a navy that was building from scratch while having at sea a completely different navy based on antiquated World War II concepts and, what is worse, commanded by men who, in thought and concept, were already completely harnessed to a new era of naval warfare. The Israel Navy of 1967 was a strange combination of highly advanced concepts with very retarded and obsolete weaponry."

That was something of an understatement. At the beginning of the three-week waiting period between the Egyptian move in force into Sinai and the opening shots of the war, most of the Navy's ships were out of commission. The Eilat was undergoing overhaul in the shipyard. The Haifa had been retired from service. In a superhuman effort by the shipyard and the naval crews, these and the other ships were prepared for action in the few available days. But nothing could be done about the missile boats on the slips at Cherbourg, or the recently acquired T-class submarines still refitting in Britain to replace their obsolete predecessors. The combined Egyptian and Syrian order-of-battle included 24 Ossa and Komar-class (Styx) missile boats, seven destroyers, 49 torpedo boats and 27 other assorted ships.

With little choice, the Navy chose a two-part strategy of deception and offense. To draw the Egyptian Navy away from the Mediterranean, the Navy transported a landing craft overland from Haifa to Eilat. Each night the LC was taken northwards on a darkened transporter, then brought in to the southern port again the following morning, after being replaced each time by a dummy. In parallel, the torpedo boats based at Eilat made a show of appearing frequently opposite the shores of Aqaba - across the bay in Jordan. The Egyptians responded to the threat of large scale landings on the southeastern Sinai coast by transferring naval units to the Red Sea. The offensive part of the strategy would fall on the shoulders of the naval commando.

On the first night of the war, 5 June 1967, a small force of naval commandos penetrated Port Said harbor, only to find that the Egyptian warships had been withdrawn to Alexandria. However, their covering force, which consisted of the destroyer Jaffa and three torpedo boats, engaged two Ossa-class missile boats that were on their way out of the harbor and scored hits on both. Meanwhile, a submarine - the Tanin - dropped six commandos close to the opening of Alexandria port, the Egyptian Navy's heavily protected home base. The commandos succeeded in damaging three ships, despite harbor patrols that were dropping depth charges. However, they did not make contact with the waiting submarine, and were forced to seek shelter in a cave outside the town.

The Tanin had problems of its own. When it returned the following night, in the hope of retrieving the commando team, it was spotted by an Egyptian frigate. With almost empty batteries, low oxygen reserves and a failed air-conditioning system, the submarine succeeded in evading the depth charge patterns laid by the frigate. On the third night, the Tanin again approached the rendezvous point but received a message that the commandos had been taken prisoner.

Meanwhile, the three torpedo boats based in Eilat, hastily reinforced by armed motor launches, were alerted to the fact that an Egyptian squadron was entering the Red Sea. An ambush was prepared, but the Egyptian admiral obviously thought better of the idea and withdrew. On the northern coast of Sinai, the landing craft prepared for a leapfrog operation - but it was canceled because of the rapid advance of the northern armored column. Nevertheless, the Navy was to have its moment of glory at the expense of its comrades on the ground. On 7 June, the torpedo boats left Eilat to give support to a paratroop column that was to take the Egyptian positions at the Straits of Tiran. When the boats arrived, the area was deserted. The force commander decided on a landing party - and the paratroopers arrived to find the Navy in possession. On the same day, the torpedo boats moved to intercept two Egyptian fishing boats that were proceeding south with indecent haste. After a couple of bursts of light arms fire, they found that they had captured 30 heavily armed Egyptian commandos.

All told, despite the heavily tilted balance of power at sea, the Navy had acquitted itself honorably. The mix of offense and deception had taken the initiative away from the vastly superior enemy naval forces. Apart from the brief appearances of three submarines off the Mediterranean coast, the Egyptian and Syrian navies had stayed close to home. However, the basic statistics of the situation had changed dramatically as a result of the war. The land frontiers, though further away from the Israeli hinterland, were in fact shorter than before. But the sea frontiers that needed to be patrolled by the Navy had multiplied fivefold - and the force that had been inadequate before the war now had to make a show of confidence over a much larger seascape.

Furthermore, the Israel Navy was assuming its new duties with equipment that it knew to be obsolete, while impatiently awaiting new tools that would be perfect for the task. To show the flag in three different arenas, the Navy elected to use three distinct force compositions. On the Suez Canal, exposed to Egyptian fire, patrols were maintained by two-man teams in rubber boats. Facing the Egyptian guns across the Gulf of Suez, landing craft and torpedo boats operated along the Sinai coastline. On the Mediterranean, with its constant threat of Styx-missile boats out of Port Said, the task fell to the destroyers and the bulk of the torpedo boat flotilla. It was obvious that the Egyptian Navy would not wait for long before challenging the integrity of the new lines.

On the night of 11 June 1967, the Eilat and two torpedo boats were on routine patrol along the northern Sinai coast when the destroyer's radar picked up an Egyptian force facing the town of Rumani. Assuming the enemy to be missile boats, the Eilat turned away to open range and ordered its much faster escorts to engage the Egyptians. As the confrontation developed, the two Egyptians - now identified as MTBs - slipped between the two Israelis and the Eilat - effectively preventing all three Israeli ships from opening fire. As the Israeli torpedo boats maneuvered back between the destroyer

and the enemy ships, the Egyptians opened fire, inviting an immediate response. In the exchange, one Egyptian boat was hit and began to limp southwards with flames clearly visible aft. Its comrade headed west for the open sea. The commander of the Eilat ordered his torpedo boats to deal with the eastern target while he engaged the other. After 30 minutes of battle, the torpedo boats' target burst into flames and exploded. Meanwhile, the Eilat had closed in on the second boat - and it also exploded. The battle ended at so close a range - 15 meters - that splinters from the destroyed ship caused minor damages to the destroyer's deck. After searching in vain for survivors, the patrol turned for home - flying brooms on their masts in keeping with an old navy custom; they had "swept" the sea clear of an enemy.

The coming months were to be marked by two major catastrophes. At 17:28 hours on 21 October 1967, while on routine patrol off the Sinai coast 14 miles east of Port Said, the INS Eilat was struck by two Styx missiles. The missile boats had been lying in wait near the entrance to Port Said harbor. With its engines and communications room unusable, the destroyer lay dead in the water, but did manage on its reserve radio to establish contact with an IDF unit in Sinai. With the ship listing badly, it was hit at 19:30 hours by another Styx which exploded the ammunition lockers. The captain ordered the crew to abandon ship. As they swam clear of the Eilat, a fourth missile struck, and the underwater shock wave caused injuries to some of the survivors. Out of a crew of 199, naval vessels and helicopters pulled from the water 152 - of whom 91 were injured. For the Navy the tragedy was augmented by frustration that the patrols were being maintained by obsolete, large crew vessels until the new ships could arrive from Cherbourg.

Three months later, the INS Dakar - one of the T-class submarines - was lost at sea with all hands while on its way home after commissioning in Portsmouth. The ship, which had departed from England on 9 January 1968, sent its last message on 24 January, off the shores of Crete. In bad weather, the navies and airforces of Israel, the United States, Great Britain and Greece searched in vain for the Dakar and its crew of 69. Its disappearance remains a mystery to this day.

Through 1968, the Navy began to receive its Saar-class missile boats from Cherbourg. The first five arrived without problems. The sixth and seventh narrowly escaped imposition of total embargo by the French government in the last weeks of 1968. And the final five were to reach Haifa one year later in an escapade that drew the world's attention to the new class of ships (see Chapter: The Cherbourg Boats). In parallel, the Navy began to acquire - at first from the United States, and later from Israel Shipyards - Hornet-class fast patrol boats. These small crew vessels, armed with 20 mm guns, heavy machineguns and depth charge racks, were to replace the obsolete and unsuitable motor torpedo boats. In 1969, when Egypt's President Nasser initiated the War of Attrition on the southern front, the Israel Navy was - for the first time - properly equipped for its missions.

As the artillery bombardments intensified across the Suez Canal, the IDF General Staff opted for a flexible and indirect response. If Nasser wanted a static war over the narrow waterway, there was no reason why the IDF had to play by his rules. The Naval Commando began operations in a minor key with two strikes - the first on June 21 1969 against a coastal station in the north of the Gulf of Suez, and the second on 11 July against an Egyptian strongpoint on the Canal line. Then, after seven IDF soldiers were killed in a forward position facing Port Taufiq, it was decided that the time had come for a more ambitious response.

Green Island, two miles south of the Canal entrance in the Gulf of Suez, was an artificial island - a heavily fortified position built on a reef. The Egyptian garrison, inside its concrete fortress, was equipped with 85 mm and 37 mm anti-aircraft guns. To the north of the island and connected to it by a bridge, was a platform that might possibly house a radar fire control center. The island was chosen as a target not only as being close to the Suez Canal, but also because the Egyptians were confident that it was impregnable. On the night of 19 July, in darkness so total that identification of the objective was almost impossible, a joint force of naval commandos and an infantry reconnaissance unit approached the island on rubber boats. The first wave of commandos swam ashore at the northern end of the island, scaled the steep walls, crossed a triple barbed wire fence and arrived at the bridge. Cutting a gap through the last fence, the commandos split into two. While one squad eliminated a sentry and headed along the bridge to the north platform, the main force assaulted the fortress.

In a bitter battle, the commandos scaled the roof of the building by climbing on the shoulders of a heavily built comrade: inevitably, as his name was Jacob, they all referred in their debriefings to "Jacob's ladder." The complex was covered with boltholes and firing positions that had to be cleared laboriously, one by one as the soldiers of the second wave tackled the heavy gun positions on the roof. Other solders were mopping up in the courtyard and the building below. As the main force evacuated the wounded to the rubber boats, a team began to lay demolition charges in the northern section of the fortress. Within 50 minutes the operation was over. As the raiding force pulled away from the island, the Egyptians laid down a heavy artillery barrage on the deserted and destroyed fort. Shrapnel tore into the engine of one of the boats, and its six occupants plunged into the water, from which they were retrieved by a helicopter. The operation, which was a total success, cost six lives. The Egyptian losses were around 70 dead.

In September 1969, the General Staff decided to put an armored column ashore on the western coast of the Gulf of Suez, with the objective of destroying coastal stations, radar posts and army camps. On the night of 7 September, naval commandos penetrated Ras Sadat anchorage to sink Egyptian vessels that could interfere with the landing or evacuation of the armored raiding party. The commandos, completely undetected, successfully attached limpet mines to two torpedo boats. Both boats would explode and sink while underway on patrol. On the way home, an explosive charge in one of the small craft suddenly detonated, killing three commandos and wounding a fourth.

At 03:00 hours on the next night, the raiding force of tanks and armored personnel carriers was brought ashore uneventfully by tank landing craft. Turning south, the column traversed 50 kilometers, attacking every military installation in its path. After ten hours, the landing craft rendezvoused with the force and took them home. The total casualties amounted to one lightly wounded soldier. Egyptian losses were estimated at 150.

The Israel Navy that emerged from the War of Attrition, in August 1970, had every reason to feel more comfortable with its situation. For the first time, the flotillas at sea did not consist of ancient World War II vintage vessels. In fact, the Cherbourg-built Saar-class missile boats were more than just state-of-the-art craft

for the 1970s; they were the only ones of their kind in the world, and had been constructed to the Navy's own specifications. And, in addition to the 12 Cherbourg boats, the Navy was already designing and building in Israel two more, with longer range and capable of remaining at sea for greater periods. Although considerable effort had been invested in the concepts of missile boat warfare before the ships arrived, the captains and crews now had the opportunity to exercise at sea. Furthermore, with the new-found advantages of the computer age, a local industry had developed - together with the Israel Navy - a tactical training center capable of putting single crews, and even all the captains of a flotilla, through their paces in realistic battle conditions of a high speed arena.

The vital statistics of the arena that faced the Israel Navy allowed no time for complacency. The combined Egyptian and Syrian fleets possessed 26 missile boats, 12 submarines, 53 motor torpedo boats, five destroyers and 17 frigate minelayers and sweepers. Against this force, the Israel Navy could muster 12 missile boats (the Israeli-built Reshef and Keshet would be launched in mid-1973), two submarines and 35 patrol boats. In addition, the removal of the PLO, lock, stock and barrel, from Jordan to a new base of operations in Lebanon, meant that the threat of terrorism from the sea could not be discounted. On the other hand, the IDF could now rely on the Navy to take its share in deterring the terrorists.

In February 1973, a seaborne force, which included the naval commando, assaulted terrorist bases at Tripoli on the northern Lebanon coast. On 9 April, in the most spectacular operation yet against the terror organizations that had staged the Munich Olympics massacre and other strikes, a combined army and navy force was transported by missile boats to Sidon and Beirut. Put ashore in rubber boats, they achieved total surprise in reaching their inland targets, where they destroyed the headquarters of one terror group and demolished sabotage materials workshops of another. Upon successful completion of the entire operation, the force was returned to base by the Navy.

On 6 October 1973, when the armies of Egypt and Syria crossed the 1967 ceasefire lines in a surprise attack, the Israel Navy was the only branch of the IDF that was ready for the next war, both conceptually and technologically. The Navy's mission in the Yom Kippur War was eminently clear: to defend the sea frontier and prevent it from becoming another battlefront. Obviously, the best way to achieve that objective was to take the initiative - and the Navy was ready to do just that. The war began on Golan and in Sinai at 13:50 hours. Shortly after 14:00 hours, a force of five missile boats was already on its way north from Haifa. Their intention was to bring the war to the Syrian Navy off its home coast before it could materialize along the Israeli shores. To do this, the flotilla would pass Lebanon and seek a confrontation 200 miles from home with an enemy that was probably expecting the Israeli ships. In addition, this would be the baptism of fire for weapons platforms that represented great faith in an as yet untried concept.

The first contact was made at 22:28 hours, facing Cyprus, with a craft that was identified as a Syrian torpedo boat. As the Syrian sped eastwards, the Israeli force closed up the range and a duel began between the guns on both sides. At 22:48, the torpedo boat - which had been hit and was slowing down - was finished by gunfire. Ten minutes later, the flotilla encountered a Syrian minelayer. The honors were accorded to the INS Reshef - the Israeli-built boat that had been commissioned weeks before the war; its first Gabriel missile sank the Syrian. As the minelayer went down, five Styx missiles closed on the flotilla. They boats evaded the incoming projectiles, but were now aware that the situation had been set up. The torpedo boat was obviously a picket, while the minelayer was the bait of a trap set by three Syrian missile boats which were now maneuvering for a flank attack on the flotilla. The Israeli boats turned south towards the three Syrians and began what was to be the first ever missile confrontation at sea. This was to be the test between the Saar-class and the Soviet made boats - and between the 22 kilometer range Gabriel and the 40 kilometer range Styx.

At one point in the battle, with eight missiles incoming, seven were off target and the eighth was shot down a few yards away from one of the boats by a medium machinegun. Two of the Syrian boats sustained direct hits from Gabriel missiles, and exploded. The third turned and raced for its home port, but ran aground on a reef where it was dispatched by gunfire. At the end of the action, which had lasted 90 minutes from the first sighting of the torpedo boat, Syrian coastal batteries began to fire. The Israeli flotilla retired to sea and headed for home. The first naval battle between missile boats had ended in a score of five to zero. The Syrian Navy had lost a sizable proportion of its order-of-battle, and the years of work on new tactics, conceptions and hardware had been proven correct.

Although the battle of Latakia cooled the Syrian Navy's fervor to seek action at sea, the Israel Navy still had a task to perform in the northern theater of operations. Since the Syrians were using surface-to-surface Frog missiles against civilian targets in northern Israel, the Government authorized the IDF to act against strategic targets on the Syrian coastline. On the night of 10 October, missile boats bombarded port installations at Latakia and a fuel depot at Banias. Shore batteries responded, but the Syrian Navy was not prepared to do more than foray out of port, fire missiles and race back to the protection of merchant shipping in the harbor. Nevertheless, the attacking force did hit two Syrian missile boats. This encounter wrote its own unique page in naval history when a ship's cook shot down a Styx missile with a machinegun. The next night, the missile boats struck at the fuel tank farm at Tartus and chalked up two more Syrian missile boats on the tally. The Navy also operated on the nights of 20 and 23 October, under coastal gunfire, but the Syrian Navy did not attempt to intervene. The Israel Navy and the IAF together had deprived Syria of 70 percent of its electric generating capacity and fuel storage.

On the Egyptian front, the first naval action took place on the night of 6 October 1973. In a clash between flotillas off the coast of Rumani, one Egyptian missile boat was sunk. On the night of 8 October, a missile boat force, that was assigned to limit Egyptian naval initiatives, encountered four Ossa-class boats off Damietta. As the Israeli force split into two, the Egyptians fired missiles - all of which either missed or were shot down by machineguns. Having fired, the Egyptians turned west and raced for the protection of Alexandria. The Israeli boats gave chase, closed the range and sank three of the Egyptian vessels. The encounter at Damietta was more than just a naval battle. For the rest of the war, the Egyptian Navy stayed in port apart from two appearances by submarines that were easily driven off.

In the Mediterranean theater, the Navy made use of its freedom of the seas to bombard military targets along the coast as far as the Egyptian frontier with Libya. However, the fact that the Egyptian Navy stayed in port was not good enough reason to ignore them. On the night of 16 October, a small force of naval commandos penetrated the heavily defended harbor of Port Said, and disabled a missile boat, an MTB equipped with rocket launchers and a landing craft.

In the Red Sea, the Navy was heavily outnumbered. The Egyptians had missile boats, destroyers, submarines, MTBs, landing and patrol craft facing six landing craft and six Hornet coastal patrol boats based at Eilat and Sharm e-Shekh (the flotilla would be reinforced during the war by three more Hornets brought overland to Eilat). On the first day, 6 October, two Hornets that were on patrol in the Gulf of Suez were ordered to attack and destroy any enemy craft in the area of Ras Zafrana and Mersa Talme. There were no targets at Ras Zafrana, but they caught a Bertram-class patrol boat and two rubber boats loaded with Egyptian commandos preparing to depart from Mersa Talme. Though both Hornets ran up on a reef - and extricated themselves - they succeeded in destroying all three targets, and prevented a raiding party from crossing the Gulf.

In response to information that the Egyptians were preparing seaborne landings across the Gulf of Suez, the Naval Commando staged a series of penetrations of the western anchorages - entering one port no less than three times - and disabled or sank missile boats and fishing craft that were being fitted to transport troops. In the Red Sea theater, the Hornets and the naval commandos had totally paralyzed the Egyptian Navy. So successful was the effort that the Hornets were able to reinforce the encirclement of the Egyptian Third Army by preventing seaborne resupply. The sole limitation on operations had been the inability of the small craft to break the blockade imposed by the Egyptian Navy on the Bab el-Mandab Straits. The Hornets simply did not have the range.

The Yom Kippur War had done more than provide the first ever naval missile boat battles. It had made of the Israel Navy a force to be reckoned with in terms of its leadership in modern technologies. The thought that had gone into design and arming of the Saar-class boats - and the Israeli-built second generation - had proven justified in war. But something else - no less important - had happened. Electronic warfare was taking its place in the naval armory. In previous wars, the role of electronics had been restricted to communications and target location and identification - by radar and sonar. The use of advanced electronics in fire control and the defense of ships against sophisticated weaponry had been in its infancy. And where it existed, it was restricted to large vessels. The advanced and unconventional thinking of Israeli naval officers now combined with local industry to provide the electronics hardware and software needed to turn the small platforms into much more than simple carriers of guns and missiles. In years to come, this partnership was to produce anti-missile and other protection systems that were arguably the best of their kind in the world.

If the Israel Navy had previously been engaged primarily in preparation for, and the fighting of, full scale wars against other navies - the mission was now changing and expanding. The PLO's move from Jordan to Lebanon meant that the terrorists could operate by sea with much greater ease. The civil war in Lebanon, which began in 1976, left the terrorist organizations with absolute control over the southern Lebanon coastline. This new situation meant that the Navy had to keep a close watch on all traffic off the Israeli Mediterranean shore. Since there was absolutely no intention of restricting civilian use of the sea, hundreds of small boats and yachts were free to wander in and out of the marinas and along the beaches. Fishermen operated out of all the harbors along the coast. In addition, the north-south lanes, further out to sea, carried a heavy traffic of merchantmen between Arab ports, any of which could drop off small craft facing the Israeli shore. All of this had to be protected or, alternatively, checked and watched.

Using a combination of Hornets close inshore, missile boats further out to sea and air patrols - flown by IAF pilots and manned by naval radar crews - the Navy took on a 24-hour-a-day, all weather task. To seal the coastline hermetically against terrorist incursions would have been a major undertaking by itself even if the sea was free of other traffic. To do so without restricting pleasure, fishing and merchant craft required not only a high level of professionalism, but considerable talents in diplomacy, tact and courtesy. It also required flexibility. The terrorists could be coming straight in from some Arab merchant ship miles out to sea, or could be attempting to creep along the shores from Lebanon in rubber craft.

There was also a morale aspect to consider. Encounters with terrorists on the frontier, or air strikes against their bases, almost

inevitably resulted in headlines for the soldiers or airmen. The sailors, on the other hand, spent long days and nights at sea in often uneventful patrols far from public recognition and appreciation. And their successes, some of them very dramatic, were for very good reasons rarely reported in the media. It took a high degree of determination and dedication among the captains and crews to maintain constant awareness, despite weather and fatigue, in the knowledge that their considerable achievements would have to be kept to themselves.

Operation Peace for Galilee, in June 1982, differed from preceding wars fought by the Israel Navy. The missile boats gave supporting fire to the ground forces and the Hornets prevented the escape of terrorists by sea - but the star performers were the landing craft. Unlike the 1978 Litani Campaign, which was aimed solely at rolling the terrorists back from close proximity to the frontier, Peace for Galilee was designed to destroy the terrorist infrastructure in southern Lebanon. At 11:00 hours on 6 June, three columns entered Lebanon on the ground, one of them along the coast road to Tyre, Sidon and Beirut. The progress of the westernmost column was slow and deliberate, in order to allow the civilian populations of Tyre and Sidon ample opportunity to get out of the line of fire.

By noon on the same day, three landing craft - the INS Bat-Sheva and its smaller sisters, the Ashdod and Achziv - were at sea, facing the coast of Lebanon. The three ships, protected by missile boats and Hornets, were loaded to capacity with paratroops, tanks and armored personnel carriers. The mission of this task force was to cut the terrorists' communication and supply lines with Beirut, and to lower their will to fight. As darkness fell and a full moon rose over the sea, a small force of naval commandos landed from rubber boats on a beach facing a palm grove just beyond the Awali River bridge, north of Sidon. As the commandos secured the beach area, two vehicles with dimmed headlamps approached. The beach party opened fire, killing the terrorists on both tenders. As a second wave - of paratroops - came ashore, the force moved to widen the beachhead and the commandos began to check for appropriate landing points. A nearby position opened fire with anti-tank weapons and machineguns, but the return fire drove the terrorists away.

Suspecting that something was happening, PLO units began to lay down Katyusha and artillery fire in the area. On board the lead landing craft a radio came to life: "Beach ready!" As the "prepare for landing" lamp lit, the LCT moved into the shore and dropped its ramp. Within seconds the paratroops and tanks dropped into the water and raced on up the beach. The LCT pulled back and waited while its companions came up in quick succession to drop their loads. There was one anxious moment as, with shells dropping alongside, a tank engine refused to turn over. But it came to life and rolled ashore as the last landing craft raised its ramp and pulled away from the beach. While the landing force seized the Awali bridge and headed for the ridge overlooking Sidon, the landing craft turned for home and their next cargo.

The next landing on the Awali beach was in broad daylight on 7 June. Despite the crews' expectations of a hot welcome, the first landing craft dropped its load of APCs and tanks as though it was taking part in a peaceful exercise. The bombardment began as the LCT moved back out to sea, and the second slid up to the beach in its place. Again, the operation was completed in minutes, and the craft headed home for another run. For two more days the landing craft kept up their shuttle service, bringing in more troops and taking out wounded - who would be transferred to helicopters out at sea. By the time the operation was completed, the LTCs had transferred armored and infantry brigades sufficient to seal the enemy rear and turn northwards to Damour at the entrance to Beirut. In a fitting postscript, the landing craft would be called on 15 months later to transport tanks and APCs from the same bridgehead back to Israel, on the day of the withdrawal to the Awali line.

Throughout the duration of the IDF's stay in Lebanon, the Navy kept up constant patrols along the coastline. Perhaps its most satisfying moment was during the PLO evacuation of Beirut, when the Israel Navy's tiny craft moved confidently through the towering ranks of US 6th Fleet battleships and carriers to ensure that the terrorists did not break the terms of their agreement not to remove heavy equipment. The removal of the terrorists from southern Lebanon did not cause any relaxation of the Navy's vigilance. Most of the ongoing patrol function continued to be performed without public fanfare. However, the few encounters that were released to the media included eight major interceptions of terror teams in the period April 1985-December 1987, following the IDF's withdrawal to the international frontier.

The missile boat flotilla - of Saar 2s, 3s and 4s, armed with Gabriel and Harpoon missiles, Vulcan-Phalanx cannon and machineguns - has been reinforced in recent years by two hydrofoils. The Saar 4 also carries a helicopter to enhance its beyond-the-horizon vision. The new procurement plans include larger - Saar 5 - missile boats. Increases in size reflect the fact that each additional weapon and electronics system translates into both weight and space. The multi-purpose conception remains, and the boats will carry sophisticated detection systems, cannons, sea-to-sea missiles, anti-submarine equipment and a variety of protective systems - including an anti-missile missile that fires vertically and promises all-round defense. The Barak 1 a-m missile is an Israeli designed and made system that has aroused considerable interest in other navies. The shopping list also includes long range submarines and more sophisticated coastal patrol boats. With these tools, the Israeli Navy remains confident that it will be able to carry out its primary missions - of protecting the coastline and maintaining the initiative at sea - into the next decades.

THE
CHERBOURG
BOATS

During its first two decades, the Israel Navy operated with converted immigrant ships and a handful of World War II surplus vessels. It came a late third in the order of priorities for procurement - after the Air Force and the ground forces. The tasks were immense and the available ships were few with large crews, so that the Navy was hard put to be everywhere it needed to be, with the small manpower at its disposal. It took some years to convince the General Staff that the protection of the coastline, in coordination with the Air Force, was not the Navy's only task. Israel's neighbors would obviously acquire Soviet-made missile boats and the other trappings of modern navies. The answer had to lie in small boats with massive fire power, capable of coping with any kind of threat or mission - and fast enough to deploy over large areas of sea, or concentrate into a powerful striking force at short notice. The conception of the multi-purpose missile boat - as opposed to the single-purpose Soviet craft - took shape in the minds of Israel's naval planners.

In the early 1960s, the IDF General Staff was ready to humor the Navy, which hoped to be able to purchase a platform for weapon systems to be designed in Israel (the mainstay of which would be the Gabriel missile), and supported by systems existing in the world market. But the conception of a boat such as the Israel Navy needed did not exist anywhere in the world. A survey of available knowhow that could be adapted to the Israeli conception led to one conclusion - West Germany. The first contacts with the Ministry of Defense of the Federal Republic were made in March 1963, but the problems seemed insurmountable: secrecy, initial doubts about feasibility, non-existent technology and budgetary concerns. Solutions were found, the Germans had become wildly enthusiastic, and production was about to begin when, in early 1965, the Federal Republic found itself in a diplomatic crisis with the Arab world. Arms sales to Israel were discontinued, and the production plans for the ships were frozen.

At the insistence of the Israel Navy, Germany accepted the proposition that the jointly-developed plans must be made available to another producer. Given the friendly climate of relations between

Israel and France, Rear Admiral Mordechai (Moka) Limon, special envoy of the Ministry of Defense to Europe, was asked to investigate the possibility of building the boats in France. Moka approached the French Ministry of Defense, received a positive answer, and was put in contact with the French Navy, which recommended a Cherbourg shipyard as the best suited to perform the job. The owner had no previous experience in building vessels of the required type, but was extremely willing to learn and to master the new technologies - a willingness that would in later years put France in the forefront of manufacturers of missile ships, and indeed encouraged the country to develop its own sea-to-sea missile, the Exocet. A contract was signed in May, 1965 for the delivery of six boats, with an option for an additional six. This in itself was a considerable act of faith in an as yet untried concept.

In June 1967, the government of General Charles de Gaulle imposed an embargo on the delivery of arms to Israel, as a result of the General's conviction that she should not have fought the Six Day War against his advice. However, the embargo did not extend to spare parts, nor did it include the boats which were, after all, only being constructed in France from plans that originated elsewhere, and were to be supplied without any armament. The first five boats were supplied, and reached Israel without incident. Then, following a raid by Israeli paratroopers on Beirut Airport on 28 December 1968 (no casualties - only a few planes destroyed), de Gaulle declared a total embargo on all arms to Israel. The sixth boat was in Gibraltar en route to Israel. The seventh was in the French naval base in Cherbourg undergoing sea trials, and due to sail for Israel the following month.

Moka learned from a friend close to de Gaulle of the President's decision before the appropriate orders were issued to the French customs authorities. With the help of the holiday season, and the normal inefficiency of French telegraph services, it was arranged to delay the new order to Cherbourg customs for 48 hours. Moka immediately called the Israeli duty officer in Cherbourg, and told him that the seventh boat must sail immediately.

The following is the account of Commodore (Res.) Hadar Kimchy who, in the dramatic months that followed, was the commander of the missile boat flotilla, including the vessels being constructed in Cherbourg.

It was a Saturday. We had the one boat undergoing sea trials. The possibility of extension of the embargo had always hovered over us, and we knew that we could encounter difficulties in taking the boat out. So we had kept her fueled up and with an adequate crew at all times. The moment we got the message that the embargo was to include the boats, we asked Cherbourg customs down to the yard to sign the necessary manifest on the grounds that "the weather was fair out at sea" (a rare occurrence in winter), and we intended to take the boat out.

A customs officer came aboard to fill in the required forms. It was a pure formality because this craft, like her sisters, was in a kind of administrative limbo. New ships, when launched, become subject to seaworthiness regulations, insurance certification and so on, all of which are the legitimate concern of port authorities. No civilian ship may put out to sea without satisfying the harbormaster that both vessel and crew are insured. But warships need neither insurance nor seaworthiness papers. All we needed as clearance was for the customs to record that the engines from Germany - were "imported for re-export" so that the pending files could be exempted from duties. The official, motivated by the desire to help his country's exports, promptly recorded all necessary details, and we were free to go. By the time that information of the embargo finally reached Cherbourg from Paris (after the weekend), we were already out at sea.

At Gibraltar, I arranged with the Royal Navy to refuel not just the one boat that had arrived one week before, but both - and then flew back to Cherbourg, confident that the sixth and seventh members of our precious flotilla were well on their way home. On previous occasions, we had consulted French naval meteorological services in Cherbourg, particularly since the Bay of Biscay crossing could be treacherous, and had taken ceremonious leave of the local naval commandant. We were, after all, guests in the naval anchorage, where we enjoyed space for our essential stores, the use of the naval barracks and canteens and so on. But this time we couldn't take that risk. Consequently, a hot reception awaited me at Cherbourg.

I was summoned to the office of the naval commandant and, in the presence of all his staff officers, was treated to a tirade of fluent

French, the gist of which was that we had behaved in un-
gentlemanly fashion. True, there was nothing illegal in what we had
done, but we must not assume that he did not fully understand that
our hasty and unceremonious departure had been prompted by prior
knowledge of the embargo decision. I asked him if we could discuss
the matter in private. When his officers had departed, I asked him
what he would have done in my place. He replied that, had he been
out of uniform, he would gladly have told me how much he would
have enjoyed being in my place, however... After a short pause, he
went on to declare that the French Navy did not want to be
involved in affairs of this kind, and that he was not prepared to
accept any kind of responsibility for our behavior. Therefore, we
were requested to remove ourselves, lock, stock, and barrel from the
naval anchorage within 24 hours.

We had no boats in the water and no crews in the barracks, so
all we had to do was shift a few spare parts and other stores over to
the shipyard adjacent to the civilian port. The naval boycott was not
to be total. As the months went by, they generously lent the
shipyard the rafts that were essential mooring for our ships; because
of the heavy Atlantic tides, we could not tie up directly to the
quayside. In fact, the move would prove to be a blessing in disguise,
since we could come in and out of the civilian port at will, without
having to cross any naval boom at the entrance.

That had been Christmas week, 1968, and we entered the new
year wiser in two respects: firstly, the civilian location allowed more
freedom of movement, and secondly, law and bureaucracy work in
strange ways. Embargo meant that no customs officer would sign
release papers, but there was nothing to stop work being done for
us. There was nothing even to stop a ship putting out to sea, and
leaving territorial waters, as long as no documentation was being
requested. Aircraft sitting on an airfield inside the country were a
different proposition, but we were not subject to any specific
authority as long as we did not request formal permission to leave
French waters for good. Over the coming months, the work in the
shipyard proceeded on schedule. One after the other, our boats were
launched and underwent sea trials with our crews on board - but
there was no sign of the embargo being lifted, and we needed the
vessels badly. Then, in late 1969, with the pressures building both at
home and in France, things began to happen in parallel.

The shipyard was in trouble financially. Over 1200 families in Cherbourg were dependent on the yard for their livelihood, and the owner could not be paid in full unless the boats were delivered. It was a Gaullist town with a strong lobby in Paris, and nobody wanted to see the yard close down. On the other hand, it was only a matter of time until officialdom woke up and took notice of the anomaly of our presence. And that might lead to unpleasant developments in the "sleeping embargo." But salvation was at hand for both Paris and Cherbourg. A prospective buyer turned up at the yard with an attractive offer. The buyer, a Norwegian representing a company in the oil exploration business, needed fast boats to service its rigs. Of course, the company would prefer something a little more heavy-duty - and it didn't really need 13,000 horsepower in a 250-ton hull. However, he was in a hurry, and nobody else had anything suitable to offer. So if the shipyard was prepared to make the sale within four weeks, he would be happy to take the five greyhounds of the sea off their hands. After all, everybody knew that in the oil business whoever gets there first with producing wells stands to make the profits.

The owner of the yard was ready to clutch at any straw, and the government, so I assume from reading between the lines, was willing to kill two birds with one stone: firstly, the deal would solve the Cherbourg problem and, secondly, it would remove one obstacle from the path to improvement in the somewhat strained Franco-Israeli relations. There was one problem: Israel had to agree to waive her rights to the boats - but she couldn't have them anyway, so it was worth a try. The approach was made, not in writing but by telephone, to Moka Limon. Moka took his time over replying. One week later he came back with a reluctant "yes." Of course Israel would prefer to have the boats, but in the present stalemate we might at least cut our losses with a sale to a respectable customer - and this Norwegian buyer did seem serious and solid.

There were some overlooked details. Had the eager sellers looked closely at the buyer's letterhead, they might have noticed that the Norwegian address was a post box serving a company registered in Panama. The Norwegian, whom Admiral Limon had known for quite a while, was convinced, at a secret meeting at Oslo Airport, to lend the name of his company, Starboat. He sincerely believed in Israel and was deeply affected by the injustice of the French embargo, with its dangerous implications for Israeli security.

It hadn't been quite that simple. For months, all the alternatives had been considered and checked out. The OC Navy had looked at the possibility of getting American-built boats, but they were geared for much larger craft. Meanwhile, our boats had been launched at regular intervals and we had been finding faults persistently during the sea trials in order to postpone the formal acceptance - at which point we could hardly have justified maintaining crews in Cherbourg. The yard was not receiving payment for the finished boats, so the nervousness there was adding to the right psychological frame of mind for the deal. At home pressure was being brought to bear on the General Staff to accept the view that, one way or another, the Navy had to have its boats.

We had thought, at one stage, of simply taking the boats and running, but Defense Minister Moshe Dayan vetoed that suggestion. In spite of the total embargo, spare parts for the IDF were being shipped out of France by diverse ways and means. Therefore Dayan and Prime Minister Golda Meir decided that there was too much at stake for them to allow the illicit escape of the five boats. It became obvious that if the boats were to be taken out of France, a legally foolproof plan would have to be drawn up. It was Moka who prepared the elaborate paper work. Over the following weeks, our friendly Norwegian's frequent business trips from Oslo to London were slightly rearranged to bring him quietly in and out of Paris to finalize details. Then the deal was offered - and snapped up.

The joy of the shipyard owner was not yet complete. The buyer wanted fast delivery, otherwise the sale might fall through. There were sea trials to be completed, and somebody had to make the actual delivery. Where on earth could crews be found at such short notice - unless of course the Israelis were prepared to do a favor to their friends; after all, we had come a long way together. Moka was most helpful and understanding: "Of course we could help out - but you do realize that it would have to be in civilian clothes - not in Israel Navy uniforms."

This was where our problems began. We were in a battle against time. We had to complete sea trials and assemble everything we needed for the final stage quickly and quietly, and be out of Cherbourg before anybody put two and two together. The shipyard owner, who I think did understand but preferred to say nothing, knew we were in a hurry. However, the fifth and last boat was only due to be launched on December 14, and it normally took at least a month to complete sea trials - so the date should be mid-January. But that didn't suit us at all. The period leading up to Christmas is not exactly a time when bureaucrats want to make close studies of stacks of paperwork. As they come back to work, with clearer heads, after New Year's Day, it might be a completely different story. So our deadline was set for the early evening of Christmas Eve - on the assumption that this was the least likely day of the entire year for anyone to be paying attention to us. And there was a lot to be done by then.

First of all, we had to ensure that the boats remained in the water; it would have been only natural to store them high and dry on land during the winter storms. That was easily overcome by continually finding minor faults that needed adjustment at sea. We had been assigned an amiable old yacht captain to keep an eye on us. But he felt queasy in high seas and, in any case, only appeared on the quayside at 9.00 a.m. The naval day starts much earlier than that, so he would turn up at the port only to find that the boat due to go out that day had already slipped its moorings at 8.00 a.m. At first, he would sit on the quay until we returned at 12.00 or 1.00 p.m. But as the weeks and months went by, and we always returned, he contentedly retired to a waterfront bistro to linger over a drink until the boat came in.

We became really nervous just before the fifth boat was launched. The French Navy launched their first nuclear submarine - in the navy yard at Cherbourg - and the ceremony, complete with visiting dignitaries, took place right across the water from our four craft. We were sure that, with the Minister of Defense and press there in force, somebody would show interest in the obviously military-style boats moored in the civilian port. But the dust settled and nothing happened. However, the shipyard decided to delay launching because of a problem with the fourth engine on boat number five. Once a month, on the 14th or 15th, the tides at Cherbourg reach a height of six meters, and this was the only time when the slipway was sufficiently covered with water to allow launching. If we missed December 14, then there was no way to get the boat into the water before January 14. It took all our powers of persuasion to convince the yard that we could run in the engine and solve the problems in the water. The truth was that it would be far easier on the yard's test bench - but we couldn't allow that. The boat was duly launched and our engineers went to work against the clock to have the obstinate engine - and everything else - ready for the 24th.

There were logistic problems to solve, and the most critical of all was fuel. We calculated that we would need full tanks on departure and two refuelings at sea. Obviously, we could not fill the tanks of five boats that were only engaged in short sea trials without arousing suspicion. The technique was simple: the faults that needed correcting each day always happened to be in the boat that was moored closest to the raft that was lashed to the quayside. To get the boat out, all the others had to slip their ropes and maneuver out of the way, with their engines running. Each day we would order a tanker to top up the few tons of fuel oil expended - and each time we would take a few more tons than we had actually used. The level in the fuel tanks was steadily rising when Christmas came to lend a hand. The regular driver of the tanker asked a favor of us: the holiday was coming up fast, and he would appreciate some free time - so would we mind particularly if he brought bigger loads twice or three times a day? That way, he could have Christmas off. Our quartermaster officer, who handled the orders and payments, was delighted to oblige.

The refuelings at sea were not so simple to arrange. First of all, the help of the Israel merchant marine had to be enlisted. Without letting too many people in on the secret, we would need two merchant ships, each with skilled naval refueling crews on board, and the ships had to be fitted up with the necessary equipment - pumps, hoses and fuel tanks - and the entire operation had to be drilled at sea. The whole exercise was explained away as a secret naval investigation of the possibility for extending the range of operations. One ship chosen was a phosphate carrier that regularly visited French shores. A month before the deadline, it was fitted up with the necessary equipment at Haifa. The refueling techniques were carefully rehearsed, including the problematics of rough seas in the Bay of Biscay. Then it sailed to Ashdod and was loaded with phosphates and clean diesel oil - our boats needed a purer variety than that usually burnt by merchantmen - and ordered to sea at deadline minus 14 days, with instructions to linger at Gibraltar until needed.

The second vessel, the Dan, was a Mediterranean line passenger ship that usually spent the winter months in port. The Navy's first problem was to find the necessary fuel tanks and install them. As luck would have it, a local fuel company was busily installing a new depot outside Tel Aviv, and had some eminently suitable tanks at hand. The company executives, who could not be told what it was all about, were very annoyed to receive a Defense Ministry requisition, and the size of their bill for the loaned tanks reflected that annoyance.

The next problem to overcome was a tricky one indeed. The civil harbor in Cherbourg faced a row of homes on the waterfront. The local families were sensitive to noises generated in the port. One night in November, we started a shipboard generator and the police promptly arrived to announce that the neighbors were complaining. But electric power would be essential to pre-heat engines for at least two hours before we put to sea. There was only one thing to do. The next night we summoned the police and took them on board a freezing boat to see our boys huddled in blankets and turning blue. The police promptly called in the harbor electrical engineer to see whether he could get a land line with the capacity that we said we needed for heating the men and the boats. It could not be done, but the police did recognize our need - so they undertook to explain to the irate neighbors that we must have the use of one of our generators at night. The complaints died away as the residents of Cherbourg grew accustomed to the noise. Meanwhile, we hoped that force of habit, plus Christmas festivities, would prevent them from complaining to the police on the big night when we had twenty engines to warm up.

We were going to need food for five crews for a week or ten days, and we could hardly buy that kind of quantity in one store at one time. A survey was made, and a list drawn up, of all the supermarkets in the Cherbourg area. We had seven Israeli families who had taken apartments and houses in the town. Each family was given a copy of the list, and of the order in which they were to be visited. Then, for seven days, the seven families each bought what would seem to be a normal amount of provisions for a family over the holiday week. The resulting 49 purchases were delivered to the quartermaster officer, who divided them up into more or less equal shares for each of the boats.

The sea trials had been carried out with skeleton crews. We needed more seamen, but the French police seemed to be paying particular attention to Israelis registering in French hotels. It was decided that we could cope with 20 men per boat instead of the full complement of 40 - but we still had to get them in. Over the 72 hours before Christmas, in small groups, missile boat crewmen from Israeli Navy bases were put aboard every available flight to London that was stopping over in Paris: international airline regulations allowed a 24-hour stopover. From Paris, the men were dispatched, two up front and two at the back of every train to Cherbourg. They were given precise instructions: Cherbourg is the last station - so don't ask questions of fellow passengers; no Hebrew language newspapers or books, and don't talk if you don't have to! Carrying suitable identification, they were picked up from the arrivals platform and taken to Israeli homes in the town. For the last three days, every available square inch of floor space in our seven families' homes was taken up by mattresses and sleeping bags. The boys were given a list of restaurants where they could eat, according to a strict rota to ensure that never more than two Israelis sat together in any public place.

One remaining detail had to be arranged. An experienced Zim Israel Shipping Lines captain, who did know what was going on, was dispatched from Israel to Antwerp, carrying written orders that allowed him to take command of any Zim ship. There he commandeered the MS Tiberias and put to sea. He was to heave to off the coast of southern England and wait to give assistance if we needed it. If anything went wrong, he was to tow the boat in trouble into an English port: better that than return to France!

The owner of the shipyard knew, more or less, that we were ready for sea - although he had obviously kept to himself any thoughts he had about the Norwegian deal and our insistence on having the fifth boat in the water. He was quite a character. He had been a pilot in World War I, and had set up a plant to make planes after the war. One day, a strike had occurred in the plant, so he closed it down. His wife had some land in Cherbourg, and there he had set up his shipyard to build yachts. It had developed into something much bigger by the time the Israel Navy had arrived, direct from our German interlude. The whole idea of our boats and the advanced technology they involved had caught his imagination and appealed to his sporting instincts. And it was perhaps those instincts that made him keep his own counsel through those long weeks.

On Wednesday the 24th, we sat down to lunch - Moka Limon, three boat commanders, myself and another officer - in the Cafe de Paris, a famous Cherbourg restaurant. We had taken a small room in which to celebrate our imminent departure - and in walked the old man. It must have been obvious at once; all these officers had rarely been together in Cherbourg. He came straight over to us and said: "So we can celebrate? If you are all here, you must know what you are doing!" He joined us at the table. We kept up the pretense as best we could: our job was to deliver the boats to Norway; the weather was stormy - no time for sailing - and it was Christmas. In the course of the conversation, somebody asked him about the traditional present given by a shipyard to a customer when a new ship left: "And what will you give us when the time comes?" When we first arrived in Cherbourg, the yard had loaned us an as yet nameless sailing boat to use whenever we wanted. We had promptly named it after the shipyard owner's daughter. He announced that he was going to Paris, and "...might not be around when you leave." Having said that, he phoned his foreman in charge of yacht production, and told him to load our sailing boat onto a cradle and place it onto one of the boats. I intervened and said that we would worry about shipping it later - not to bother loading it aboard now.

We were as ready as we would ever be - and then the weather struck with full Atlantic fury. Zero hour was set for 8 p.m. on Christmas Eve, an hour when we could confidently expect the respectable burghers of Cherbourg to be sitting at their heavily-laden Christmas tables, eating to their hearts' content and drinking heady French wines. At eight o'clock, there was a gale blowing with Force 9 winds reported in the Bay of Biscay. There was no way we could put to sea in that, nor any sign of it abating in the hours to come. And we could hardly ask the French Navy for their weather forecasts. I ordered our departure delayed to 10 p.m. and sat a number of seamen at radio sets to listen to the met reports from the BBC, French radio and so on. But it was all the same: strong westerly winds with a barometric depression moving in from the

Atlantic. I postponed to midnight, but there was still no change. We had to be well away in the dark, and if we didn't go that night, how on earth would we be able to conceal all the equipment and the crews? At 1.00 a.m. on Christmas Day, the BBC, bless their hearts, reported that the depression was turning north for Ireland, Scotland and Scandinavia - and the winds were now northwesterly. This meant that the seas would still be high, but the winds would flatten the waves. This was it - at 2 a.m. we would go.

All five generators had been running all evening - and no one had complained. Now there only remained one minor detail to take care of. All seven families in Cherbourg were running their own cars. They were asked to bring them down to the quayside and park them "inadvertently" across the entrance. Then, if the police got wind of 20 twenty marine engines starting up, they would have a long walk up the quay and we would gain precious minutes. As it turned out, the police never appeared. The engines turned over and gained power, the last mooring ropes were slipped off - and we were on our way home.

Christmas Day in Europe is a quiet day - no newspapers, nothing to disturb the family atmosphere. If anybody missed us, we didn't know about it until we reached our first refueling rendezvous off southern Spain. There we heard a brief BBC report that we had left Cherbourg - nothing more. Much later, we were to find out that a furious President of France had ordered a naval squadron to sea to hunt for us, but the mayor of the town where the naval base was located ordered his harbormaster to lower the boom at the port entrance - "because of the storm."

We did have visitors. A local customs man came out on a fishing boat from a nearby Spanish harbor, circled a couple of times to see what was going on, and headed back to port. Either he said nothing, or the Spaniards weren't interested, for, there was absolutely no noise about us out of Spain. A helicopter circled overhead during the refueling, but that turned out to be the local Lloyds man whose duty it was to keep statistics on ship movements - and to him we were obviously only a statistic, or perhaps five of them.

On the afternoon of the third day, we slipped through the Straits of Gibraltar close to the Moroccan coast. The five of us, in line astern, passed scores of ships of every conceivable nationality. Nobody paid any attention. So far, the reports about us said that we

were heading for Norway. On the next morning, the news bulletins reported us in the Mediterranean and from here on, everybody was looking for us. Out at sea, we knew very little of the fuss in the press - it was only later that I was handed a bunch of newspaper clippings: one report stated that Royal Navy Gibraltar cabled a reply to a French Admiralty request for information: "We did see five unmarked warships pass through the Straits." In response to the inevitable supplementary question, the Royal Navy added, obligingly if tardily: "That was about 12 hours ago."

The first inquisitive soul we saw was a French aircraft which circled and went away. Then a small plane from Malta came head on towards us. As he flew overhead, we heard on a live BBC broadcast, an excited reporter crying: "I can see them, below me now!"

We met with the MS Dan, for our second refueling, south of Malta in the shadow of the island of Lampedusa. From here on we were in waters where somebody might try to stop us by force, and we were unarmed. I had issued strict orders about emergency procedures. In the Atlantic, the boat commanders were told, if in trouble, to make for Lisbon. Each boat carried a street map of the city and local money, so that if anybody had to be taken to hospital, it could be done with a minimum of questions asked of the locals. Gibraltar was the second possibility. We would not be unwelcome there. In the Mediterranean, we had likewise selected other possibilities. Luckily, there was no need. The only medical problem happened to be on the boat carrying our doctor, and technical problems conveniently occurred only where there was a senior engineering officer to help out.

We were under orders from the OC Navy not to resist if challenged by French naval units, but they never came anywhere near us. I was not overly concerned about the Libyans or Egyptians. We were running with heavy seas behind us and, moreover, they didn't then have anything fast enough to match our speed. The only tangible danger was from a submarine lying in wait at the entrance to the Aegean, and that was highly unlikely. To be on the safe side, I split the force in two with orders to reform south of Cyprus, then take as northerly a course as possible, to keep distance between us and Egypt.

The weather was bad all the way - high seas and rain squalls. Normally we might have cursed our bad luck, but this time the poor visibility and the waves running with us were exactly what we needed, up to the last leg. Then, since we would have entered Haifa at midday if we maintained speed, we were ordered to slow down and only enter port after dark. Now the heavy seas became a nuisance, particularly since two of the boats were only running on three engines. But we held on for six hours. Then, in the late evening of New Year's Eve, we slid stealthily into Haifa harbor - only to find that the world was waiting for us on the quayside.

The French government made the best of what was for them a bad job. The boats had been legally purchased - for oil exploration work. By agreement with Paris, they spent their first six months, unarmed, performing as specified in the sale contract. Rear Admiral Limon left France a few days after the five boats arrived safely at Haifa. The French authorities could not pin on him anything that violated French law. However, they asked the Israeli Government to recall him from Paris. A small price to pay for the victories of Damietta and Latakia in the 1973 war. The sailboat given by the shipyard owner of Cherbourg was quietly loaded on board a Zim merchant ship, and arrived in Haifa one month after its bigger sisters. The Israeli fuel company executives, in atonement for their annoyance over the requisition of their fuel tanks, turned up in Haifa port with 120 bottles of champagne for the 120 seamen who had made the Christmas voyage from Cherbourg.

NOT BY
THE SWORD
ALONE - THE
NAHAL

There was no doubt in the minds of the fathers of Zionism that a nation cannot exist without physical bonds to its land. The conversion of Jews returning to their traditional homeland into farmers and laborers held an almost mystical promise of a final break with the Diaspora traditions of merchants and tailors - trades that could be carried across borders in the endless search for sanctuary. Land and the ability to work it with the sweat of one's own labor were themes that drove intellectuals and ideologists, professors and students to face the hardships of rocky hillsides and malarial swamps. And throughout the early Zionist endeavor ran the thread of need to protect the new farmers against marauders and thieves, attracted by the livestock, crops and equipment of settlements that were struggling for survival in a backward and lethargic environment.

Amid the struggle to reclaim marginal land, purchased with pennies dropped into Jewish National Fund collection boxes all over the world, and to defend the homesteads against mindless violence, the images of the Hashomer watchman and the kibbutz and moshav farmer, with plow and rifle, became synonymous with the rebirth of the nation. In the absence of overt defensive forces, the Jewish community of Mandatory Palestine subscribed to the proposition that the agricultural settlements would determine the political and security borders of the homeland when it achieved sovereignty.

One tragic event, in March 1920, was to have a profound effect on the determination to defend the agricultural communities. A band of Bedouins, ostensibly searching for a French customs officer, gained entry to the settlement compound of Tel Hai in the Upper Galilee Valley - then within the territory mandated to France. Once inside, they turned on the settlers and killed eight of them. Tel Hai was evacuated, but it gave birth to a resolve never again to abandon a settlement. Through the Arab riots of the 1930s, new kibbutzim were established by first erecting a stockade and a watchtower. So profound was the national commitment to co-existence of agriculture and defense that each of these "tower and stockade" settlements was erected - within hours, for fear of British interference - by hundreds of volunteers who flocked in from all the neighboring areas.

The lesson of Tel Hai was not lost during the War of Independence in 1948. Prime Minister Ben Gurion insisted that the outlying communities were not be abandoned in the face of the invading armies. Though not all of them could be held for long, some of the kibbutzim played a vital role in the war. Yad Mordechai, in the south, held for five precious days, and delayed the Egyptian advance on Tel Aviv long enough to allow Givati Brigade to prepare a defense line twenty miles from the city. Ramat Rachel, immediately south of Jerusalem, effectively prevented a link up of Jordanian and Egyptian forces in the city. Degania, in the Jordan Valley, stopped the Syrian Army while Gesher, a few miles further south, performed the same feat against the Iraqi Army. Through the early months of 1948, dozens of settlements repulsed attacks by local Arabs, the Palestine Liberation Army and the invaders from Egypt, Syria, Iraq, Lebanon and Jordan.

The philosophy was later summed up by Yigal Allon, who had commanded the Palmach in the 1948 war: "The true frontier of Israel moves and forms according to the movement and location of Jewish workers of the soil. Without Jewish settlement, defense of the country is not possible, even if we double the force of the army." In 1941, when the Palmach was founded as the first regular force of the Hagana, its platoons and companies were quite naturally based in the kibbutzim. There, they combined military training with their share of the agricultural work and guard duties. Apart from the advantages of being relatively well concealed from prying British eyes, the soldiers were in fact paying for their keep by the work they did on the farms.

The Palmach was dismembered during the War of Independence. First, its pilots were transferred in April 1948 to the Hagana Air Service. Then, the Palyam was absorbed into the Israel Navy and its "Arab Department" was transferred to IDF Intelligence Branch. Though the Palmach brigades continued to operate under the IDF General Staff, their independent headquarters was disbanded on 7 November 1948; Ben Gurion did not want any "politically-oriented armies within the army" (the Palmach was clearly affiliated with the left wing labor settlement movement). However, much of the Palmach tradition of informality, equality and innovation was bequeathed to the IDF. Despite the fact that the force was never more than 5000 men and women - of whom 999 fell in the war - its influence was so profound that it provided three out of the 12 majors-general, 20 out of the 45 colonels and 40% of all lieutenant colonels and majors of the IDF in the 1948 war. In later years, four chiefs-of-staff and more than 40 majors-general were former Palmach officers.

On 8 September 1949, the Knesset enacted the Defense Service Law, Section F of which reads: "The first 12 months of regular service of a male, and the 12 months service of a female, after basic military training, will be devoted primarily to agricultural training as shall be determined in regulations, excepting recruits sent to serve in the Air Force or Navy." In other words, all members of the ground army were to fulfill the philosophy of the founding fathers. In presenting the law to the Knesset, Ben Gurion said: "An efficient army will not arise in this country... if the youth, and especially the immigrants, do not first accept the agricultural training which will give them roots in the homeland, will accustom them to physical work, will give them a language, cultural habits and a routine of discipline... A year of agricultural preparation is intended to build the nation, to crystallize this dust of man collected together from all the ends of Earth into one national entity."

Although the Defense Service Law has been amended from time to time, Section F has never been repealed. It was, however, never enforced. In the early 1950s, three-quarters of Israel was wilderness, only 12% of the labor force worked in agriculture - and the population of hungry mouths had doubled within months. The IDF General Staff did set up, temporarily, two farms to grow potatoes for civilian and the army's own needs. But the idea was not exactly popular among the new recruits, nor did it appeal to the generals who were facing severe manpower problems. The answer to Ben Gurion's dream lay elsewhere, in an army formation that already existed.

On 11 June 1948, at the beginning of the first truce of the War of Independence, the Negev was cut off and Western Galilee was in enemy hands. It was common knowledge that the truce was no more than a temporary respite, and that the Jewish community had tapped the last of its military age manpower reserves. When the war resumed, as it would within 28 days, its outcome would resolve the fate of the newborn State of Israel. The Provisional Government convened and, among other desperate decisions, resolved to mobilize all the 17-year-olds for two months intensive training as a last reserve that could be sent to the frontlines. The resulting mobilization order became known as Order 31 - for these were youngsters born in 1931.

Among the thousands of schoolchildren who abandoned their books, and apprentices who downed tools, to report to the Gadna ("Youth Battalions") training base were a few hundred members of youth movement groups. It was, and still is, a common practice within the Zionist youth movements, for boys and girls still in school to form "garinim" (social nuclei) with the intent of settling on the land. Some of these garinim eventually join existing kibbutzim, while others elect to build their own settlements on sites chosen in coordination with the Jewish National Fund and other authorities. Concerned that the exigencies of military service would destroy the coherence of these nuclei, on 10 August 1948, eight youth movements jointly submitted a plea to Ben Gurion not to break up the groups. On 16 August, the Prime Minister responded in writing: "Your intent to preserve the nuclei for imminent settlement on the land is fundamentally correct, and the Defense Ministry will instruct the military staff in this matter. Obviously, as long as this war is not over, the needs of war and victory must take precedence, but unless absolutely necessary the groups will not be dispersed..." The letter went on to refer to a distinctive frame for the groups as Noar Halutzi Lohem ("Fighting Pioneer Youth").

On 12 September, within a proclamation defining the structure of Gadna, Chief-of-Staff Yaacov Dori included the following provision: "To preserve the pioneering element of settlement, a special frame will be organized within the Gadna. This framework will contain all the organized settlement nuclei of the youth movements that are subject to enlistment under Order 31, or any subsequent Order, and will be called 'Noar Halutzi Lohem' (Nahal). These groups include girls." The first battalion of Nahal was constituted from seven settlement groups. As the tide of war turned, the 17-year-olds were not committed to battle - but, in 1949, the Nahal participated together with other youth in a major engineering project: the Gadna constructed a strategically important road along the shores of the Dead Sea from Sodom to Masada and the oasis of Ein Gedi. Nahal groups also descended to Eilat, in the same year, to help prepare the defenses of the new desert outpost on the banks of the Red Sea.

That same year, the settlement authorities approached the Nahal Battalion with a demand for two groups for specific, tough and urgent missions. Firstly, somebody had to resettle the derelict community of Tselim in the Negev and, secondly, a group of Palmach veterans that was going to create a new kibbutz at Rosh Hanikra, on the Lebanese frontier, needed reinforcement. With some trepidation, the Nahal agreed. Later in the same year, there was no hesitation about a sudden move made by another ex-Nahal group. This particular garin had settled in Ein Gev - a kibbutz on the eastern shores of the Sea of Galilee, under the guns of the Syrians on the Golan Heights. A few miles to the south stood a hill called Tel Kasr which, though in Israel, was within the demilitarized zone under the recent armistice agreements. On 6 November 1949, acting on their own initiative, the Nahlaim - as they had become known - ascended the hill, carrying reels of barbed wire, fence posts and tools on their backs. Quickly fencing in an area for their encampment, they proceeded to erect a few huts. Their kibbutz, Tel Katzir, was joined within weeks by Haon, on the shores of the lake between their hilltop and Ein Gev.

Life in these settlements was not a picnic. While some of the youngsters cleared land of rocks in order to start farming, others worked in nearby settlements to earn enough income to keep their own kibbutzim going. Water was not readily available, and had to be carted in. It was some time before they had electricity, and then mostly from small generators that only worked a few hours a day. Tel Katzir in particular was hard hit by a drought that killed off a whole year's crop. And, as though that was not enough, fire gutted the communal dining hall and kitchen. But neither the trials and tribulations of nature nor Syrian sniping from the hills above could drive the settlers off their hill.

The concept of Nahal was so different from the other echelons of the IDF that a special department - "Youth and Nahal Branch" - was created within the Ministry of Defense. And it fell to this Branch to find a formula to cover the military service obligations of these young settlers. The result was a provision that was to be unique to the army: "Unpaid Service." Under this formula, members of the garinim who settled in border areas where there were specific security problems, were exempted from completing their full conscript service. In return, they made a commitment to remain at least five years in the settlement. Their kibbutzim were part of the regional defense systems, and the members were trained, with periodic refreshers, in the necessary military roles. Each kibbutz was also required to supply its quota of cadets for non-commissioned and officers courses. For the most part, the kibbutz could make its own selection of candidates, though in specific cases it was not unknown for the IDF to bring pressure to bear in order to get what it considered to be promising material for high command or, for example, pilots' courses. Unpaid Service, with minor variations, was to remain a cornerstone of the Nahal as it moved into the next stage of its development.

On 24 November 1949, after enactment of the Defense Service Law, the General Staff ordered the reorganization of the Nahal as a fully fledged regular unit of the IDF - no longer an offshoot of the pre-military Gadna. Within the two years conscript service common to all soldiers, the male soldiers of Nahal would spend nine months in agriculture. The girls in the garinim were to remain in the settlements when the boys went off to perform the military part of their duties. Army huts were erected in 50 kibbutzim that were to get the groups, and which were in some cases the places where they intended to live after their army service. Although the Nahlaim were to share in the work and cultural life of the communities, they were soldiers and a part of the military and social entity of the Nahal, even when serving their months as farmers.

The Youth and Nahal Branch was responsible not only for negotiating where Nahal garinim were to be placed, but also for formulating the contracts between the army and the settlements that received the groups. There were a number of rigidly enforced provisos. The Nahlaim could not be employed in service occupations: they were there to train as farmers - not cooks or laundrymen. During their time in the settlements, they were to spend five days a month in military training and one day studying and attending lectures. The settlements were committed, under contract, to supply their Nahal group with services that included water, electricity, landscaping of the camp, food, laundry and even haircuts once every three weeks.

Because of the general manpower situation, the Nahal was restricted to volunteers belonging to settlement groups that had formed before enlistment, with a small sprinkling of new immigrants to help them find their feet in their new country. At this stage, their military training was to be as infantrymen, although - unique among IDF formations - medical profiles were not a prime consideration in acceptance into Nahal. Those who were fit to be infantrymen trained as such, while the others learnt the military support trades that the formation needed: medical orderlies, signalers, quarter-masters and so on.

There were problems emanating from the nature of the groups and the ideologies and life styles that they intended to adopt as kibbutz members. In an army that has never been famous for parade ground spit and polish, the Nahlaim's insistence on wearing their shirt tails flopping loose and scuffed, unshined boots was to set new standards of individualism. When the wearing of rank badges became mandatory, Nahal groups debated whether it was really necessary to salute officers. In keeping with Palmach and kibbutz traditions, they argued that standing at attention when talking to an officer was sufficient sign of respect without giving in to the exaggerated behavior patterns of other armies. Controversy arose over the precise boundaries of authority between their officers and the coordinators of their settlement and agricultural activities. The arguments were resolved in favor of military authority, but the officers learnt to live with compromises as far as the coordinators were concerned.

This new experiment was beneficial both to the settlements and to the Nahlaim. The garinim not only lightened the work burden in a period when farmers were struggling to produce sufficient food for a population that had doubled overnight, but the presence of trained soldiers added a new dimension to nightly guard duties and the protection of workers in the fields. For the Nahlaim, it was a chance to become accustomed to farm work and learn agriculture, while soaking up the atmosphere of communal living. It also strengthened the coherence of the group. Previously, their experience had been restricted to after-school and holiday activities. Now they were learning to live with each other on a day-to-day basis, prior to starting out on their own.

By the end of 1950, the Nahal could already list the beginnings of serious achievements in permanent settlement after army service: four new kibbutzim, three groups that had gone to rehabilitate or reinforce struggling farming communities and seven garinim that had joined kibbutzim created earlier by their own youth movements. In addition, 140 Yemenite youth had been specially trained to work with immigrants from the Yemen in the transit camps that were springing up to house the influx of mass immigration. By May 1951, the Nahal was ready to hold its first reunion of veterans and serving soldiers. The gathering was greeted by Prime Minister Ben Gurion as: "The strangest formation of the strangest army in the world." Ben Gurion and Chief of Staff Yigael Yadin were then treated to a display that included sports events and a hint of things to come: Nahal soldiers erected in double time a model settlement of their own. The Prime Minister and Chief of Staff were witnessing a dress rehearsal for the Nahal's next step - one that was to change the map of Israel.

In the early 1950s, the unpopulated gaps in the frontiers of Israel beckoned to marauders and smugglers. Southern Israel was becoming a playground for "fedayeen" - Palestinian Arab terrorists employed and operated by Egyptian Army Intelligence in the Gaza Strip. The IDF had neither the manpower nor the means to seal off every inch of the frontier. Settling civilians along all the borders was not a solution. The new immigrants who were beginning to work on the land were more suited to the cooperative life of the moshav than they were to the communal living of a kibbutz. But the moshav structure of individual family units, each settler's involvement in his own plot of land and their refugee background, made the immigrant "moshavnikim" unlikely to function as an effective defensive unit. Conversely, the kibbutz oriented youth movements could not provide enough settlement groups to seal all the gaps. And, had they been able to speed up the process of creating new kibbutzim, few of the critical areas offered the possibility of establishing immediately viable economic units. The national networks could not provide electricity, water or even road systems at anywhere near the rate that major civilian settlement projects would require. Much of the potential farm land needed to be cleared of rocks and other obstacles. In some areas, particularly in the southern desert, agricultural knowledge was not yet sufficiently advanced to give answers to all the problems.

In June 1951, a company of 100 new recruits assembled, after two weeks basic training, to prepare for a special assignment. This was not a regular garin, but rather a collection of individuals, mostly new immigrants, none of whom particularly wanted to set up an army agricultural station. Faced with their obvious unwillingness, the company commander decided to impose strict discipline throughout the month that he had to knock them into shape. On 25 July, he led a convoy of trucks to the foot of a hill overlooking Egyptian positions on the Gaza frontier, in an area where infiltrators had been laying mines on the roads, stealing livestock and murdering farmers. The soldiers ascended the hill, rifles in hand, and began to dig in. While they waited for their supply trucks, an Egyptian convoy deposited soldiers on the facing slopes. The Nahlaim waited hours in their foxholes under the blazing desert sun until their equipment arrived. They erected a fence and some tents, then settled down for a nervous night. Few of them slept, but the only occurrence was a machinegun burst from an equally nervous Egyptian on the hill opposite.

In the days that followed, the reluctant farmers erected a camp and began to work the land. They were joined by a couple of veteran kibbutzniks who led them in digging a four kilometer long trench to bring water to their first fields. They made mistakes: their first attempt at growing onions failed because they planted the bulbs upside down. But gradually the farm took shape and their enthusiasm grew. The Nahal had added a new term to the compendium of settlements in Israel - "heachzuyot" (holding points). For want of a name, the place would be called "Nahlaim A," but that would soon change to "Nahal Oz." The Charter of Nahlaim A, deposited under the cornerstone of the first permanent building, read: "We are putting down a first peg in the creation of a soldiers' settlement on the frontier. We face a long border and wildernesses waiting for redemption. The frontiers and the soil, the voices of our many brothers, cry out to us: 'Put down a firm peg! Turn the border into a living wall defending this land!' We, new immigrants and sons of this land, from east and west, north and south - wherever our nation is dispersed - have gathered here at the orders of the IDF and take upon ourselves the protection of this land... In this place, there will be a community teeming with life, creating life and guaranteeing life. Let this be a sign to us and to the nations that our intent is peace and creation..."

Three weeks after the ascent to Nahlaim A, the Nahal erected its second "holding point." Nahlaim B - later to be known as Gonen -

was located on the eastern edge of the Upper Galilee valley, just above the swampland that was being drained under continual Syrian harassment and mere yards from the Syrian frontier at the foot of the Golan slopes. The garin was provided with a budget for irrigation piping to cover 75 acres - all of which had to be cleared of rocks and stones - given two tractors and promised the guidance of veteran farmers from the neighboring kibbutzim. Nahal Oz, Gonen and the heachzuyot that would follow them, were staffed by garinim that came, did their required period of agricultural service, then moved on. When the settlement was close to economic viability, the last garin assigned would be the one destined to convert the place into a civilian settlement. Both Nahal Oz and Gonen reached the point where they were self-supporting in 1953, and were handed over to their last groups as independent kibbutzim.

Nahlaim C and E were not only different from their predecessors, they were pioneering settlements in a completely new environment - the deep rift valley of the Negev Desert. But that was where their similarity ended. Nahlaim E was set up in January 1953 at the oasis of Ein Gedi, famous enough for its fertility in antiquity to have won honorable mention in the Song of Songs. Situated on the western banks of the Dead Sea, 2700 feet below sea level, the settlement clung to a shoreline never more than a hundred yards wide under the towering cliffs of the Negev mountains. It was a recipe for claustrophobia, enhanced by isolation from other human beings. Ein Gedi's nearest neighbor was the Dead Sea Works - the potash extraction plant at the south end of the chemical-saturated lake. However, deep in a cleft in the mountains was the spring that had turned the place into a flourishing oasis. In later years, Ein Gedi would become a major tourist attraction because of that spring and the nature reserve that surrounded it.

Nahlaim C - Ein Radyan, founded in October 1951 - was the antithesis of Ein Gedi. The site had been a waystation on trade routes from time immemorial. Its name was an Arabic distortion of "Ad Dianum," after a Roman temple that had stood in this legion outpost. Twenty five miles north of the Red Sea, and some one hundred miles south of the Dead Sea, Ein Radyan sheltered under the hills on the west edge of the five mile wide Arava Valley, which was bisected by the international frontier between Israel and Jordan. On a clear day, from the hill immediately above the Nahal camp, it was possible to see thirty miles north or south across the desert. Eastwards, the valley ended in the towering Edom Mountains of southern Jordan. The nearest neighbors were a copper mine ten miles to the south and, 25 miles further north, a Public Works Department camp responsible for periodically leveling and grading the dirt track that passed as the main road from Beersheba to Eilat.

Unlike Ein Gedi, the Nahlaim at Ein Radyan were not isolated from human contact. Truck drivers regularly carried supplies on the eight or ten hour drive from Beersheba to Eilat. A bus ran to and from Tel Aviv twice a week, and occasional archaeological missions, geologists and water engineers looked in on the settlers. But the Eilat road was not a main highway frequented by private traffic. In fact, travelers southwards were warned by huge signs on the outskirts of Beersheba: "If you are on your way south, check fuel, oil, water, arms and ammunition - and inform the police!" The message was clear: traffic on the road ran the risk of ambush by terrorists and roving Bedouin, and nobody took that risk unarmed.

Both settlements enjoyed the potential advantage that the desert climate would let them send fruit and vegetables to market ahead of season: the high prices commanded by out-of-season products would compensate for transportation costs. But Ein Radyan faced a double disadvantage. Their land was high in salt content, and the local wells could only supply brackish water. Some crops could survive in a salty environment - and even tasted sweeter because of it - but irrigation inevitably left a white salt crust on the surface. Rather than improving, the land could only deteriorate, particularly because the desert sand was devoid of the bacteria so essential for plant life, and crops ploughed back in to supply nitrogen did not decompose. The Nahlaim tried hoeing before and after watering, they alternated between sprinklers and water channels - but the white crust remained. Then, in one of those accidents that leave scientists wondering why they overlooked the obvious, the soldier whose job it was to open the water valves in the fields had a headache. Usually no one strayed beyond the perimeter fence after dark, because the camel caravans that smuggled arms to Jordan and drugs back to Egypt through the Negev wadis were far too large to risk a chance encounter. But the young soldier was ready to risk anything rather than take his throbbing head out into the blazing sun. He turned the sprinklers on in the early evening and came back to close them late at night. Next morning - there was no white crust. The agricultural experts who had been pondering the problem, and offering advice, had simply forgotten that water does not evaporate at night.

Not all the problems were that easy to solve. For example, it was obvious from the wild date palms growing around a pool of brackish water on the desert floor that this fruit would flourish. But there was no source of young palms to start a plantation. It so happened that the Jordan Valley settlements far to the north were also in need of planting stock. Through a net of devious deals, young date palms were smuggled out of Iraq crated in boxes labeled "fresh fruit," and transhipped in Cyprus. Part of the consignment was sent south to Ein Radyan, where land had been leveled and prepared weeks in advance. As luck would have it, the semi-trailer that brought the precious cargo overturned on the desert road fifty miles north of Ein Radyan. Every available pair of hands was mobilized to race north and reload the plants on army commandcars before they perished in the heat.

The problems of Ein Gedi and Ein Radyan were so different from other settlements that, in 1954, the kibbutz movement put together two groups of volunteer veteran kibbutzniks - 15 in each - to go south and spend a year or two with the Nahlaim. The work done in these two settlements was destined to open up the possibilities of agriculture in the whole of the Arava Valley. Indeed, the research into cattle husbandry in desert conditions, performed by a young Nahal corporal who had graduated in agriculture from a New Zealand university, formed the basis for dairy farming and a milk products industry at Ein Radyan - and won him an offer of a Fulbright scholarship to the University of California at Davis. Ein Gedi was transferred to its last garin as a kibbutz in January 1956. Ein Radyan, renamed Yotvata, was to become a kibbutz on 1 January 1958 and, henceforward was the model to emulate for all the settlements that sprang up along the Arava Valley; and 12 of those were to start as heachzuyot of the Nahal.

These were just four of 130 Nahal holding points, each with its own story, established by 1987, 85 of which had already become civilian settlements. There were a handful of heachzuyot that were abandoned for various reasons, but even this had its positive aspect. It was far easier to remove Nahal farms from Sinai as the IDF withdrew in 1982, than civilian farmers who might have formed an

emotional attachment to their homes and land. In addition to the Nahal's own settlements, its demobilized soldiers established another 34 kibbutzim and moshavim, reinforced the population of close to 200 older settlements and rehabilitated 60 more. All told, over four decades, the Nahal has absorbed, trained and passed on to settlements, new and old, more than 2800 garinim. But its efforts were not restricted to agriculture alone. Recognizing that some of the new development towns, with their largely immigrant population, were struggling socially, educationally and culturally, the Nahal sent some of its groups to spend part of their service time working with the townspeople of Kiriat Shmoneh, Shlomi, Maalot and Hatzor.

All of this effort inevitably aroused the interest of developing countries, for whom the concept of Nahal offered solutions to some of their own problems. Delegations came from all over the world to see for themselves - and to ask for assistance. As a result, Nahal officers have been sent to 21 African states, five in Asia and ten in South America to help organize and implement Nahal-style initiatives among the youth of those countries. As one senior IDF officer put it: "Nahal, as an instrument of agricultural and social development, has over the years become one of Israel's most important 'export products' to the developing nations." However, all of this enterprise was only one aspect of service in the Nahal. The Nahlaim were, after all, soldiers - and their split role was not without its critics.

The IDF had accepted a revolutionary concept by agreeing not to break up peer groups of youngsters, but the price was expensive. Some of the best of Israeli youth were members of Nahal garinim - and they were excluded from the normal selection processes by which the IDF chose candidates for elite units and specialist roles. Perhaps even more significantly, many of the Nahal soldiers would have been prime candidates for officers' courses. In the eyes of some senior officers, the sin had been compounded by allowing these groups to spend nine months of their two years' service in agriculture. Although the Nahal were performing an important role in regional defense, they were not available to the limited pool of combat troops - and this meant that the burden of ongoing security was unfairly distributed. In the small army of the 1950s, with growing problems of terrorist incursions and every sign that Israel's neighbors were building up their military power for another war, these arguments could hardly be ignored. And when the Chief of

Staff weighed in with a statement that "I need soldiers - not tomato farmers," the Nahal quite naturally felt that its future was threatened.

The best way to draw the teeth of the opposition was to better them at their own game. In 1955, the Nahal joined the paratroops. Despite doubts about the ability of Nahlaim, who were not renowned for military discipline, to make the grade in the tough training regimen of the airborne, the experiment succeeded. A battalion of Nahal were able to add the coveted red berets and brown boots to their uniform, with its sword and sickle shoulder tag. Their first test came on 2 November 1955, when they were assigned the task of removing Egyptian Army units from fortified positions that they had seized in the Nitzana demilitarized zone. The Nahal unit chosen for the task was the squad commanders' course. They staged a classic infantry assault, ending in close combat with bayonets. Five weeks later, Nahlaim participated in an operation to neutralize Syrian positions that had been shelling the Jordan Valley settlements. By October 1956, the Nahal had participated in four major border clashes.

On 29 October 1956, the first day of the Sinai Campaign, the Nahal Airborne Battalion crossed the frontier at Kuntilla and made a 170 mile dash to link up with their comrades of 202 Parachute Brigade, who had parachuted down at the eastern end of the Mitla Pass. The link up was achieved by the night of 30 October. At noon of the next day, elements of the battalion entered the Pass and found themselves pinned down by enemy fire (for a full account of the battle, see Chapter: Pages from the Diary of a Paratrooper). For their part in this action, two Nahlaim received citations and one was decorated with a medal for gallantry under fire. After the battle at Mitla, the battalion continued with 202 Brigade in a race down the shores of the Gulf of Suez to Sharm e-Shekh on the Straits of Tiran.

After the relatively quiet years of the early 1960s, two Nahal formations were attached to the infantry brigade that broke through the Um Katef complex in the Six Day War. The Nahal units trekked across five miles of sand dunes and swept into an assault on Egyptian lines that had been designed, under Soviet doctrines, to withstand the attack of a complete division. In an action that cost 11 dead and 40 wounded, the Nahlaim achieved their objective.

Meanwhile, their comrades of the Nahal Airborne took part in the conquest of the Gaza Strip and in Maj. Gen. Tal's ugda which was fighting its way from Rafiah to Qantara, on the Suez Canal. Reservist veterans of Nahal Airborne participated in the battle for Jerusalem and the southern Golan Heights.

In the years that followed the Six Day War, while shouldering an increased burden of placing heachzuyot at critical points on the new frontiers, the Nahal shared in the campaign against PLO infiltrators in the Jordan Rift Valley and in the raids designed to throw the Egyptians off balance in their War of Attrition. On 6 October 1973, when the Egyptian and Syrian armies flooded across the IDF lines, units of the Nahal were occupying some of the Suez Canal strongpoints and the southern perimeter positions on the Golan Heights. The Nahal Airborne on Golan clung to their foothold, and their tenacious resistance enabled them to guide artillery fire during the desperate days of the containment battle.

At the Pier Strongpoint, at the southern end of the Suez Canal line, 42 Nahlaim held out against thousands of Egyptians for eight days, and only surrendered after it was clear that no relief column could get through to them. As they marched out into captivity, having used the last of their water to shave and wash, the Egyptians were unwilling to believe that this tiny, proud unit was all that had held them off for more than a week. Meanwhile, the Nahal Airborne had been flown down from Golan. They took part in the battle for the town of Suez, and other actions to the west of the Canal. Nahal soldiers also fought with the Armored Corps and Artillery, and were among the first to arrive at Kilometer 101, the westernmost point of IDF advance on the road to Cairo.

In the wake of the Yom Kippur War, with the IDF in the midst of a crash program to rebuild its armored forces, the Nahal was called on to shoulder its share. For a while the Armored Corps was treated to the uncommon sight of tank crewmen wearing the red berets and brown boots of paratroopers together with Nahal insignia. Having worked hard to earn those status symbols, the Nahlaim were not going to give them up that easily. But, meanwhile, there were changes in the other aspects of Nahal service. Because of the general burden of ongoing security, the time spent in agriculture was reduced and the groups volunteering for the Nahal were called on to make a commitment for extra service: four months for the boys and two for the girls. In addition, though the heachzuyot policy was continuing, the Nahal was also establishing camps that combined both its roles. In the new "maachazim" (holdings), the farm work was done by those Nahlaim with lower medical profiles, while the combat qualified soldiers engaged in military duties. The compromise enabled the IDF to perform its tasks on the eastern and northern frontiers without the necessity for calling up reservists for line duties.

The Nahal Airborne took part in the 1978 Litani Campaign, together with the Paratroop Brigade, and shared in the police duties of the area across the frontier until UNIFIL moved in to replace withdrawing units of the IDF. In 1982, the Nahal was involved on all sectors of Operation Peace for Galilee. In the west, units took part in the battle for Rashadiya and the seaborne landings above the Awali River. A Nahal column moved out from the Awali bridgehead to Damur and was the first unit to reach the eastern suburbs of Beirut. On the central sector, Nahal units led the armored column that clashed with Syrian tanks and commandos at Ein Zahlta, and went on to Behamdoun on the Beirut-Damascus highway. Nahal Airborne participated in the final stages of the battle against the PLO, and took the terrorist positions in Burj el-Burajne on the southern outskirts of Beirut. Since 1982, the Nahal has shared with the other elite infantry brigades in ongoing security duties on the northern frontier.

For the Nahal, its own awareness of its combat heritage and settlement achievements was recognition enough. It could even take pride in the fact that its own entertainment troupe had already acquired wide popularity by the mid-1950s, and the songs that had originated in the Nahal had become popular folklore - and an expression of the family spirit of this community of farmer-soldiers. However, for Israeli society, the Nahal's quiet satisfaction with its own record was not enough.

Every year, on Independence Day, the President of Israel presents the Israel Prizes for science, medicine, the humanities, biblical studies, literature and the performing arts. These prizes are the greatest recognition that the country can give to outstanding achievement. In 1984, on Israel's 36th Independence Day, the eminent scientists, authors, biblical scholars and doctors were joined on the stage of the Jerusalem Theater by an IDF officer and a civilian from one of the oddest branches of the Ministry of Defense. The Master of Ceremonies stepped up to the podium and began to read: "The Israel Prize for a special contribution to society and the State, for an enterprise that brings together the realization of principles of ingathering of the exiles, security, settlement and the values of Judaism and Zionism, is awarded to the Nahal - Fighting Pioneer Youth..." For the Nahal, and indeed for the entire IDF, the Israel Prize was a symbol of the army's involvement in the life of the nation of Israel - an involvement that goes far beyond its commitment to the defense of that nation.

WOMEN
IN THE IDF

In September 1949, six months after the War of Independence, the Knesset wrote into the National Service Law a provision that women would be subject to conscription together with the men. That, incidentally, made Israel the only country in the world to maintain conscription for women. But the Knesset was only legislating a frame for an already established fact; it was not resolving the debates about the nature of women's service, some of which preceded the Law while others were to continue to the present day.

As early as May 1948, David Ben Gurion touched on the essence of the debate: "There is a fundamental difference between the Hagana and the IDF. Until November 1947, the Hagana was for local defense. There was a need to defend the place of settlement, and the call to defense included everybody who was capable. But an army is a totally different thing. In war, an army's main task is to destroy the enemy army - not just defend. When we protected the home with rifle in hand, there was no difference between boy and girl. Both could take shelter, and everything that he knew - she knew. But in an army and in war, there is a reality of inequality in nature, and it is impossible to send girls to fighting units. Yet an army also needs non-combat units. And women are needed for appropriate professions to strengthen the nation's fighting force by releasing men from those tasks for combat."

In the jargon of the 1980s, that declaration would probably be condemned as male chauvinism - but this was the 1940s and Ben Gurion was not alone. However, under the pressures of invasion by five Arab armies, the Prime Minister's view moderated to condone some necessary, if temporary, compromises. Women had fought, and sometimes commanded men, in the pre-State Palmach, Hagana, Etzel and Lehi. And they continued in combat roles in the 1948 war. Women escorted convoys in the "War of the Roads" and took their full share in the defense of besieged kibbutzim and moshavim. But, after some discussion between opposing schools of thought, a Hagana committee charged with "special staff assignments" concurred with another of Ben Gurion's perceptions and, in March 1948, decided on the creation of a separate branch for women. The committee did not publish any recommendations about the function of the branch or the role of its members. It did, however, reflect a World War II conception, by declaring the name for the women's branch as the "Auxiliary Corps" - following the British pattern of "Auxiliary Territorial Service," in which the women had functioned as drivers, clerks and support echelons, but not as fighting soldiers.

The Corps was officially created on 1 April 1948, and its first two staff officers were typical advocates of the opposing philosophies about women in the army. Shoshana Gershonowitz had been one of the first Hagana women to volunteer for the British ATS in World War II. Shorika Braverman was a member of a kibbutz and the Palmach, one of a group that had volunteered to parachute into Nazi Europe: she fought with the partisans in Yugoslavia. The Palmach women, represented by Shorika, bore arms, fought alongside the men - and were steeped in the underground army's informality and predilection for improvisation. The ATS veterans had experienced the discipline, organization, hierarchy of rank and paperwork of a regular army. While the one group took integration into units with the men as the natural way of things, the other was used to the concept of a women's army as a separate support entity.

The result was an obvious compromise. Shoshana took charge of the mobilization of women and their organization into military frames. Shorika was in command of training under a regime that assumed that all Israeli women should be able to defend themselves - and that ability to use weapons and function in the field were essential components in the forging of character.

The first officers' course, given in early May 1948 to past commanders of the ATS and the Hagana-Palmach, came as something of a culture shock to both groups. The ex-ATS, who had never handled weapons, suddenly found themselves issued with grease-coated Sten submachineguns that needed to be cleaned, oiled and fired. The Palmach graduates, used to the informal khaki shorts and shirts of their kibbutz-influenced background, were stunned by their new uniforms that included "bourgeois" items like neckties and stockings.

On 16 May 1948, two days after the graduation of the new officers and, incidentally, the declaration of Israel's independence, the women's army received its first intake of 400 recruits. Their induction and training did not lack for signs of the times. On the day they arrived at their base, the camp was bombarded by artillery and their first military duty was to dig foxholes. Their passing-out parade was also punctuated by falling shells, but they completed the swearing in ceremony and the singing of the national anthem before they took cover.

The women were initially organized in separate battalions to operate alongside the units where they were needed, with their own administration and services. However, this could not last for two reasons. Firstly, the duplication of logistics and administration that had seemed appropriate for a corps that started with 2600 women, was no longer suited to the 12,000 who were in service by the end of the 1948 war. Secondly, and perhaps more importantly, the women themselves were identifying with the units where they served rather than with the Corps. A young woman soldier, asked where she was posted, was likely to answer "I'm in the artillery" rather than "I serve in the Auxiliary Corps." So, one year after its inception, the branch became an administrative and advisory headquarters, attached to IDF Manpower Branch, while its legions of women were dispersed among the units where they were needed, and where they proudly wore the shoulder flashes and cap badges of those units.

As the years have gone by, the women have become very much a part of every unit of the IDF. Nevertheless, the Senior Women's Officer and her headquarters have retained a status and importance that cannot be defined in the normally clearcut terms of military organization. Were this a civilian world, the closest - though not absolute - parallel might be that of a trade union, with responsibilities vis-a-vis the employer regarding welfare, conditions of employment and advancement. The basic training of women, for example, is the direct domain of the Women's Corps (the name was officially changed early in the 1950s), though the commanding officers of the training bases report both to the Corps and to IDF Training Branch; policy and changes in training programs emanate upwards and are resolved in friendly consultation, which takes into account the messages that the Corps wants to project and the needs of the IDF as discerned by the Branch.

Conditions of women's service, wherever they may be assigned, have remained very much the responsibility of the Senior Women's Officer. Though the women are subject to the hierarchy and discipline of the battalion, brigade or branch where they serve, that hierarchy always includes a Women's Corps officer responsible for their welfare and problems - and prepared to argue their case where necessary. Thus, the Corps hovers in the background as supervisor, and acts in the foreground as advisor to the Head of Manpower Branch on the overall role of women in the army. It sounds like an invitation to schizophrenia - but it does function remarkably well.

The viewpoints of the first five Senior Women's Officers, all of whom had served in the British ATS, were to set certain standards of organization, discipline and performance, but the precise role of women was influenced by the expectations of the society of which the IDF is very much a part. After the dust of the 1948 war had settled, the view was expressed, both in the IDF and in society at large, that women should not fight because, if a girl is injured or killed, the blow to unit morale would be almost intolerable. Another commonly accepted view held that, knowing the enemies against whom we fight, the thought of women being taken prisoner is unconscionable. The IDF, therefore, operates on the principle that women will not serve in combat roles. This is less an arbitrary and chauvinistic view taken by the army, than a compliance with society's demands.

The tasks performed by women, and the heights to which they can rise, must therefore be measured in terms of the basic parameters of non-combat duties. Since a woman cannot be a combat soldier, it follows that she cannot aspire to command a brigade or division in the field - tasks that are never assigned to men without combat experience. Conversely, the variety of trades open to women in the IDF has steadily widened, both horizontally and vertically. Even though the IDF did sentence one young girl officer to a month in prison after the Six Day War, for deserting to the battle front (she served only one week of the sentence), women are finding ever greater acceptance for essential roles in combat echelons - short of actually holding a weapon on the firing lines.

Nevertheless, a significant limitation is imposed by military or manpower economics. Conscript service for men is three years, followed by reserve army duties up to the age of 50. Women serve two years and, though theoretically liable for duty up to the age of 24 if unmarried, are rarely called to the reserve. Consequently, calculations of the length of job training as against payback time must influence the choice of military professions open to women in the IDF. This in turn creates a clear distinction between opportunities for conscripts and for regulars - a distinction that is less obvious among the men, for they can progress up the professional ladder at any stage in their service. For this reason, the two categories of women's service must be viewed as separate entities, though both start from the same recruit training.

There is one other reservation. The National Service Law, that called for the universal conscription of women, did stipulate certain exemptions. The IDF does not call married women for conscript service, though this limitation does not apply to the regular army. The Law also recognizes that women with deep religious convictions might find service in the IDF in conflict with their upbringing and beliefs. Ultra orthodox women are brought up to avoid the company of men. It was also accepted that army life might hamper the observance of some religious ordinances for women, even though the IDF goes out of its way to maintain kashrut in its kitchens, to observe the religious festivals and so on. Though the right to refuse service is written into the Law, a high proportion of young women from religious homes do not exercise the option. The choice is that of the recruit herself, but it is often the result of parental influence. In a society committed to its own defense, many parents also believe that the two years of service is important in shaping character and love of country.

The Beginning

The IDF maintains two installations for the basic training of women recruits. Training Base 12 is devoted exclusively to the Women's Corps; and also trains squad commanders and officers. Base Camp 80 doubles as the training depot for the Nahal Brigade. With the exception of young women destined for service in the Nahal, the choice of where the recruits are sent is purely arbitrary, according to the day of the week on which they report for induction.

There is virtually no unwillingness to serve, or resentment at being called. There are, in fact, cases of young women rejected by pre-army medical boards who insist on signing volunteer forms. Sociologists would probably indicate two components in this phenomenon. Firstly, Israeli youth tend to be highly motivated and aware of the need for personal sacrifice for the sake of national security. Secondly, there is peer group pressure. The whole of the class from school is enlisting. For the next two years the talk at social gatherings is going to be about the army and how "the Chief-of-Staff can't run the IDF without me": nobody wants to be the wallflower in the corner with nothing to contribute.

Basic training, which lasts three weeks, is a period of adjustment to a new lifestyle and regime. Its first objective is to teach the young women what belonging to the army means, how to express themselves and something of the dynamics of the system. They learn some elements of soldiering: how to use an Uzzi submachinegun, an introduction to elementary first aid, basic CBN (Chemical, Biological, Nuclear) self-defense and the meaning of discipline. As much as time permits, they are taught the combat heritage and history of the IDF.

Sex education occupies only a small part of the curriculum, primarily because most Israeli youth grow up in a co-educational environment, and are relatively free of inhibitions and obsessions by the time they come to the army. However, classroom time is devoted to the status of the woman, as an individual, within the army system and the rights and obligations of soldiers. Emphasis is placed on understanding the implications of the oath that they will be swearing, upon completion of the course, to the IDF and to Israel - an oath that demands absolute devotion to the service of the State and the Zionist idea.

Young women who have volunteered for the Nahal Brigade undergo six weeks of training. Because of the nature of their service, which might place them in outlying Nahal settlements, they receive more intensive weapons training on M16 and Galil carbines. During their week of fieldcraft, they are introduced to the principles of map reading and navigation. The difference between them and the other recruits is in the assumption that their role is going to be closer to that of combat soldiers, and might require of them participation in the defense of the settlements where their groups are posted.

Theoretically, much of what is taught at recruit camp could be learnt from textbooks read at home. However, this would neglect the psychological and emotional transition from civilian and school life to the army. From the moment of arrival at the IDF induction base, the 18-year-olds are trading their jeans and T-shirts for a uniform that is not particularly flattering. Perhaps for the first time in their lives, they are being told that they may wear only one ring, earrings that do not extend below the lobes and no colored nail polish; field units are sometimes lax about these regulations - but recruit camp makes no concessions. In other words, they are giving up what they see as their individual personalities.

For 18 years they have been partially free to do as they please, in homes that have not only given them considerable leeway, but might have spent the last year or so catering to their every whim - precisely because they are soon to go into the army. Now they are about to be told when to get up in the morning, what to wear and do and even how to talk. The potential for trauma is obviously immense, and it is enhanced by the total change of environment. The three weeks of basic training is, therefore, an abrupt switch from childhood or adolescence to a world that demands mature responsibility.

It follows that, even though the young women come to the army willingly - and have in fact been aware that they are going to do just that through the whole of their lives to date - this first encounter with new faces and situations can cause adjustment crises. Some of the young women, from less sheltered backgrounds, adapt within three or four days and begin to talk and behave like soldiers. Others - those with dominant bonds to the society from which they have come - find the process harder. A part of their fear is the unconscious reflection of doting parents, who worry about what their child is eating and how cold she must be living in a tent (particular care is taken over the standards of cooking in the base kitchens, to ease the comparisons with "what mother makes"). The two training camps are perhaps over-endowed with public telephones to satisfy the compulsion to call home - not necessarily because the young lady needs to, but because her parents expect it.

Family anxieties, where they exist, surface in full force if the daughter has to spend a weekend in camp. Suddenly, the parents don't feel well, or there's a problem with grandmother, or some family function that absolutely necessitates her presence. This phenomenon demands all the patience, tact and firmness of the training staff in dealing with the families. After all, the point of the exercise is to acclimatize the young women to the new way of life that they will lead for the next two years, and any compromise here can lead to misery later. It also dictates the availability of experienced officers and psychologists, throughout the recruit training period, to discuss any problem and help in overcoming any adjustment trauma.

The ultimate objective of producing young soldier women who will fit into, and feel at home with, the military frames in which they will serve, obviously necessitates the sensitive application of reward and punishment. In addition, it requires a relationship between recruit and instructor substantially different to that of the training bases for men. There is less distance between the young women and their squad commanders, who may be only six months apart in age. On occasion this causes the instructor to identify with the recruits and argue their case instead of that of the system. Consequently, the senior staff put as much effort into on-the-job sensitivity training for the instructors as they do for their charges. Punishments - for example, for constant lack of punctuality - may be recommended by the squad commanders but are set by the platoon and company officers.

The adjustment process is relatively fast, though it differs from individual to invidual. One of its elements is the initial uncertainty about what they are going to do in the army. Upon induction, the recruit's serial number is fed into the Manpower Branch computer, which retrieves her scores in the pre-army registration tests - physical fitness and intellectual capacity. These are then matched against the current IDF requirements and availability of places in professional courses. On her second or third day at the training base, she is given a personalized dossier which lists the available openings in her score category. Representatives of the various branches of the IDF speak to the young women about the different jobs and what they entail. Each recruit then marks her order of preference for the trades she has been offered. Classification officers from the IDF Induction Center talk to them separately, go over their preferences with them - and then refer them on to representatives of the requested branch for personal interviews. This process takes place in the now familiar surroundings of the training base. The interview results are returned to the IDF Induction and Classification Center, where the final postings are decided. Generally, more than 50% of the recruits will be assigned to one or other of their first three preferences.

The choices made by the young women confound one fond belief of Israeli society - that they are influenced by proximity to home: for some, their two years service is a chance to "go out on their own," while others want to be with the family every night. It sounds plausible, but research shows that they are mostly interested in doing something worthwhile and important - that they can look back on with satisfaction - and less concerned about location.

However, there are initial misconceptions about the relative importance of jobs: it has been known to happen that a young woman who wanted to be a medical orderly has felt acute disappointment at being posted to a far more interesting function, appropriate to her qualifications, in - for example - Signals and Electronics Branch. In cases such as these, and they are not very frequent, considerable persuasion needs to be used to overcome preconceptions and sometimes mistaken imagery. Again society and its conceptions is not without influence: the job of company clerk in a line battalion on the Golan Heights is popularly considered more prestigious than some highly responsible clerical jobs in the headquarters of a senior General Staff officer. However, most of the recruits either achieve their satisfaction immediately, or come to appreciate the choice when they start their professional training.

One other common public misconception relates to the prestige of serving as an instructor training male combat soldiers. The job is vitally important, and women do it extremely well. Yet many of them prefer the mud, grease and camaraderie of an armored company on the line to the sterile surroundings of classroom simulators and mock-ups in the brand new, spick and span installations of the Armor School. Though it defies commonly-held views of neatly dressed and well turned out women, the sloppiness of dirty fatigues and wind-blown hair has its own appeal to 18-year-olds.

One paradox in preferences results from the basic training itself. The job of instructor for combat soldiers is a popular choice, but few want the task of remaining at the base to train new intakes of young women. In the recruits' minds, their instructors are not only the people who "nag" them into shape, but they also have to get up at the same time and live with the same schedules: thus, it appears that their instructors are living through recruit training time and again. The same is true of instructors who train the boys, but somehow it seems different. The Women's Corps needs picked young women for its own training program, since their effort and sensitivity is going to set the tone for two years of service.

Consequently, the Corps has to make its own choices and overcome initial resistance.

Attempts are made during the training period to identify future candidates for commissions as officers in the various branches of the IDF. The scores of these young women on psychometric tests given towards the end of the three weeks are included, with the evaluations of the training officers, in the files forwarded to the branch where the prospective candidate is assigned. From here on, though they are not aware of their scores, their performance will be assessed and, if satisfactory, they will be offered officers' courses.

Two Years

The prohibition on women in combat does not extend to combat support roles. On occasion, it has not prevented women from being present on the battlefield, though not on the firing lines. In the 1956 Sinai Campaign, women served with the ground forces as medics and radio operators and flew with the IAF; one woman lieutenant was co-pilot of the lead plane that dropped paratroops at the Mitla Pass. Women also functioned in combat support roles in the Six Day and Yom Kippur Wars - close to, but not on the front line. During the 1982 Peace for Galilee Campaign, however, strict orders were issued to prevent women soldiers from entering Lebanon, though a loophole was created to permit some 20 women to serve at Sidon headquarters.

The original intent, after the 1948 war, was to exclude women entirely from combat units. This situation was reversed in 1953 for reasons that had as much to do with preserving the social and human atmosphere of the line battalions as it did with filling manpower loopholes. Inevitably, the first jobs to open up to female conscripts in the fighting units were battalion and company clerks, telephone and radio operators. The clerical postings were, and still are, very popular assignments since the job entails much more than just typing and answering telephones. A good clerk is almost as essential to the efficient running and morale of the unit as the commanding officer and the sergeant major - and some say more so.

Two other roles in line and other units that are the exclusive prerogative of women are the "Education" and "Conditions of Service" NCOs. The former is responsible for all educational and cultural activities - an area in which the IDF is extremely active. The latter job is something of a misnomer. She is less concerned with the conditions of army service than with the problems that the men and women of the unit might have outside the army. Her job demands that she becomes acquainted with each of the soldiers and his or her home environment. If there are medical problems of parents, or shortage of income because the son is serving, she will arrange postings near home or family allowances. For immigrant soldiers, who have no family in the country, she will find foster homes and obtain housing allowances. Both jobs are vital to unit morale and are regarded as choice assignments by the young women themselves - even though they entail longer service than the two years that the National Service Law requires.

To overcome the job limitations imposed by the shortness of service for women, the IDF instituted a program of pre-army courses for trades that require extensive training. These are purely voluntary and are offered to the young women, in a detailed brochure which is mailed to all pupils in the twelfth grade, upon registration for service. (Many schools have made a point of inviting alumni from various IDF branches to talk to twelfth graders about their army occupations.) The assumption is that some of them will be willing to give up a part of their last summer vacation to pre-empt their occupation for the next two years. Any young woman who applies for this program will be invited to take various tests and be interviewed by representatives of the branch that she is requesting. If accepted, she will receive part of her training before induction and part after basic training. Basic training for these recruits is only two weeks, and is much easier because they are already familiar with the army and are free of the uncertainty of not knowing what they will be doing.

The two assignments of Conditions of Service and Education NCOs both fall within this category. For Conditions of Service, the course before induction is 11 weeks and the applicants sign a declaration of willingness to serve an additional five weeks - to ensure continuity as one intake finishes and another replaces them; among other things, the course gives psychological and sociological preparation for dealing with human beings and their problems. The Education NCOs undergo a two month course before basic training, then return for another month.

The pre-army program offers wide choices. Some will equip the young women with a useful profession for civilian life after the army, while others give invaluable on-the-job experience in trades already learnt in secondary or technical high schools. The length of courses differs and some trades carry an obligation of a few months or years of service in the regular army. For example, electronics and electro-optical technicians take a pre-army course, with another six months after basic training - and give an extra half year of regular service. Computer programmers take a seven month course, all of it after induction, and sign on for four years extra service.

The Navy and the Air Force offer their own selection of pre-army choices, all of which can lead to commissions as officers for women who are interested and display the appropriate qualifications. By this means the Navy seeks coastal radar operators, sailors for support craft, telegraphists and radio operators; the Air Force accepts young women for courses as aerial photography analysts, meteorologists, aerial intelligence analysts, flight and operations controllers.

Ground forces options within this program include squad commander/instructor for the Women's Corps itself, counselors to work with the Gadna "Youth" Battalions, physical training instructors, photo analysts for Intelligence Branch, psychotechnical evaluators and interviewers, medics and dental technicians. One special category is that of soldier teacher to work with underprivileged youth, who will be upgrading their primary education during their conscript service. This particular job attracts a great many religious young women, who could claim exemption from conscription.

Two IDF branches - Maintenance and Adjutancy - accept officer candidates at the pre-army stage for a fast route of progress up the ladder of promotion. This is obviously a career decision, rather than a choice of conscript service employment. The women who choose this route for the Adjutancy Corps are destined for service as reserve officers - responsible for the contact with reservists, and their mobilization for training or active service - or as unit adjutants, who deal with or supervise all aspects of the relationship between the soldier or officer and the IDF, and form the chain of communication between the commanding officer and his unit. Maintenance Officers are in charge of the regular and efficient running of unit logistics - food, transport, fuel, ammunition and all the other aspects of supply and services.

The variety of tasks to which young women who have not made a pre-army choice can be assigned is virtually endless. Among the

most sought after are jobs as instructors for combat troops. The Artillery Corps had women gunners in the 1948 war, when the calibers and size of projectiles were somewhat smaller than the present generation. As artillery progressed, and in keeping with the no-combat rule, the Corps cut back. However, it was the first branch of the IDF to accept the principle that its gunners could be taught by women. Not satisfied with teaching alone, women have carved a niche in gunnery control. They also operate the artillery simulators on which reservists get their refresher training.

The Armored Corps was not far behind the Artillery. Virtually all the instructors at the IDF Armor School, where tank crewmen learn the basics of their trade, are women. Perhaps not unnaturally, these young women do have one gripe: "We are allowed to teach tank crews - but they don't let us fight!" The general trend in the IDF is to integrate women more and more into training functions. Infantry, pilots and naval crews receive part of their instruction from women. This has been known to create initial problems with their 18-year-old trainees, some of whom arrive in the army with macho images - but they are soon overcome as the young women demonstrate total command of their subject and absolute professionalism. The way is open for outstanding instructors to take officers' courses and return as supervisors to the various schools. However, many of them prefer to function directly with the men they are training, and have a disdain for the "paper pushing" function that comes with a commission.

The Engineering Corps not only employs women as instructors, but has qualified a few to work as mine sweepers and bomb disposal crews: at IDF Officers' School, women trained by the Combat Engineers instruct, among other things, the handling of explosives and sabotage materials. In the Ordnance Corps, there are occasional lathe operators and metalworkers and conscript young women are responsible for quality control in the plants of outside contractors. Other technical trades that have ceased to be all male domains include aircraft fitters and aero-engine mechanics in the IAF.

A couple of the professions "conquered" by women are deserving of special note. The IDF is the only army in the world where all parachute packing is done by women. This is a volunteer job, and is considered the hardest physical task to which young women can be assigned. The packers and the clerks of the Parachute Brigade have the option of taking the jump course, if they so desire - and many of them do. A function traditionally reserved for men was that of Operations officer or sergeant of brigades on the line. The assumption was that combat experience was essential in control of the movements and tasks of fighting troops. Not without some senior command resistance, the conscript young women recently began to infiltrate this "elite profession," only to find that they were quickly accepted at face value by their colleagues. Although they are far from holding a monopoly in this field, the point has been made.

Perhaps to the chagrin of the male chauvinists, experience has proven that some tasks are best assigned to women. For example, the powers of sustained concentration of 18-year-old women are higher than those of their male counterparts. Consequently, some jobs at computer or radar screens are almost reserved occupations. The achievements of women radar operators in the navy, in detecting terrorist incursion attempts, have won them one of the most prized jobs in coastal defense - on board the aircraft that fly patrols out at sea. Airsickness is a constant hazard of bad weather flying, and their crewmates have to carry some of their equipment out to the planes for them - but nobody grumbles.

Career Soldiers

If feminist arguments about equal opportunities for women are at all applicable to the IDF, it is not in recruit training or the two years of conscript service - other, of course, than the fundamental dis-crimination against combat roles. As a general rule, the IDF does not accept soldiers, men or women, for regular army service under the rank of sergeant major, though there may be occasional exceptions in technical trades. Up to this rank, soldiers are usually more concerned about their occupation than the number of chevrons on their sleeves. In any case, conscript pay in the IDF is hardly an issue of discrimination arguments; it constitutes not much more than pocket money, supplemented by commissary privileges and the willingness of some civilian - particularly entertainment and food - businesses to offer substantial discounts to soldiers in uniform.

Regular army pay and conditions are a different story. Though they tend to lag behind civilian scales, particularly when the working hours and days away from home of soldiers are taken into account, the differences of rank and role begin to be meaningful. Advancement and job satisfaction, though important to national servicemen and women, are much more critical for regulars. The conscript knows that his or her service is a temporary time-out which will come to an end. The regular, on the other hand, has made a career decision - in which motivation to serve is only one, albeit important, component. The pace of achievement is also critical, because the IDF - unlike other armies - has a policy and tradition of early retirement. The Chief-of-Staff, with the rank of lieutenant general, is usually a man in his early fifties. Majors general are mostly in their late forties.

Therefore, it is obvious that any feelings about equality between the sexes, or the lack of it, are going to surface after national mandatory service. Yet the consensus of opinion among women officers is that the IDF, with the possible exception of the legal profession, is the most open institution in Israeli society. The fact that the daily and weekly press see point to publishing stories about individual women who have reached the top in civilian occupations, but rarely do so about women in the army, is one sure indicator of this. That does not mean that there are no problems or prejudices, but it does imply that the army is open to persuasion.

All the occupations available to women during their conscript service - and there are hundreds of them - are open for advancement up the ladder of promotion. In addition, there are many staff, technical and professional jobs that become possible only with an officer's commission. For the most part these are postings available equally to men or women. However, there is a growing phen-omenon in recent years whereby women might have to fight for their "place in the sun" of a certain military profession - but, once there, they quickly achieve virtual monopoly. For example, the post of Town Marshal calls for all the qualities of policeman, social worker and diplomat - all with the assurance of authority. This is where families come with requests for compassionate leave, soldiers and reservists call in sick and unable to report for duty and the Military Police coordinate their searches for those absent without leave. Toughest of all, the Town Marshal is the officer who takes the dreaded notice to next of kin when an IDF soldier falls in battle, or is wounded. The officer appointed was always male, simply because that is the way it always had been. But once the first women were assigned and succeeded, the situation changed so radically that all but two of the Marshals in the towns and cities of Israel are now female.

Here and there the women encounter conservative views, which they have to break down the hard way. And they do not always succeed. For instance, little can be done in those cases where a better qualified woman and a less qualified man, of the same rank, apply for a particular posting - and the prospective commander chooses the male officer because they served together in the Six Day War, or occupied the same trench in a forward outpost. True, the "old boys' club" would influence the commander's choice if both applicants were men, but that is little consolation.

Some senior women officers argue that the women can sometimes be their own worst enemies, and there is no doubt that promotions or added responsibilities are occasionally rejected on the grounds of "I don't know what my husband might want to do, next year." This perhaps separates those women who have opted for a career with motivation from those who simply see the army as an employer. It does, however, imply that a woman's success on the ladder is very much dependent on the amount of support and understanding that she receives at home. Again, a similar argument could be developed around male officers who have always served in staff functions - as opposed to their colleagues who spend years with line units, with frequent changes of location and duties.

Some jobs in the IDF are no respecters of an eight to five working routine. In field units and training establishments, dawn to midnight can be normal - and even in the General Staff, high level meetings are often scheduled into the evenings. For a woman with children, her husband's willing cooperation becomes very important. It is perhaps understandable that the ones who climb highest are those whose husbands are, or were, high ranking officers who know what is involved. On the other hand, well-meaning male displays of consideration can be infuriating. Faced with a new commanding officer's solicitous question, "how will you manage with the children," many a woman officer has had to choke back the obvious retort: "You think I didn't consider that when I applied for this post!"

The top of the pyramid of rank for women officers has steadily been pushed upwards. In 1986, the Senior Women's Officer was promoted, for the first time, to brigadier general. The promotion was as much a recognition of the growing role of women as it was a personal achievement of the incumbent. As the base of senior ranks - majors, lieutenant colonels and colonels - steadily widens, there is growing pressure for acceptance of the principle that some branches of the IDF can equally as well be commanded by high ranking women. Where the need for combat experience is a prerequisite, it is an obvious stumbling block. But that does not apply to a great many intelligence, logistic and staff departments. The overall picture is one of constant progress, even if the women do have to prove their point anew in each post. However, the plain fact is that the women of Israel are needed in the IDF, and even the most conservative of male officers recognize that reality.

EDUCATION CORPS - AN OBLIGATION TO SOCIETY

T he IDF's role in education began, like many other aspects in the shaping of the image and identity of the army, before the State was born. In 1941, with Rommel's Afrika Korps almost at the gates of Palestine in the south and Vichy France holding Syria and Lebanon to the north, the Hagana - then a locally based part-time militia - created the Palmach, with British blessings, as its first regular unit, able to operate anywhere in the country. The Palmach's first institutionalized step in the direction of non-military education was taken with the appointment of a "Hasbara Officer" in 1944. "Hasbara" is a Hebrew term that translates approximately as "explanation and dissemination."

The nature of duties of the Hasbara Officer owed a lot to the personalities of the first men who held the position, but their basic conceptions have withstood the test of time and still underlie the foundations of the IDF Education Corps and its work. They, like the High Command that appointed them, believed it essential to foster an informed motivation among the men and women of the Palmach. Although, in the shadow of World War II, the temptation to nickname these officers "politruks" was too great to ignore, they were anything but Red Army model "political commissars" always prepared to quote from "Chairman Mao's little red book." Motivation was to come from knowledge, which was best supplied by lectures, talks and open debates that strengthened personal conviction while avoiding brainwashing.

There was immediate recognition that the best candidates for this role had to be the commanders who led their men in their military duties. The first officer assigned to hasbara and cultural activities, handled these duties as additional to his normal role as commander of a support weapons platoon. And the participants in the first course for hasbara officers were mostly officers with command duties: the subjects taught them, in classroom lessons, lectures and discussions, were: analysis of Zionist policies; relations with the British and Arabs; Hagana and Palmach history; teaching techniques for use in their platoons and companies; the commander as educator; and the place of culture and social events within the unit calendar. The bottom line, which would survive transition to the

IDF, was that motivation and education activities were inseparable from the role of commander.

Full-time service was, inevitably, a break in the education of the adolescent. Consequently, it was incumbent on the command to do everything that circumstances permitted to continue the educational effort for its men and women. This early understanding of a need was to lead the Palmach, in late 1945, to a series of two-week educational seminars, devoted at this stage to the history, geography and development of Palestine - subjects that were already being taught in study days and tours of the country. The seminars, in turn, led directly to the establishment in 1948 of the IDF's first Army School of Education at Camp Marcus in Haifa.

Camp Marcus was initially dedicated to a prime problem of Israel - and the IDF - in the early years. Wave after wave of mass immigration was bringing people who did not know the language of the country - Hebrew. They had to be taught if they were to function in the army and in society, and that teaching brought with it recognition that some of the immigrant populations were in sore need of primary education. In parallel, and in keeping with the statement by the second IDF Chief-of-Staff, Yigael Yadin, that "we cannot treat the distress of our recruits without treating the distress of their environment," the army began to assign young women who had completed their secondary education, from each annual intake of recruits, to fill gaps in the educational system in the immigrant transit camps and development areas. From these initial, perhaps piecemeal steps, the IDF educational system has developed into a unique effort and the envy of other countries.

The Officer as Educator

"Since the National Service Law decrees that the IDF will be the cradle of maturity of Israeli youth, we are obliged to educate - to bridge the gap between adolescent and adult identities. And the larger that gap - the larger the responsibility imposed on us as commanders."

Brigadier Nehemia Dagan - Senior Education Officer

At the age of 18, all the young men and women of Israel are subject to conscript service in the IDF. Just at the point where in other societies, teenagers are making their final decisions about what to study in which university, Israelis are donning military uniform. The men will wear that uniform for 36 months, and at intervals thereafter up to the age of 50. The women put aside their own careers and ambitions to serve the nation for 24 months. Since this is, of necessity, a long break in the learning process, the IDF feels obliged to continue broadening the horizons and stimulating the minds of its young soldiers.

It follows that IDF commanders are responsible, not only for the lives and welfare of their men and women, but also for their education both as soldiers and citizens. In purely military terms, the soldier's success in carrying out his mission is in direct relationship to the content, forcefulness and clarity of value messages transmitted by his officers. Whether or not he or she will leave the army with a better understanding of the responsibilities of being a citizen is also dependent on what the army educational system can supply, and this too must be affected by the tone set by commanders. Therefore, any consideration of the educational effort and content must begin with an understanding of the training of IDF officers as educators.

The Education Corps caters for the needs of commanders, both noncoms and officers, at two facilities created for the specific purpose - the School for Leadership Development and the Jerusalem Education Center. All command courses, at each rung on the ladder of promotion, include seminars at the School with programs that bring the officer up-to-date knowledge in psychology, management and human relations. This is a supplement to professional military training, to assist the students in the transition from simple soldier to junior commander, then from NCO to officer, by giving - among other things - the skills to understand and cope with each new role.

The School has three departments: the Commander Training Institute, the Staff Training Unit - each staffed by psychologists, sociologists, educators and experts in organization - and a Hasbara Team to supply enrichment theme content. All three combine personal knowledge of IDF service with professional skills, in a process that takes place in a building complex donated to the IDF by the Soldiers' Welfare Committee, and especially designed to provide ideal study conditions, free of routine chores.

The basic assumption is that the commander's responsibility for development and enlightenment of his men necessitates knowledge

and preparation. The Commander Training Institute programs are based on active participation rather than frontal lectures, and rely on the students' own experiences as well as supplied situations - played out in simulations together with the instructors of courses from which the groups are drawn: this way, the exercises in student participation can be applied directly to their actual professional training. The trainees come from all echelons, from squad leaders to senior officers, for a five-day course of skills in military leadership, awareness of the nature of their own roles and behavioral principles that will help in leading men: interpersonal communication, command style, group categorization, care for the individual, etc. Two days of each five, organized by the Hasbara Team, are devoted to enrichment of the student's own knowledge of basic issues that include democracy, society, Jewish-Arab relations, religion, nationality and state; the teaching methods utilize guided tours, debates, lectures and independent research.

The Staff Training Unit hosts all IDF echelons, though its main concern is with the development and organization of training staffs of IDF recruit bases. The subjects covered in its three-day workshops, chaired by appropriate professionals, include: processes of specifying objectives, role definition, establishment of work procedures, evaluation of professional functioning of existing staff, interpersonal relationships, decision-making, etc.

While the School's activities take place as part of other courses, the Jerusalem Education Center is devoted to refreshers for officers relieved from ongoing military duties to attend the program. The courses, of either a few days or weeks, give the officers educational tools, enrich their own knowledge of subjects fundamental to the existence of the IDF and Israeli society, and enhance their skills in the fields of personal example, care for the individual and human relations. The focus is on problems of security, state and society. The Center does not profess any single viewpoint, but rather endeavors to present the full spectrum of opinions prevalent in Israeli society regarding social and national issues on the current agenda of every citizen.

In the Center's lectures, debates, event analysis, simulation, role playing, human relations workshops and guided tours, the officers are encouraged to formulate their own personal conceptions. Main lecture and debate themes are the development of the Zionist

movement, Jewish communities abroad, immigration and absorption and the link between the Jewish People and Israel. Workshop sessions examine values and dimensions of tolerance, pluralism, social involvement and national commitment within Israeli democracy, and selected stress centers of Israeli society, including the Arab-Israel conflict and possible solutions of the Judea-Samaria-Gaza issue. Since the Center is in Jerusalem, the officers' familiarity with the city is enhanced by guided tours of the city and by review of its history, holiness for Jews and other religions and place in IDF heritage.

Warrant officers and sergeants-major undergo special three week courses, with colleagues from their own branch of service, on current social problems and their implications, democratic government, principles of tolerance and co-existence, realization of the Zionist ideal, etc. A special two-week refresher, given from time to time for a few dozen warrant officers drawn from all over the army, seeks to strengthen the senior NCOs' identification with the IDF, their self-image as commanders and their ability to cope with their private lives in the light of their demanding military duties.

Army School for Education

"Since IDF unit commanders are viewed as the educators of their soldiers, it follows that the work of the education staff distributed throughout units of the IDF, and serving as the right hand of commanders in the educational sphere - is the torch that leads the way."

Standing Orders of the Education Corps

The Education Corps trains its own personnel at the Army School of Education. And here, since the bulk of the field work has to fall on the shoulders of 18-year-old women soldiers, and national service for women is only 24 months, the Corps had to face an objective problem: if the training of teachers and instructors was to be a part of that two years, little useful time would be left to ply their trade. The answer was found, to this and other problems of women's service, by offering the young recruits a chance to choose their profession of service before enlistment - in return for their willingness to give the army a few weeks more than the National Defense Law requires. Thus, young women who opt to serve either as teachers, or as "education and knowledge of the country instructors" - after screening to assess their suitability - enter an eight or nine week course before induction. Upon enlistment, they undergo a shortened basic training, then return to the School for another month of preparation for their duties.

To be accepted for either of the two courses given at the School, the young women need to be secondary school graduates of high individual quality. The interviewers who process candidates are looking for characteristics that are not measurable by regular test techniques: a strong desire to influence the level of society in the IDF and Israel, highly developed social awareness and a flair for guiding, educating and motivating people.

The three month program for "Education and Knowledge of the Country" Instructors comprises comprehensive courses in teaching methods appropriate to the routine activities of IDF units, and hones the personal skills necessary to promote an appropriate value-oriented educational atmosphere among soldiers. During their course, the instructors acquire knowledge of key cultural and educational enrichment themes. They also learn how to organize study days, tours, commanders' evenings, participatory games, simulations, debates and other tools for achievement of their roles. At a later stage, after eight months of active service in the field, some of them will be brought back to the School for a course as Education Officers, which broadens their talents for command, guidance and professionalism in special subjects.

Instruction in the Units

> "A human being adds another layer to his personality every day: study, experience, assimilation, conversation, debate, impression, successes and failures. For all these to come together into one, complete identity - the foundations are more important than anything else. We can give these only as the first base of Education Corps instruction."
>
> Standing Orders of the Education Corps

Within the units where they serve, the education NCOs and officers use as much time as can be created in the schedules of military activity, to enrich the soldiers in a variety of subjects. It is not uncommon on a trip around the country to encounter platoons of

soldiers being led through an archaeological dig, a battlefield or a museum by a young corporal or sergeant, while she explains one or other aspect with a familiarity that would not shame a professional historian. In camp, she organizes lectures, workshop days and debates, arranges educational film shows and brings entertainers, both civilian and army.

The instructors' daily work also includes consultation with, and collection and preparation of material for, the unit commanders in their educational function: "CO's evenings" on specific themes, weekly current events' briefings and open discussions. The instructors' youth, which could in theory have been an obstacle, presents no special problems. The officers' own training as educators prepares them to accept advice from the young women, while the soldiers themselves have certain expectations stemming from the prior knowledge that the educational system exists.

Organizationally, the instructors are supervised by education officers at the various levels of command: battalion, brigade, division, regional command or branch. These officers work both to an annual program, in which educational themes change every two months, and in short-term responses to significant events in Israel and the IDF. Since they are part of the unit command structure, the educators participate in routine exercises and maneuvers, and accompany their unit on active duty and in war.

The main thrust of educational content is aimed at forging the individual and national identity of IDF soldiers, as the link between military service and an aware, responsible and involved civilian experience. Soldiers are encouraged to clarify for themselves the place of Jewish religion and the Zionist movement in the existence of Israel, by study of chapters from Jewish and Zionist history and the customs and traditions of different Jewish communities - while sharpening awareness of current problems such as immigration, emigration and the present-day attainment of Zionist objectives. As a side effect, soldiers for whom the IDF may be the first contact with people from backgrounds different to their own, begin to get an appreciation for the way the other man lives.

As an aid to the soldier's personal ability to cope in a modern day complex environment, the Corps gives intensive treatment to the growing polarization of the Israeli political system: the borderlines between religious and secular; relations with Palestinian Arabs; the

IDF's problems in Judea, Samaria and Gaza; and the danger that intolerance can blur commitment to democracy. Though the Corps treads warily wherever conflicting political opinions are involved, IDF soldiers participate in democratic, political and social dynamics designed to bring them ultimately to recognition of the advantages of democracy as a bridge between viewpoints, to strengthen their negation of extremism while enhancing their mature personal conceptions of the social and political complexities of Israel.

Combat heritage is obviously an inseparable part of military training and an essential component in the ongoing improvement of the army's performance, both moral and operational. This entails imbuing soldiers with the IDF's value system - adherence to mission, personal example, the brotherhood of arms and morality in combat - and the basic values that have become a trademark of the IDF: "Follow me!," evacuation of casualties, mutual dependency, personal responsibility and esprit de corps. Special "lesson kits" help officers in tactical discussion of various battle moves and the significance of the values inherent in them. Soldiers learn about deeds of individual and unit heroism, acquire knowledge of the history of the army and their own units and are initiated into the lessons learnt by the IDF from its successes and shortcomings, through tours of battlefields, films and encounters with soldiers who took part in the particular actions.

Instructors have almost endless opportunities to apply knowledge of the country to actual landscapes during routine maneuvers, navigational exercises, briefings, even operational actions - in addition to tours, walks and lectures on nature, geography, archaeology, etc. These interludes and outings are extremely popular with the soldiers because of their active and social aspects. Apart from physical acquaintance with an area, the soldiers' exposure to nature, history and culture deepens their awareness of ecological, social, demographic and economic aspects. A close cooperation between the Corps and the Society for the Protection of Nature, the Nature Reserve Authority and the Israel Archaeological Society, also emphasizes values of nature preservation and archaeological heritage.

In addition to the basic enrichment themes, the Corps' work program includes deep background subjects that relate, in the short or long term, to the military function itself and the constant effort to improve performance of the army and its soldiers. For example, a project was initiated to prepare regular and reservist units for the tensions and inner conflicts arising from operational duties in Judea, Samaria and Gaza: working in a hostile environment, inappropriateness of missions in these areas to the combat training of the soldiers and their personal viewpoints. These units participate in seminars on the characteristics of the areas and their populations, the type and nature of required missions and the problems likely to arise.

Special courses are organized for specific audiences. One refresher for officers covers IDF regulations and policy and the role of the officer in the campaign against drug abuse. An IDF prison reform, aimed at rehabilitation, caused the Corps to mobilize psychologists and professional educators for group therapy activities to assist prisoners in combating deviant tendencies: the prison educational program is put over to the prisoners by Military Police instructors, who thereby double as jailers and educators.

The instructors are supported by the professional departments of the Senior Education Officer's headquarters. The professionals - both national servicemen and women like themselves, and long-term regulars - supply a constant flow of slides, tapes, broadsheets, booklets and teaching aids for the instructors, commanding officers and their audience. The Corps' film unit makes movies for its own needs and supplies equipment and personnel to IDF units that need specific subjects of their own. The unit also acquires from outside producers, and - by arrangement with Israel Television - duplicate TV programs of educational and cultural value for soldiers who did not have an opportunity to see them first time around.

The reservists assigned to the Education Corps include intellectuals, academics and senior personnel in the public and private sectors, who are available to lecture, lead workshops and chair discussions even in the remotest of bases and outposts. The basic premise is that all soldiers are thinking human beings who should be challenged to contend with intellectual complexities. The lecture subjects listened to by soldiers include: Judaism, Zionism, sociology, government and scores of enriching themes taken from science, culture, nature and current events. Because of the military framework, lecturers are prohibited from expressing personal political opinions, other than in the context of dialogue between opposing viewpoints. However, many lectures are devoted to controversial

issues, with the intent of enhancing the soldiers' maturity, understanding and critical faculties.

Another keenly anticipated tool is the "hasbara seminar" - a concentrated educational program for the unit as an entity. These periodic seminars allow soldiers and their officers a week-long break from their military routines. They are given by Hasbara Teams based in Galilee, Jerusalem, on the Coastal Plain, in the Negev and at Eilat - in installations equipped with the necessary teaching and information aids for themes key to the IDF and Israeli society: national, state, army and social concerns; knowledge of the country and combat heritage; enrichment in subjects such as history, science and industry. The emphasis is on enjoyable "experiences" in field trips and tours, debates and games, visits to sites and institutions and entertainment. Apart from getting to know the country, the seminars strengthen the social bonds of the unit - precisely because they are doing something together, free of their daily military duties. One such seminar, at the Corps' Carmiel Base, is given to all new recruits of combat units on the theme of "adapting to army service."

The Education Corps makes arrangements with institutions, museums and sites considered of educational importance, under which education officers and NCOs can bring groups of soldiers. The criteria for selecting these sites are the relevance of their purpose and content to basic issues in the army's educational program, and their ability to put across their message as an interesting "experience." Although entry vouchers are also available, under certain conditions, to individual soldiers, Education Corps instructors use the facility to bring groups from seminar programs. The sites include, for example: places of historic relevance such as the Diaspora Museum, Holocaust Memorial, Ghetto Fighters Museum; archaeological excavations - the Western Wall, David's City and the Citadel in Jerusalem; combat heritage themes at Ammunition Hill and the Underground Fighters Museum in Acre; nature - Banias Nature Reserve and the Stalagmite Caves; culture - Tel Aviv Museum and the Israel Museum.

Culture in the IDF

"We in the IDF are involved in culture because of the deep sense that, for the three years in which we supply all the needs of the young men and women who serve, we must also supply their spiritual needs. For many soldiers the years of their army service provide their first encounter with the performing arts - music, theatre and dance. The IDF's cultural activity is, therefore, important in encouraging Israeli society to be a cultured society."

Standing Orders of the Education Corps

The conviction of the IDF that it has a duty to stimulate the minds of its soldiers also extends into the cultural field. The army's motivation is not only to provide entertainment for the sake of morale, though that is in itself important enough, but also to cultivate an appreciation that the soldiers can take with them into civilian life. Israel is rich in cultural institutions and audiences for them, and the IDF can claim its share of the credit on both counts. The Education Corps both encourages young talents, during their national service, and uses professional musicians, singers, actors, composers and theatre directors in the reserve army, to appear before soldiers and to serve as mentors for their young colleagues in uniform.

Special attention is paid to talents that, if unused, might easily stagnate during military service. Promising musicians, for example, are posted to the Senior Education Officer's headquarters, where their daily routine is divided in two: in the mornings they perform regular duties - and then spend the afternoon with their music. They play in one or other of five chamber music ensembles, each of which gives a weekly recital for IDF soldiers in their own camps, accompanied by music appreciation commentary. In addition, once a week, 30 of these gifted musicians gather together in a chamber music orchestra as an added chance to develop their talents - alongside a golden opportunity for young conductors (not necessarily soldiers) to work with a high-quality orchestra.

These recitals, by soldiers of their own age, and concerts by reservists from Israel's orchestras, give the men and women of the IDF the chance to become acquainted with the rich world of classical music in a planned and explained manner. Wherever possible, soldiers are exposed to the performing arts by bringing the event to the audience. Here the accent is on performances, that are, by their very nature, easily mobile, without need for elaborate auditoriums and stages. The performers are not restricted to Israelis: both in times of war and relative peace, some of the world's best musicians and entertainers have volunteered to appear before IDF soldiers in base camps and on the frontlines.

Five army entertainment troupes, usually composed of some 14-15 national service men and women, and each belonging to an army corps or regional command, perform regularly for soldiers. Their mobility and simplicity of staging - free of the need for heavy props - enables them to appear wherever there are soldiers: camps, outposts and under the open sky, for audiences as large as a brigade or as small as a platoon. The songs and skits of these troupes have become a part of IDF and Israeli folklore; hardly a day passes without some of them being aired on Israel's radio stations. Indeed they are so popular that the army receives frequent requests for performances on national and local occasions. The majority of Israel's popular singers, actors and musicians made their debuts in uniform before army audiences.

The IDF Theatre, composed of 14 soldier actors, enables the Education Corps to bring plays to places where other theatre companies do not go. The repertoire is chosen from the best of Israeli and international theatre, with the inclusion of original works written by leading Israeli playwrights to deal with the experiences of soldiers and youth, along themes selected by the Education Corps. To ensure universal access, the plays are staged with a minimum of props. Through intensive work with the best of Israeli directors, the Theatre offers soldiers subject matter close to their own hearts, which can serve as a basis for other value-oriented educational activities and debates - from the essence of democracy and through to issues of army life, command and leadership.

Each Sunday morning, thousands of IDF soldiers return to base after weekend leave. Under a recent Education Corps decision, instead of standing at bus depots, soldiers wait for their organized transport in auditoriums, where they enjoy events that cannot easily be brought out to them: plays, dance theatres, concerts and musical shows, painting and sculpture exhibits and films. These "Sunday Culture" activities include direct confrontation between the soldiers and the participants and talks on the particular art form. Thus, for example, in addition to seeing a play, the soldiers will talk to the director and actors about processes of production, the actor's work, the history of the theatre and so on. The program also extends to Israel's universities, where the Sunday morning wait for transport is spent in listening to lectures on subjects designed to awaken the soldier's interest.

Books have a deep significance in Jewish culture and Israeli society, and the Education Corps purchases tens of thousands of them for the libraries that exist in every IDF camp. Once a year, Hebrew Book Month gives soldiers a special opportunity to purchase the best of Hebrew literature at token prices, and to meet with authors for discussions of their work. In addition, Tarmil ("Haversack") Books, published by the Senior Education Officer, today lists more than 200 original Hebrew and translated works, which are sold to soldiers at a specially low price and distributed to unit libraries.

IDF Media

"In this modern age, which provides us with the full basket of means to transfer up-to-date information rapidly and to a huge audience, the electronic media have an influence unmatched by any other. It would be a mistake not to harness this power to the function of army education. On the other hand, it is extremely important that the control over use of the media will be strong and accompanied, as far as possible, by an open and meaningful channel for public supervision".

Standing Orders of the Education Corps

In September 1950, Prime Minister and Defense Minister Ben Gurion announced the establishment of Galei Zahal - "IDF Radiowaves" - the IDF's radio station. As a national network, recognized by the Broadcasting Authority Law, the station broadcasts, 29 hours a day on two wavelengths, educational, cultural and information programs to soldiers and civilians alike. Galei Zahal is staffed by conscript servicemen and women reporters, music programmers, announcers, interviewers and producers - and by regulars and civilian employees, some of whom started with the station as serving soldiers - who supply managerial, professional and creative talents. For many of the conscripts, Galei Zahal and the public reputation that it brings them, is all the reference they will need to find work in the civilian media - radio, television and printed - after release from the service.

Though part of the military establishment, the station zealously preserves its editorial independence, and the high standard of radiophonic performance set by its staff has been rewarded by constant popularity in public opinion polls. So much so, in fact, that one IDF Chief-of-Staff bent on closing the station's newsroom - as part of a budget cut campaign - was dissuaded by members of the Knesset on the grounds that the IDF's radio was the most objective source of reporting available to them and the public.

In times of emergency, Galei Zahal reporters cover events from the forward lines, and forge a fast and reassuring link with the families at home - often in the form of broadcast personal messages from soldiers. In more peaceful times, the station maintains its close links with the army through programs on military and defense affairs, special broadcasts for soldiers on the frontlines and entertainment for serving men and women. Israel probably listens to news broadcasts more than any other country, and Galei Zahal has responded to public demand by giving news flashes on the half-hour to supplement Israel Radio's hourly bulletins. It broadcasts throughout the night, when civilian stations have shut down, gives radio coverage of the evening TV news for soldiers who have no opportunity to watch, supplies radio newsreels at regular times during the day and shares with educational television an afternoon current affairs program.

The station devotes regular schedules, original programs and special broadcasts to cultural, educational and social themes. Its commitment to the closing of social gaps is no empty slogan: a "Broadcast University" series has, over a decade, brought the audience more than a hundred lecture courses by top ranking academics. Tens of thousands of books have been sold to back up the lectures. The station also gives prominent place to original Israeli creativity. Each Saturday, for example, Galei Zahal broadcasts ten continuous hours of Hebrew songs. Each day, time is devoted to correcting Hebrew usage by demonstrating common mistakes and how to cure them (with a high proportion of immigrants in the population, the national language is not necessarily the mother tongue of all listeners). Other programs are devoted to the works of Israeli writers and poets and to critiques of art and theatre.

Galei Zahal considers itself committed to scheduling that appeals to most of the Israeli public. The result is a rare media mix of

classical, Israeli, pop and folk music, interviews, news, current events and documentaries, that offers its listeners a vast choice of programs and content. To gain extra broadcast hours, the station recently began to separate its FM and AM broadcasts at certain times during the day, to enable direct coverage of important Knesset debates, national and international sports and outstanding cultural events, without disrupting normal programming.

Bamachane - "In Camp" - a weekly magazine for soldiers, is published by the Education Corps to acquaint soldiers, officers and civilians with a variety of subjects. The magazine competes for the leisure time of its audience by maintaining high standards of journalistic reporting, depth of insights, credibility and variety of content. At the same time, because it is financed and published by the IDF, and read by soldiers, Bamachane imposes on itself two significant restrictions: the subjects covered in its pages do not stray beyond the bounds of public consensus; there is no attempt whatsoever to preach a particular social or political viewpoint. Apart from a wide selection of army and security subjects, current social and political events, culture and the arts, science and technology - Bamachane occasionally publishes supplements and special editions for defined audiences - reservists outside the country, the children of regular army personnel, demobilized soldiers, youth awaiting enlistment, etc.

Once a month, the army education system provides IDF officers with an academic forum in the form of Skira Hodshit - "Monthly Roundup" - a journal that publishes articles by professionals and academics, interviews and debates. The journal deals in depth with current and historic events and processes in policy, security, society and economy of Israel, the Jewish People and other countries. To select articles and authors, the editorial staff are assisted by a board composed of academics, whose task it is to evaluate submitted work solely in its professional aspects while avoiding political and other prejudices. Because of its uncompromising high standards - Skira Hodshit is much sought after by secondary schools, universities and private homes in Israel.

While Bamachane and Skira Hodshit, although available to the public, are primarily internal publications for the army, Maarachot Publishing House produces a journal and series of books for the general audience. Its main themes are military history and

philosophy and comparative studies - and the level is academic.
Writers appearing in the journal and books include senior officers and
lecturers from Israel's universities.

Formal Education

"Knowledge is the essential base for social processes: how to
read and write, understand the written text, ability to contend
with the supply of science, technology, culture and the arts
and, most important, stimulation of modern man's appetite for
learning - all these are acquired by a process of enlightenment.
For Israeli society, the IDF is the last institutionalized chance
to give its citizens all these."

Standing Orders of the Education Corps

General Staff Regulation 37.0102, dated November 1977 and
incorporated into the National Service Law by the Knesset in the
early 1980s, obliges all soldiers who have not completed primary
education in the civilian system - or who did so abroad, and have not
attended school in Israel - to acquire the basics during their military
service. The subjects stipulated by the Regulation are Hebrew, Bible,
Geography and History of Israel, Citizenship, Arithmetic and
Geometry, General Geography and History, Nature and English.
And the required level is that of a Ministry of Education recognized
Primary School Leaving Certificate.

Youngsters identified as deficient in primary education, upon
reporting for IDF induction, are taken to the Yigal Allon Education
and Enlightenment Center. Here they receive, together with their
basic army training, elementary education up to the level of eight
years' schooling, and guidance in improving their personal and social
performance prior to assignment to units. In some cases, where the
educational deficiency is only identified at a later stage, soldiers are
sent to the Center at mid-service for the basic education course
alone.

These recruits generally dropped out of the school system as
children for a variety of reasons: they may have had learning
problems with which the education system was not equipped to deal;
those from large families might have been withdrawn from school
because of economic pressures at home. Some of them are unable to
read and write, or express thoughts of more than a few basic words.

Many of them display a chronic inability to adjust to any social frame - including the IDF. Their first two weeks at the Center are, therefore, deliberately spent in accustoming them to fundamental ideas of self-discipline: getting up in the mornings, wearing uniform, functioning in a group and respecting officers and instructors.

The military instructors are hand picked among volunteers from the elite infantry brigades - paratroops, Golani and Givati - and receive special sensitivity training. They are told, for example, to display extraordinary patience and restraint in the face of insults and dumb insolence - and even to recruits who resort to street habits of drawing switchblades. In those cases where a young recruit runs, on the assumption that he is suffering acute adjustment problems, nobody chases after him, since this would only aggravate his mental distress. Neither are the Military Police called in to bring him back as "Absent Without Leave." Instead, officers and instructors from the Center call on the family, to persuade them and the recruit that the education he is going to get is for his own benefit. Perhaps because of the special regard in which the IDF is held in society at large, the gentle persuasion usually works. Visits to the families are, in any case, a normal procedure: better results are achieved if teachers and instructors are familiar with the home problems and environment from which the recruit has come.

If the underlying principle of recruitment was only the manpower needs of the army, the IDF - like most modern armed forces - would have rejected these recruits and left them to wallow in their social and educational distress. Since the purpose of this, and other programs, is to exploit the conscript army frame as society's last chance to recover drop-out youth, the Center's conceptions of normal military punishment are tempered to the predicament of these youth. Where, in other units, serious disciplinary infractions would result in sentences to a military prison, the commanding officers at Allon Center recognize that imprisonment will return the recruit to first base in the enlightenment process: the inevitable result would be a deepening of the youngster's self image as a failure who can never make the grade. Consequently, though carrot and stick techniques must be applied, the "shape" of the stick makes allowances for this particular audience - and prison is not a normal disciplinary option. The initial adjustment problem is usually overcome within the first two weeks - and the education phase begins in week three.

The integration of basic military training and schooling in one base provides disadvantaged soldiers particularly comfortable conditions for their adaptation to army frames. The recruits are housed in buildings that offer most of the amenities of home - or perhaps even better for some of them. The training and learning process is gradual and controlled. Strict military discipline, unhesitatingly applied even in the classroom, initially guarantees the cooperation of the pupils and eventually brings them to active study participation. Each group is assigned a military instructor and two Education Corps teachers, allowing a personal approach to each soldier, individual tutoring and consideration for social and psychological problems. Bearing in mind that the original reason for dropping out of school may have been the inability of teachers to give individual attention in classes of thirty or more, the Center's classes are held to ten at most, and sometimes as few as three pupils.

Apart from acquiring basic learning in subjects such as Hebrew, mathematics, history, Bible and citizenship - on which the pupil is graded for his graduation certificate (at the accepted levels of the civilian school system) - the soldier, during the course, enhances his ties with Israel, Israeli society and the IDF through enrichment activities: tours, lectures, entertainment evenings, movies, etc., relating to current events, culture, IDF combat heritage and knowledge of the country. When they leave the Center for assignment to army units, their commanding officers are given guidance on how to ease their integration and adaptation.

The Allon Center's activity is not restricted to new recruits. Towards the end of their three year conscript service, IDF soldiers - mostly from combat units - are directed to the Center to round off their basic education. This is followed, with their agreement to an extra half-year of service, by an opportunity to upgrade their education to the normal compulsory level of ten years' schooling. They can also be guided onwards, if they wish, to a full secondary education - with matriculation certification - in academic preparatory courses after their military service. In parallel, those soldiers who wish to do so are directed to trade schools to gain a profession that will serve them in civilian society.

New immigrants, arriving in Israel from all over the world, study before enlistment in a three-month course which, apart from giving them a working knowledge of Hebrew, enhances their familiarity with the history of the Jewish People, the country and citizenship. This course is designed to strengthen their personal bond to country and to stimulate them for their active service in the IDF. A special project for Hebrew language has recently been developed for Ethiopian Jews. This is a pre-army course, given in the frame of Gadna ("Youth Battalions"), which includes primary education as well as language. The Center also holds Hebrew courses for minority groups that enlist in the IDF, in order to ease their military and personal function in the service. These courses are attended by Druze and Circassian soldiers whose knowledge and understanding of the language, and ability to express themselves in it, is wanting.

The achievements of the Allon Center have been proven by examination of education levels and language fluency of the soldiers, and by the number of pupils who successfully complete military service with an education.

Absorption of Culturally Deprived Youth in the IDF

"Conscript service in the IDF is a primary tier in the shaping of identity of the Israeli citizen. Therefore, it is incumbent on us to give every youth who wants to serve all the help and support to enable him to pass through this significant experience - especially since the person who does not serve in the IDF carries a stigma for all his life... For he who has not succeeded, this is the last opportunity to try and complete his education and enlightenment as an adult citizen."

Standing Orders of the Education Corps

One of the first questions asked by a prospective employer in Israel is "where did you serve?" A job candidate who cannot show army service is likely to be suspect: if the army didn't want him, there has to be good reason... In social circles, when conversation inevitably comes around to experiences in the conscript or reserve army, the man who didn't serve is neither treated as belonging, nor feels personally comfortable with the thought. Though the IDF is not directly responsible for this social attitude, it cannot ignore the situation. Neither can it reject the implied moral responsibility.

In sociological terms, education problems do not begin and end with children who dropped out because of learning problems alone.

For the past ten years, in response to requests from civilian authorities, the IDF has been recruiting underprivileged youth within a special framework. The Center for Advancement of Special Populations, which functions as a part of the headquarters of the Senior Education Officer, deals with delinquents and low social motivation groups. The guiding principle of work with these groups has to be the placing of benefit to the individual, and his maximal personal and social advancement - before the needs of the army. The treatment of these populations involves easing adaptation to the system by a special basic training, completion of education, professional or trade instruction and preparation for integration into society upon demobilization.

Staff from the Hashomer Farm, where these youth will be introduced to army life, visit their homes a month before enlistment, in order to become acquainted with their family and social situation - and to enlighten the family and recruits about the program soon to begin. Upon processing at the IDF Induction and Classification Base, staff members escort them directly to the Farm, where they undergo a ten-day induction program developed specially for them. The program takes into consideration the difficulties of these youth, in a gradual introduction to army life, with its demands, concepts and procedures.

Following the ten-day introduction, the recruits begin a basic training program, in companies divided by education level: their studies may be directed at completion of education in Hebrew, arithmetic, nature and citizenship, or may be devoted to enrichment alone. As do all new recruits, they learn to function in military behavior patterns - obeying orders, punctuality, orderliness. However, for most of them, these principles are a new experience which they find hard to accept. So their basic training - every new recruit's first encounter with the army - is spread out over a period of four months in "almost home" physical and human conditions, designed to help them adjust as easily as possible.

The instruction staff at the Farm are guided primarily by the need to develop learning habits, thought processes and understanding, alongside training soldiers for absorption into the ranks of IDF units. Platoon and squad commanders, drawn from various IDF units, and the education officers and teachers - who in part double as squad commanders - receive special training for their roles. Psychologists and sociologists accompany the program, both to advise the instructors and teachers, and to deal directly with the problems of the recruits.

Social involvement in their environment is fostered by a project in which the recruits assist in rehabilitation and renewal of distressed civilian neighborhoods. They also become acquainted with IDF values, units and history, and are helped to uproot their delinquent tendencies.

Teaching methods include classroom, tutorials and self-study, based on classes that never contain more than 10-12 pupils. The teaching staff, trained for this specific function, is composed of young women soldiers, doing their two-year conscript service and who have volunteered for the pre-army preparatory courses as teachers. This group is characterized by high personal standards, exceptional capacities for work and a strong sense of mission. Since most of these recruits come from broken homes or very large families, their soldier teachers are in many cases the first human beings to really pay attention to them and their problems. Many of these teachers are young religious women, who could have been exempted from conscript service, but opted to enlist for a most exacting teaching job - either at the Allon Center or the Hashomer Farm.

At the beginning of their service, or the end - dependent on their individual characteristics - the graduates of this program are given a two-month primer for trade training: basic professional knowhow, various enrichment themes and deeper insights into their own traits and talents. These soldiers go on to take regular army courses as automotive mechanics and electricians, metal and woodworkers, or courses specially for them: fork lift operators, heavy earthmoving equipment drivers and technical warehousemen. These are the trades in which they will serve during the remainder of their three years in the army, and all are selected for applicability to civilian employment.

Following their basic training and education, the soldiers are assigned to IDF units by their trade attainments, individual levels and needs. Commanders are encouraged to accept them and continue the educational process, in classes that take place during their active service. A network of professional officers maintains constant educational follow up. In addition, their commanders receive special refreshers as "educational counselors," which give a grounding in assisting the soldier personally and professionally in his integration, guidance on instilling work habits and the importance of personal example with which the soldier can identify.

For these special populations, and for some other categories of soldiers, lack of a warm home and family atmosphere causes loneliness, insecurity and alienation - and consequent difficulties in daily performance of military duties. Homeless soldiers - orphans, children of broken families, new immigrants and those whose parents have left the country - are placed with foster families during their military service. The warmth, attention, encouragement and advice extended them by the families, assist in improving their personal feelings and military performance. The Adoption Department of the Center for Advancement of Special Populations carefully matches each soldier - taking into consideration his age, past and difficulties - to a foster family from a pool of Israelis who have volunteered to help. This is not formal adoption, but rather the acceptance of the soldier into the family for his leaves and religious holidays. The chosen family takes care of most of his material and emotional needs, and offers him warmth and the sense of belonging. Once a month, the Adoption Department meets with the families to counsel them in their welcome activity.

Secondary Education

A matriculation certificate is universally accepted as advantageous for integration into civilian life. A great many soldiers, both conscripts and regulars, take advantage of a six-month course given in the IDF Secondary School, either full time or in evening classes, to be able to sit for Ministry of Education external examinations. As an independent body, the School is assisted by the use of civilian school buildings and professional academic teachers - both IDF civilian employees and NCO teacher-instructors - in providing all the required subjects. In return for a token payment, and after entrance examinations to determine his personal level, any IDF soldier wishing to complete his secondary education or achieve better grades, can study in the School.

The number of subjects studied is determined by the soldier's own abilities. The number of students accepted is regulated in accordance with the IDF's work program and available resources. Institutions for secondary education, which serve as branches of the School, are spread all over the country, and these allow study without excess travel hardship and permit the soldier to enter civilian life with the right credentials.

The responsibility of professional echelons for the IDF's capability in routine duties and as a fighting force, and their command status vis-a-vis many other soldiers, makes of the warrant officers and sergeants-major of the IDF a primary and stable target audience for education: a large share of the effort directed at them takes place in Education Corps courses to upgrade their schooling to ten years. The initial classification of student population among warrant officers is done by the IDF Adjutancy Corps, which can order them to schooling. Basic tests in Hebrew and mathematics determine the length of course - three or eight months. Each year, large groups of senior NCOs complete their compulsory education levels, under the tutelage of professional teachers and the Corps' education NCOs. Professional advancement, improved pay scales and continued education to matriculation in a one-year course of the IDF Secondary School and Haifa University, open up to the warrant officer who has completed ten years' schooling.

Preparation for Demobilization

In the long process of handling soldiers with difficulties, the IDF's real test comes when they have to face the challenge of integration as citizens in society. The IDF Demobilization Preparation Center grooms soldiers who have no trade training for work in industry, or for studies: in a month of theoretical studies and guided tours of plants and work places, soldiers come in contact with the labor market, get to know the possibilities for study and trade training, develop learning skills and enrich their knowledge of nation and society.

If they are prepared to agree to an extra six months' national service, the IDF gives them courses in civilian trade schools. The courses are designed to move along at the level of the soldiers, in small classes - in order to avoid the classic problems of students struggling to keep up. Graduates receive accepted civilian trade certification for building, textiles, automotive occupations, metalworking and the hotel industry - and help in finding jobs. Women NCO instructors, who serve as the soldiers' direct commanders and enrich their general knowledge throughout the programs, are integrated into the professional teaching staff of the schools. Soldiers with exceptional difficulties are given a three-month "technology primer" course before entering the program.

Work Groups

The spiral of social alienation among drop-outs begins long before enlistment age. In coordination with the Ministry of Labor and the networks of trade and professional schools, the IDF literally combs the streets for 14-18 year-old idle and unemployed youth and offers them study and work groups in army camps, for their personal and social rehabilitation. Under the supervision of the camp commander, a social counselor, a trade instructor and NCO teachers from the Education Corps, these youths receive formal trade and general education in schools on the bases, and spend a number of hours of apprenticeship each day in workshops around the camp. In parallel, the groups get courses and individual tutoring in work habits and discipline.

The preparation of these disadvantaged youth for renewed integration into society, is also helped by strengthening their sense of belonging to country and state in a week-long seminar given them every summer in field schools of the Nature Protection Society. This is, for many of them, their first encounter with the scenery of the country - and it is also a way to prepare them, by discussions, tours and certain military oriented activities, for their eventual conscript service in the IDF.

The scope of Education Corps activity is constantly threatened by the budgetary problems that face the IDF. However, there is a strong public awareness of, and interest in the army's personal and cultural enrichment programs. Faced with the recognition that the programs are vital for society and constantly imperiled by budgetary considerations - that must place the IDF's security obligations above education in the order of priorities - Israel's citizens have shown a remarkable willingness to shoulder a share of the burden. The Soldiers' Welfare Committee, among its much wider activities, has helped with facilities that it has donated to the IDF - including, among others, the home of the School for Leadership Development and the Hashomer Farm. An additional fund, Libi - a Hebrew acronym for "For the Sake of the Security of Israel" - was created by public subscription, from Israel and abroad, specifically to support the educational effort. Israeli society's determination to keep all the programs running, has served as a reaffirmation to the IDF of its special relationship with the People that it serves, and a reconfirmation to the Educational Corps of the value of its efforts to produce enlightened citizen soldiers.